Reconciliation Through Truth

South Africa, as a symbol and exemplar of global injustice, commanded world attention for decades. Now it is attracting attention in a different way. And the new country is taking stock of the old, in ways that retain a global significance. This book is about the process of transition.

The South African transition, while widely billed as a miracle, has not yet received the same systematic treatment as political transitions elsewhere. The book serves as a primary text in the new South African politics, presenting for the first time the new country's view of its old self. It scans the key issues and debates of the transition.

The new South Africa has established the Truth and Reconciliation Commission as a mechanism to ensure a collective coming-to-grips with the prior system. While many such mechanisms elsewhere have focused on providing amnesty or exculpation for former human rights abusers, the South African mechanism combines amnesty provisions with procedures for making reparation to victims, and is mandated to sum up the historical sweep of the South African past.

In addressing these issues, the book breaks new ground. It drives home the depth and strength of allegiance that the old regime commanded from its beneficiaries. It emphasises the long-standing ideals that held sway among those who resisted apartheid. And it makes clear that, in Nelson Mandela's words, a long walk remains, even now, en route to freedom.

The authors compellingly demonstrate how the old system violated the world's basic human norms – and how the new country is raising and enhancing the status of the international norms on which apartheid trampled.

Kader Asmal was exiled in Ireland for 27 years, where he taught law and became Dean of the Faculty of Arts (Humanities) at Trinity College, Dublin. Formerly professor at the University of the Western Cape and an ANC negotiator in the South African transition to democracy, he is now a Cabinet Minister in Nelson Mandela's government.

Louise Asmal, a lifelong civil rights campaigner and former honorary secretary of the Irish Anti-Apartheid Movement, was a central participant in the international sanctions campaign against apartheid and in the global movement for solidarity with the South African majority.

Ronald Suresh Roberts, from Trinidad, is a graduate of Balliol College, Oxford, and Harvard Law School, and author of Clarence Thomas and the Tough Love Crowd: Counterfeit Heroes and Unhappy Truths (1995). He has lived in South Africa since the 1994 elections, when he co-ordinated election monitors.

FOR THE PEOPLE OF SOUTH AFRICA AND THE WORLD
WHO UNITED TO DEFEAT THE CRIME OF APARTHEID

RECONCILIATION THROUGH TRUTH

A Reckoning of Apartheid's Criminal Governance

Kader Asmal, Louise Asmal & Ronald Suresh Roberts

"The Government should be in the dock, not me. I plead not guilty."
– Nelson Mandela at the Rivonia Trial, 1963.

"All right, let us forget about moral guilt."
– Percy Yutar, Rivonia Trial prosecutor, 1964.

DAVID PHILIP PUBLISHERS
Cape Town & Johannesburg

in association with

MAYIBUYE BOOKS
University of the Western Cape

First published 1996 in southern Africa by David Philip Publishers (Pty) Ltd,
208 Werdmuller Centre, Claremont 7700, South Africa,
in association with Mayibuye Books, University of the Western Cape,
Private Bag X17, Bellville 7535, South Africa

Mayibuye History and Literature Series No. 74

ISBN 0 86486 324 1

Grateful acknowledgment for the use of copyright material is made to the following: (on page
28) to Professor Michael Chapman for "Concrete Poem – The Chameleon Dance" from *The
Paperbook of South African English Poetry* (Jonathan Ball / Ad Donker, Johannesburg); and (on
page 44) to Mark Behr for the extract from *The Smell of Apples* (Little, Brown UK, London, and
Abacus, London).

Printed by Creda Press (Pty) Ltd, Eliot Avenue, Epping, South Africa

Contents

Acknowledgments

A book of this nature is not the product of a few months or even years of research; its essence has been distilled from a life-time of experience and debate in the liberation struggle, and in the solidarity movement. We single out a few names, but emphasise that they do not exhaust our moral and intellectual debts.

We express our gratitude:

to the late Rosalynde de Lanerolle, dear friend and fellow-exile, whose insights into the need for truth contributed so much to the ideas contained in Kader Asmal's 1992 lecture on the topic of this book;

to Oliver Tambo, the late and much-loved President of the ANC, who at the Children's Conference in Harare in 1987 talked so persuasively against any urge for revenge, which he believed could be successfully averted in a post-apartheid society;

to Albert Luthuli, 1960 Nobel Peace prize winner, whose anti-racist and at the same time deeply traditional African culture were the very essence of ubuntu;

to Professor Richard Falk, for his insights into the moral issues relating to individual responsibility;

to the Rev. Terence McCaughey and the many friends in Ireland whose solidarity and views helped over the years to inspire and shape the ideas expressed in this book;

to Zukile Nomvete whose comradeship during the dark days of the emergency epitomised the good humour and determination of the South African resistance to apartheid;

and to Rafiq and Adam Asmal who suffered the vagaries of their parents with equanimity, deflated their pretensions, and remain unfailingly supportive.

The authors also wish to thank Robert Shaw for his research assistance and Patti Smith for her patient endurance of the writing process.

One of the real delights of our new democracy, for me personally, has been the vibrant culture of public debate that is slowly emerging. We have come a long way since our public intellectual life was blighted by apartheid's regime of censorship, described in this book.

Even in prison, I avidly read any newspapers we could obtain. They gave us little joy though, not only because they often disclosed such harsh facts but because of the absence from their pages of large areas of pain and suffering. As I read about apartheid South Africa in its own press, I knew that new chapters of its history were being passed over, sometimes wilfully, sometimes unconsciously, and sometimes deliberately obliterated through the actions of the censor.

Today it is my hope that, in facing up to our past, we can ensure that never again will South Africa's children have to remain content with accounts of our country that are known to be false.

The elections of April 1994 did not set us free - but we did achieve the freedom to be free. There are new dilemmas in our new democracy, and real problems which our institutions and the media face. There are new responsibilities and new challenges. Nevertheless, few would now dispute our newly won right to debate and argue about our response to those challenges. This is one of our country's real achievements.

The Truth and Reconciliation Commission is a milestone on the freedom road, and this book will illuminate the journey. It presents a necessary perspective on our unfolding future. Like all useful contributions to any country's new awakening, it will spark lively debate.

Such debate is essential if our rainbow nation is to draw the full range of lessons from its past. Our country has been through a long dark night of anguish, which we must now put behind us. The most important question is how best to achieve that goal. So I welcome the book's emphasis on identifying the nature and scope of past wrongs and taking methodical steps to remove them.

I believe that joining hands in that task is a central aim of reconciliation. I am often asked how it is that I emerged without bitterness from so long a time in prison. This question is intended as a compliment, and I can appreciate the motives of those who ask it. Nevertheless, it must be said that millions of South Africa's people spent an even longer time in the prison of apartheid. Some were imprisoned by the apartheid laws in a condition of homelessness and near-despair. Others were imprisoned in the racism of the mind. These are places where some still languish.

In such circumstances, personal bitterness is irrelevant. It is a luxury that we, as individuals and as a country, simply cannot afford, any more than we can afford to listen to special pleading from the privileged. Instead we must insist with quiet resolve on a firm policy of undoing the continuing effects of the past.

It is another personal delight for me today to watch how the divisions of the past are giving way to the beginnings of a new South African sense of belonging, shared by all.

Books which confront the difficult issues that face us, as does this book, contribute to that process of new beginnings.

Nelson Mandela
President
Republic of South Africa

June 1996

Introduction

"One name for another, a part for the whole: the historic violence of Apartheid can always be treated as a metonymy. In its past as well as in its present ... one can always decipher through its singularity so many other kinds of violence going on in the world. At once part, cause, effect, example, what is happening there translates what takes place here, always here, wherever one is and wherever one looks, closest to home. Infinite responsibility, therefore, no rest allowed for any form of good conscience."
  – Jacques Derrida, *Spectres of Marx* (1994) from his dedication to the slain Chris Hani.

What is happening there translates what takes place here, wherever one is. What happened in the old South Africa showed those outside it (and all three of the authors were outside South Africa for most of the apartheid period) the flaws and dangers of the societies in which we lived. Apartheid was conceived and perfected in South Africa, but it drew sustenance from indefensible political ideas and systems abroad, and in turn fed the racist inclinations of still other ideologues and governments.

So an effective examination of the apartheid past should illuminate not only the past itself, but also the present, here and elsewhere. Ruth First, a leader of the South African resistance who was detained, harassed and eventually bombed to death by the apartheid government, commented from exile in 1970 that "I don't feel specially South African. It was just where one happened to meet the issues."[1] Even for many of those at its very heart and centre, the struggle against apartheid was never a parochial exercise. It was also the best available way of trying to do something for everybody.

Now in the new South Africa we seem, more than most places, to be grappling successfully with the defining problem of the twentieth century. That problem, in eminent American historian W E B Du Bois's phrase, is the problem of the colour line.

It is subversive in the best sense of the word that a global underdog – a country of the so-called Third World – should loom so large in the globe's most pressing debates. It can credibly be said, as an American lawyer did at a 1996 Harvard Law School conference, that the civilised twentieth century began with Nelson Mandela's release from prison in 1990.

Quoting his predecessor of the 1950s and 1960s, ANC President Albert

Luthuli, President Mandela expressed, just days after his release, the belief that "here in South Africa, with all our diversities of colour and race, we will show the world a new pattern for democracy [and] set a new example for the world."[2] It was an explicit and practical grappling with the moral and political problem identified by Du Bois.

Yet clearly South Africa's new politics, its novel practice of nonracialism, remains young and fragile. Apartheid was not ended by military defeat, but through sustained resistance and peaceful negotiation. Apartheid's ideological and practical legacy therefore remains to be undone, both here and abroad. The collective exercise of facing the South African past is an important aspect of that undoing – and not only for South Africans.

The 1993 South African Constitution, known as the interim constitution, set out its hope of reconciliation for all the people of South Africa, its determination to transcend the divisions and strife of the past, and its commitment to the granting of amnesty for "acts, omissions and offences associated with political objectives and committed in the course of the conflicts of the past." It will investigate human rights abuses dating back to 1 March 1960, and afterwards will present its report to the President. Like similar commissions in Latin America and elsewhere, the South African Truth and Reconciliation Commission will attempt to assess the injustices of the past in order to inaugurate a more just future.

A meaningful examination of the South African past can only be built, as this book is, on the recognition that apartheid was a terrible evil which treated the majority of the people of South Africa – and by implication the world – as inferior beings. It produced, according to a 1989 survey, the world's most unequal society. Its implementation bred lawlessness and brought a culture of felony into the driver's seat of a country.

Apartheid's rulers casually broke their own laws, as well as international laws and norms, for their own narrow and self-interested ends. Apartheid death-squad commander Eugene de Kock (nicknamed "Prime Evil"), who learnt his grizzly trade as a member of the Rhodesian special forces and was, at the time of writing, on trial for 121 criminal charges, recently captured a central impulse of apartheid governance: "Why keep to the Queensberry rules and fight one boxer when you can kick them in the balls and kill three."[3]

International agreements like the controversial 1984 Nkomati Accord, providing for non-aggression and good neighbourliness between apartheid South Africa and beleaguered Mozambique, were no bar to the apartheid regime's continued secret support for Mozambique's rebel Renamo movement.[4] Apartheid governance was an inglorious assault by a state on the same citizens it ought to have served as guardian and on the same neighbours with whom (sporadically) it pretended to cooperate. It sought to deprive the South African majority even of its citizenship and, claiming a right to regional domination, it attacked the sovereignty and simple dignity of the people of southern Africa.

The authors do not, however, see the Truth and Reconciliation Commission as an instrument of vengeance. A spirit of vengeance would destroy the country's new politics of nonracialism. It would contradict the ideals of the resistance, specifically the nonracialism of the African National Congress, from which all three of the authors have drawn inspiration and to which two of us belong.

While the authors have backgrounds in legal practice, legal activism and legal academia, ours is emphatically not a contribution by lawyers for lawyers alone. The authors' legal backgrounds are relevant to many of the views presented, particularly on such matters as the status of apartheid as a crime against humanity. But the main concern remains the moral, political, historical and international significance of the South African past for a range of contemporary debates. We aim to show that the burdens of history comprise an invaluable ballast of common sense in charting the new country's course away from its inglorious past.

A brief explanation of the authors' backgrounds will put our views into perspective and, as it were, declare our interests at the outset.

Kader Asmal grew up in South Africa in a small town where, if he saw a white man walking in the street, he was expected to step off the pavement to make way for him. He was drawn to politics by Chief Albert Luthuli, South Africa's first Nobel Prize Laureate, and the then President of the African National Congress. His early awareness of the faraway atrocities of Nazi Germany internationalised his human rights perspective and in later life, as an academic lawyer, informed his view that apartheid was a crime against humanity. In the 1970s and 1980s, he became a specialist on the question of the illegitimacy of apartheid under international law, a subject on which he wrote widely. For many years he campaigned for a South African equivalent of the Nuremberg trials, which put major Nazi war criminals in the dock after Germany was defeated in the Second World War, but his experiences as an ANC constitutionalist during the negotiated transition changed his mind, and he became a protagonist of a South African Truth and Reconciliation Commission. He currently serves as a Cabinet Minister in President Mandela's government.

Louise Asmal comes from a family with a strong background and belief in individual rights. She was working for a prominent British civil liberties organisation in London when she met her husband, Kader Asmal, and became involved in the international resistance to apartheid and the solidarity movement in support of the South African dispossessed. For many years she was honorary secretary of the Irish Anti-Apartheid Movement, which was built on three pillars: publicising the truth about apartheid; campaigning for sanctions in order to help end apartheid before it bred uncontrollable violence; and supporting South African resistance to apartheid.

As a Trinidadian of that country's first postcolonial generation, Ronald Suresh Roberts grew up in a political and cultural environment saturated with anti-apartheid resistance. In the early post-war era the noted historian Dr Eric

Williams, who shortly afterwards served as Trinidad and Tobago's first post-independence Prime Minister, commented, with his genius for the incisive colloquialism, that "Massa Day Done." And yet, almost simultaneously, the harsh grip of J G Strijdom's *baasskap* politics gathered momentum in South Africa. For newly independent West Indians, the old South Africa was a last bastion of unabashed racism. As a student in the United Kingdom and the United States, Roberts observed how defenders of racial privilege in those countries manipulated popular ignorance of historical truths. This was a theme of his first book, *Clarence Thomas and the Tough Love Crowd: Counterfeit Heroes and Unhappy Truths*.

The struggle against apartheid unified black and white, men and women, the South African majority and people all over the world. In its new guises – its metonymous forms – it still unifies, from their varying backgrounds and different identities, the authors of this book. Apartheid was, in Nigerian novelist Ben Okri's phrase, the whole world's "howling pot of human misery." Within this horrible unmelting pot of human cultures, the world saw, in acute form, its problem of the colour line.

In apartheid South Africa, more relentlessly and for longer than elsewhere, blacks knew both the demoralising inner lash and the violent outer lash of what Okri called "the skin's anointed pain." Meanwhile, apartheid's architects and their constituency stood, increasingly frantic and violently so, with a finger in the dyke of world history.

It is difficult to climb fully inside the mindset, the cruel, empty and strained prerogatives of the skin, that sustained apartheid for four decades. Apartheid fostered in its adherents – both passive and active – peculiar senses of self, of others, and of the world beyond national borders (in rare moments when those others or that world were conceded to be of any legitimate relevance). This peculiarity was not merely an abstract process of illogic or of twisted concepts. It was not only dogma. It cannot have been; it had to have been something more bodily and visceral if it was to have lasted so long. Apartheid must have had real and strange (in)human building blocks.

Indeed, apartheid's beneficiaries put disfavoured racial castes into a zoo of being; they confined blacks to a zone of nothingness – even as world opinion put these white beneficiaries themselves in a moral and political dog-house for these very same acts and policies. It is difficult to capture and to preserve for posterity the ugly and fine-grained texture of this human divide, this relationship of zoo-keeper over the kept, that subsisted unnaturally between people and other people for so long.

It is difficult, but not impossible. We can perhaps arrive near the heart of the matter with a glance at Mrs Betsie Verwoerd, wife of H F Verwoerd and currently resident in the separatist dorp of Orania. In November 1973, Mrs Verwoerd objected that if white children of working mothers were cared for by black domestic workers, an unhealthy bond would develop between white children and their black carers. "Even the characteristic smell, which is normally repulsive to a white person, will become associated in the child's mind with the person with whom he spends most of his time. Can this later repel him when he is grown up?"[5]

What kind of world was this? In the existential belly of white supremacy, ordinary human relations were suppressed or distorted. The normal likes and dislikes of people for one another were controlled by the state and disfigured by white supremacist culture; the whole ugly process was hidden behind the soothing euphemisms of apartheid, or separate freedoms. It was a world that was upside-down.

Why Face the Past?

When President Nelson Mandela magnanimously visited Mrs Verwoerd in 1995, a new world had largely arrived. It did not seem then that the President smelt repulsive to her. It seemed she had abandoned her strange science of racial scent. Yet even after the President's visit, Mrs Verwoerd still clung falteringly to the little all-white town of Orania, that failed experiment in racial purity, an ideology that has definitively lost its way in South Africa and the world.

The challenge now is to put something new in its place. As South Africa faces its past, through the South African Commission for Truth and Reconciliation and more generally, there is an enormous challenge: we must faithfully record the pain of the past so that a unified nation can call upon that past as a galvanising force in the large tasks of reconstruction.

We have been fortunate in South Africa that virtually everyone, even Mrs Betsie Verwoerd, eventually recognised the need for change (of some sort). But now that bracketed question – change of some sort – must occupy centre stage. The question – what sort of change? – cannot remain any longer in parenthesis. In these early years of consolidating democracy, there must be a galvanising and self-critical vision of the goals of our society. And such a vision in turn requires a clear-sighted and constantly debated grasp of what was wrong in the past. More than one eminent international observer has remarked on the fact that contemporary South African academic and media commentary seems to lag behind the broad and swift sweep of change that has gripped the country. With notable exceptions (some of which we mention in this book), there has so far been, at best, only a sporadic presence of the intellectual ferment that can accompany moral and political transition.

Ten years ago, at the height of the apartheid dictatorship, no-one imagined that democracy and reconciliation would come so quickly to the country. Nevertheless, if reconciliation is to remain solidly grounded, there must be a further recognition: that the old apartheid system was not just practically unsustainable, a "mistake." It was, rather, deliberately evil. It was, in the words of Willem de Klerk, brother of the former Deputy President, "darkness masquerading as light."

While there were scattered infringements of the ideals of the African National Congress by those resisting apartheid and its war machine, they were aberrations in no way commensurate with the atrocity that was apartheid. There was no moral similarity between the goals, instincts, basic values, or even the tactics, of those who fought to end apartheid, when measured against the values and conduct of those who struggled to uphold it. Not once did the ANC target any apartheid leader for assassination; the apartheid state systematically targeted its opponents.

The apartheid regime presided over a *state*; it abused the weighty prerogatives and betrayed the grave responsibilities that only states possess. In contrast, the anti-apartheid resistance comprised citizens banding together in self-defence, without the resources – and consequently the obligations in deploying those resources – that only states possess.

To label such distinctions (developed in further detail below) "moral favouritism,"[1] is to yearn for a lollipop world of superficial and childish even-handedness between an atrocity (apartheid) and its opposite (the resistance). It is to equate the deliberate evils of the Nazis with the mistakes of the resistance to them.

A large part of the morality of nations as of individuals lies in the responsibility to choose between right and wrong, between apartheid and its opposite. And so the new nation must choose. To dismiss this choice-making as favouritism trivialises the issue and threatens to bury the vibrant and self-questioning political morality that is coming alive in this country. It is simply short-sighted, not canny *realpolitik*, to ignore or suppress the moral distinctions between the battle to preserve apartheid and the battle to abolish it. South Africa cannot afford this brand of playground relativism, so what might seem obvious needs meticulous re-emphasis:

Apartheid was evil. It was a crime against humanity. It was statutorily entrenched in the years following the victory of the National Party in the 1948 elections, but its foundations ran deep, having already been laid in the colonial years, through policies pursued by General Jan Smuts and his supporters, formally the losers of the 1948 election.

There were really two political parties in apartheid South Africa: those who had the vote and those who were denied it. In 1948 and for decades afterwards, white supremacist logic and its corollary – voteless blacks deemed undeserving of the franchise – were the basic building blocks of electoral politics on both sides of the divide. This includes those parliamentarians who dissented, on a variety of grounds, from particular apartheid measures.

Institutionalised racism began at least as early as the founding of the Union of South Africa in 1910. The Land Act of 1913, which unequally apportioned the country between blacks and whites, is one of the world's most infamous acts of social engineering. It allotted thirteen per cent of the land, mostly marginal in quality, to the African seventy per cent of the country. Another cornerstone of apartheid, the vicious pass laws which controlled the movement of the black population, originated even further in the past. The South African Truth and Reconciliation Commission's terms of reference, however, require that it focus on activities dating back to 1960, not 1948 which was the electoral birth of apartheid.

7

To some extent all historical datelines are arbitrary and it would be disingenuous to deny that the arbitrary played at least a small part in fixing the 1960 cutoff point. But beyond that, the selection of an historical cut-off point for the Truth and Reconciliation Commission is really a question of what made apartheid as bad as it was.

In the first half of this century, developing countries everywhere reeled under the lash of colonialism and racist exploitation. South Africa, for instance under the Fusion Government (1934–39) and other administrations, not excluding those headed by the internationally acclaimed General Jan Smuts, was always at or near the cutting edge of these appalling worldwide trends. Even before the 1948 Nationalist victory, South African governance reflected a white supremacist consensus and a concentration on resolving inter-white disagreements in order to grapple with the aftermath of the world depression of the early 1930s.

The 1948 election heralded an intensification and systematisation of practices of white supremacy. The amateur racism and personal prejudices of the colonial period gave way to a new pseudo-scientific vigour and to the professionalisation of racist systemrs, epitomised by the Population Registration apparatus established in 1950, which attempted to supply a documentary basis for racial classification – and hence racial discrimination.

Yet the Nationalists had won with a slim and precarious majority in 1948; they were faced with a relatively independent and assertive (albeit traditional and conservative) judiciary, and there was vigorous extra-parliamentary civil protest, exemplified by the 1952 Defiance Campaign. So the apartheid executive was absorbed for the larger part of the fifties in running battles with its courts and with civic protesters. Then in 1960, after four years in the courts, the widely publicised Treason Trial collapsed as the last of the 156 originally accused, including Nelson Mandela, were acquitted. The fifties, then, was a decade of fits and starts, in which the passage of apartheid statutes by parliament advanced more quickly than implementation of the system on the ground. Despite the suppression of the South African Communist Party in 1950, many within the extraparliamentary opposition could still hope that its demands would be heard, just as the similar demands of oppressed people the world over were finally getting a hearing.

But in the 1960s this extra-parliamentary opposition was ruthlessly criminalised rather than heeded; it was brutally slaughtered, as at Sharpeville, rather than heard. Earlier assaults on free political association and expression – notably the 1950 Suppression of Communism Act and a 1953 law criminalising civil disobedience – were expanded in a manner directly targeted at the antiapartheid resistance. The Unlawful Organisations Act was introduced in 1960 and immediately invoked in order to ban the African National Congress and the Pan Africanist Congress. Violent repression of dissent through various forms of internal security legislation also intensified. As discussed below, by the late 1960s the first death squad was born, dedicated to the assassination of political opponents of apartheid.

Without overly anticipating the more systematic discussion of all these themes below, it is enough to say here that the 1960 cut-off date chosen by legislators roughly approximates to the period at which the apartheid state turned unabashedly to the view that only traitors could differ with it over fundamental policy matters, including the basic human rights of voteless black people.

So 1960 was a watershed. On its far side were indefensible formrs of authoritarianism and racism; but after 1960, by criminalising dissent itself, the regime sought to categorise resisters, by definition, as outlaws. Apartheid turned its face, finally, against the world, even against the mild conservatism of Harold Macmillan, whose speech to the effect that the "wind of change" and decolonisation was blowing across Africa was delivered before unrepentant apartheid parliamentarians in February 1960.

Those who enforced apartheid with such violent and liturgical zeal acted no doubt from a variety of motives: some out of fear, some out of greed, others out of an uncritical herd instinct or a straightforward hatred of blacks; some out of anxiety to preserve what they called "white values." Others there were, no doubt, who believed so profoundly in their cause, and were so culturally imprinted with racism, that they could honestly claim to have believed that they were acting in the best interests of their country by keeping the black barbarians in their place. Even more outlandishly, one Nationalist newspaper editor cynically suggested, in effect, that apartheid had to be tried in order to show that it would not work.

Faced with this variety of motives, the new country must hold up a mirror to the old protagonists, passive and active, of apartheid to show them their actions in the light in which these were seen by the majority of the people of South Africa, and indeed by most people of the world.

The majority of people in South Africa lived and breathed the truths of apartheid. They suffered the indignities and humiliation of statutory inferiority. They suffered the pain of being forced out of homes and off their land; away from their loved ones. They were imprisoned and detained in thousands. They require not revelations, but acknowledgment from the perpetrators and the beneficiaries. They require a collective renunciation, by society as a whole, of apartheid's acts, systems and beliefs.

Poet and Nobel Laureate Derek Walcott has commented that "history is fiction, subject to a fitful muse, memory." In moving away from the discredited governing consciousness of the past, we will need to build a new, shared and ceaselessly debated memory of that past. Without sustained remembrance and debate, it will be difficult to develop a new South African culture with its various strands intertwined in constructive friction, rather than in mere conflict and mutual strangulation.

This talk of shared memory must not be misunderstood or mystified. It is not the creation of a post-apartheid *volk* or a stifling homogenous nationhood; nor a new Fatherland. Nor is it merely a nationwide equivalent of every individual's mental ability to retain facts and arguments at the front of her consciousness.

Such analogies between individual and collective memory are unhelpful. Rather, shared memory, in the intended sense, is a process of historical accountability.

This is a workaday exercise, involving academic controversy, political debate, media revelations, processes of proof and of disproof. Even where individual perpetrators of past abuse deny or suppress individual memory of it, these processes of public debate are likely to result in exposure. A good example is that of the Japanese state's wartime regime of forced prostitution – of Korean "comfort women" – which came to light because of an alert Japanese archivist who, when public debate flared up amidst official denials, remembered having seen documentary proof and managed to recover it, forcing a modification of the official position.

Thus the process of forging collective memory is a flaring up of debate; it is the creation of a public atmosphere in which the seemingly unimportant memories and annals of the past achieve a new public importance. New incentives are unleashed so that forgotten or neglected private thoughts and evidence enter the domain of public acknowledgment. For the first time, seemingly worthless private reminiscence achieves public currency and manifest worth. This is a precise, not a sentimental, process.

Such a process of collective memory will in turn move us towards a number of crucial goals:

*it will enable us to achieve a measure of justice for the victims of our horrific past by acknowledging the atrocities that they suffered;

*it will provide a basis for a collective acknowledgment of the illegitimacy of apartheid;

*it will facilitate the building of a culture of public ethics for the first time in South Africa and it will make room for genuine reconciliation;

*it will provide a basis for the necessary decriminalisation of the anti-apartheid resistance;

*it will ensure a sound basis for corrective action in dismantling the apartheid legacy;

*it will lay bare the roots of the violence that still plagues parts of the country;

*it will illuminate the longstanding humane values of the anti-apartheid resistance, for so long distorted by apartheid propagandists;

*it will demonstrate the morality of the armed struggle against apartheid;

*it will establish and underpin a new equality of all citizens before the law;

*it will place property rights on a secure and legitimate footing for the first time in our nation's history;

*it will enable privileged South Africans to face up to collective understanding and, therefore, responsibility for a past in which only they had voting rights;

*it will offer an acknowledgment of the wrongs done to the countries of southern Africa in the name of our country;

*it will clarify the important international implications of apartheid in the past and present, as well as acknowledging the correctness of international mobilisation against apartheid; and *finally, it will allow for a necessary process of historical catharsis as the previously excluded speak at last for themselves, and the privileged caste joins the South African family for the first time.

The exercise of facing the past is no mere luxury or optional extra; nor is it merely an attempt, as some have claimed, "to lift the veil on the untold story of the 'dirty war.'" This latter idea of the Truth Commission's work – that it should be a large-scale rewrite of Jacques Pauw's death squads exposé, *In the Heart of the Whore* – is a trivialisation. The exercise of facing the South African past, no mere horror story or exercise in historical voyeurism, is rather, in multiple ways including those listed above, a cornerstone of reconstruction.

The South African process of facing the past has, in fact, a more ambitious scope and set of goals than the similar processes elsewhere. Other efforts have sought to achieve an historically accurate picture of the past, or to confer amnesty, or to compensate victimrs. The South African Truth and Reconciliation Commission aims to achieve all of these together.

It is an extraordinary exercise, global in its significance, which has not yet received the kind of careful and relevant analysis that it deserves. So some important reasons for facing the past, each listed above and going far beyond the simple drama of storytelling, will be examined sequentially in the chapters that follow.

Achieving Justice Through Truth

"At 4.30 p m on the 17th of August, 1982, Ruth, relaxed, happy and waiting to share a farewell toast to a departing colleague, was killed instantly opening a Pretoria-prepared parcel bomb." Thus wrote the late Joe Slovo at the front of a small document personally signed and distributed by him in January 1983, following the assassination of his wife and companion Ruth First. Today the man who allegedly made that bomb contentedly runs a mattress shop, unrepentant; seemingly all has been laid to rest.

In preparing his document Joe compiled expressions not merely of condolence, but also of renewed political commitment, from colleagues and friends, heads of state, and numerous organisations. A memorial meeting of uMkhonto weSizwe (MK) combatants sent a message insisting that Ruth remained alive spiritually. "*Hamba Kahle*, Mama Ruth First," they said.

Afterwards, in meticulous acts of remembrance, Joe visited Ruth's grave annually on the 17th of August. Then one year Pretoria's death squad coordinator, perversely called the "Civil Cooperation Bureau," anticipating Joe's visit, put plastic explosives in a tin can under Ruth's gravestone. Evidently they hoped to kill Joe while incidentally obliterating Ruth again. They failed and Joe lived. Ruth's gravestone survived, but he could not safely return to her buried body. Apartheid forced his remembrance underground.

Undiscouraged, Joe predicted that soon "those who rule through torture and killing will be thrown on to the rubbish heap of history" and "the lives of people like Ruth will be celebrated openly in freedom and joy." On the back cover of Joe's memorial booklet, Ruth holds a brandy glass high in her concurring, undying, gesture of celebration.

For the new South Africa to abandon accurate remembrance in these early years of its birth would be the most cruel self-slaughter. The Truth and Reconciliation Commission will prevent that. It will provide the occasion to celebrate, in the full meaning of that word, i.e. to perform publicly and duly, to observe and honour with rites and festivities, to publish abroad, praise and extol. The Truth Commission must end the long and unjust decades of marginalised tribute. Justice must come out of the closet. It is part of what has been called "the battle to disclose the dead victim's moral claims,"[1] ignored, indeed defiled and rejected, by the previous system.

So there is a legitimate place for celebration, but not triumphalism, as we look back upon the South African past. In 1996, nearly eighteen months after Joe's own death, such a celebration was held on Ruth's birthday, 4 May, at Joe's grave in Soweto. The event commemorated Joe's life's work and its culmination as South Africa's first democratic Minister of Housing.

Again the mood in this remembrance was not merely of condolence but of celebration; and of gratitude for the lively "working legacy" that Joe and Ruth both left. With Soweto residents, President Mandela ceremonially danced around Joe's grave. The memorial stone unveiled on that day was beautifully sculpted, but also deliberately jagged-edged. It symbolised all the rough edges of every person's character, and also Joe's own unfinished political work in progress – the country's work, and the world's.

In Joe's 1983 memorial document, the Director General of UNESCO commented that Ruth's "writings and actions are imbued with truth and realism that cannot be obliterated by her physical disappearance." Likewise, following the assassination of Chris Hani in the last days of apartheid, Archbishop Tutu, now Chairperson of the Truth and Reconciliation Commission, commented that "his death is not a defeat. His death is our victory. His death is the victory of truth, the truth of liberation, that liberation is stronger than the lie of apartheid, that liberation is stronger than the injustice of apartheid, of its oppression and exploitation."[2]

So despite their bombing and their attempted re-bombing of her dead body, Ruth is not gone, not yet; likewise with the assassinated Chris Hani and the peacefully deceased survivor, Joe Slovo. What can kill her and them, and all of those who fought like them, are not guns and bombs but false remembrance. Genuine remembrance must renounce the hangman in order to celebrate the innocents hanged.

Joe Slovo's home-made fragment of remembrance must now find sustenance, and public presence, in the official acts of the Truth and Reconciliation Commission. South African Constitutional Court Judge Richard Goldstone, investigator of past political violence in South Africa and United Nations chief prosecutor in the war crimes trials in the former Yugoslavia, put the point well when he said that "fundamental to all forms of justice is official acknowledgment of what happened, whether by criminal process or by truth commission."[3] And such acknowledgment necessarily must include moral acknowledgment. To ensure that thousands of private and secret home-made monuments, like Joe's small document, receive public acknowledgment, we must face the horrors of the past. It is part of our indebtedness to those who fell for freedom.

This enriched form of justice is not merely a technical enterprise for the courts. More important than criminal prosecutions (of which there have been several and will be more) is the acknowledgment of today's indebtedness to those who were wrongly vilified, tortured, maimed and killed yesterday. In particular, justice as much includes the undoing of the unjust criminal prosecutions of the past as the establishment today of new findings of criminal guilt (by the courts) or moral and political responsibility (by the Truth and Reconciliation Commission).

Additionally, while there has been a widespread perception that the require-ments of justice conflict with the priority of national reconciliation, this idea is based on a false view of what reconciliation means. Properly understood, a just and moral appraisal of the past is the true life-blood of reconciliation (this point is carried further in chapter 6).

Archbishop Desmond Tutu commented optimistically, in the dark days of 1977, that "the powers of injustice, of oppression, of exploitation, have done their worst and they have lost. They have lost because they are immoral and wrong and . . . our cause, the cause of justice and liberation, must triumph because it is moral and just and right."4

Twenty years later – twenty years! – Archbishop Tutu reflected, in 1996, of his role in leading the Truth and Reconciliation Commission, that "it would be very difficult, as someone who has fought for justice for all those years, to find myself now involved in injustice." He has also commented that "despite all appearances to the contrary," the collective faith that justice would prevail had survived the darkest hours of the past.5 It would be a chilling defeat if justice, which survived the unlikely circumstances of the lean years, were to perish now in these new times of relative ease, through a misapprehension on the part of the Truth and Reconciliation Commission about its work.

The Promotion of National Unity and Reconciliation Act, which establishes the Truth and Reconciliation Commission, should provide a useful window into apartheid and an important vehicle for arriving at justice through a clear-sighted and ethically decisive grasp of the truth about the past.

Yet this fact has not always been understood in public commentary on, and interpretation of, the Act. It is ironic that such an Act, avowedly designed to assist the moral and political rebalancing of the new South Africa, should have become bogged down in cramped interpretation and pedantry reminiscent of the old South Africa's methods of legal interpretation.

Foremost among these old-guard interpretations is the idea that the Act some-how binds the Commissioners to set aside their basic human faculties of moral judgment. The idea has arisen that the Commissioners will face moral dilem-mas, because they are bound, we are told, by an Act which makes no distinction between apartheid and its opposite. But in fact neither international practice, nor the Act itself, forbids such distinctions.

There are many precedents for making such distinctions. In reviewing the conduct of anti-Nazi plotters who inadvertently endangered or harmed civilians when they were planning to assassinate Hitler, one cannot ignore the real dif-ferences of goals and ideals between the plotters and their target. In fact, no sig-nificant historian of Nazi rule and of the resistance to it throughout Europe – in Italy, France, the Netherlands or Denmark, let alone Eastern Europe – even sug-gests such an equivalence. Those who oppose differentiating between apartheid and the resistance to it have yet to state a convincing moral or legal basis for adopting such an approach in South Africa.

14

It is far easier, for those bent upon perverse doctrines of indifferentism, to equate Auschwitz with Hiroshima (where, unlike Nagasaki, there were few significant military targets to justify extraordinary civilian death tolls) than to equate apartheid with its opposite. All such schematic balancing acts must be rejected in facing the South African past, just as the attempts by US President Reagan and German Chancellor Kohl, in 1986, to equate their visit to SS graves at Bitburg cemetery with their simultaneous remembrance of Holocaust victims, caused a justified worldwide uproar at the time.

At the level of statutory interpretation, it is wrong to argue that the Act, in adjudicating what counts as a human rights violation, makes no moral distinction between apartheid and its opposite. In fact the Act provides, in its section governing the actions of the Commission when dealing with victims, that "victims shall be treated equally and without discrimination of any kind, including race, colour, gender, sex, sexual orientation, age, language, religion, nationality, political or other opinion, cultural beliefs or practices, property, birth or family status, ethnic or social origin or disability."

This is a narrow and simple requirement of fair play in listening to people who have suffered in the past. It means that individuals who suffered collateral injury or human rights abuses at the hands of the resistance should not, on that basis, receive discriminatory audience from the Commission. The victims in question will generally have been private citizens; in some cases they may, rightly or wrongly, have been accused of spying for the benefit of apartheid. In no case should the prior occupation or alleged occupation of victims lead the Truth and Reconciliation Commission to discriminate against them as it hears their story.

However, such a right of non-discriminatory audience is hardly a sufficient peg on which to hang the view that the Commission is prohibited from making value judgements between the causes in the advancement of which serious mistakes were made or abuses committed, and indeed between the different circumstances that gave rise to the misdeeds. (The real differences between the two sides of the conflict constitute a major theme of this book.)

In setting out the objectives of the Commission, section 3(1) of the Act provides that it shall establish "as complete a picture as possible of the causes, nature and extent of the gross violations of human rights which were committed . . . including the antecedents, circumstances, factors and context of such violations, as well as the perspectives of the victims and the motives and perspectives of the persons responsible for the commission of the violations, by conducting investigations and holding hearings."

Presenting a full picture of the perspectives and motives of both sides is not the same as abandoning relevant moral judgements between them. In fact it is the exact opposite of that.

Clearly one can, for example, attempt to present a full picture of German Nazi perspectives and motives in order to demonstrate the reasons for condemning them. Indeed, any truly complete picture of Nazi motives and perspectives will demand condemnation. To decline a moral condemnation when the full facts scream exactly for that is to join in a business of exculpation; it is to put on, intentionally or otherwise, the garb of the apologist. It is to enter upon not merely a moral dilemma, but actual immorality.

Fortunately, press reports have suggested that most of the Commissioners are aware of such realities and are "flabbergasted" by assertions to the contrary. The idea that the Act imposes moral dilemmas on the Commissioners as they evaluate apartheid is perverse; properly read, the Act imposes no such fetters.

In fact it actively calls for the opposite. The Preamble and the Act itself repeatedly require a "restoration of the human and civil dignity of victims of human rights violations." This task surely cannot be achieved by suggesting to victims of apartheid abuses that the thing they were fighting against was morally indistinguishable from what they were fighting for. The world was certainly under no such illusion. The Western-dominated United Nations Security Council itself reaffirmed, on the day following the 16 June 1976 Soweto uprising, that apartheid was "a crime against the conscience and dignity of mankind and seriously disturbs international peace and security."

Moreover, where the victims were injured by the resistance, it is an insult to them to suggest that the restoration of their dignity hinges upon an historical rehabilitation of apartheid and its apparatus of violence. *No victim of human rights misdeeds of the anti-apartheid resistance has made this claim, or would make this claim.* It is instead advanced in a self-serving fashion only by the old pilots of apartheid, taking renewed advantage of the pain of innocents.

It would be helpful that such victims understand what exactly drove the resistance towards measures that inflicted collateral casualties. They need to understand the unpredictable nature of resistance and the difficulties of preserving command and control structures while also on the run from the very state that ought to be a secure home.

As detailed below, the apartheid regime deployed its massive resources with deliberate and systematic violence. By contrast, the anti-apartheid resistance committed sporadic lapses, due to its material deprivation and refugee status, as well as the fear and paranoia induced by the regime's battery of "dirty tricks" and its tactics of infiltration. Ordinary tactics were not an option for the resistance; the regime, which had that option, rejected it and instead intentionally embraced abnormal measures.

These truths will be lost if the Truth and Reconciliation Commission's final report blurs them behind imprecise language and moral indifferentism, driven by a mistaken view that the relevant law creates statutory moral "dilemmas."

A related misconception is the idea that applicants to the Truth and Reconciliation Commission have almost an automatic amnesty right under section 20 of the Act. This section provides that the Amnesty Committee "shall" grant amnesty if "it is satisfied that" the amnesty application "complies with the requirements of this Act," that the act was associated with a political objective, and that the applicant has made "full disclosure of all relevant facts."

This section has given rise to the view that the Truth and Reconciliation Commission has no discretion to decline a grant of amnesty should a particular perpetrator fail to show remorse or contrition in respect of the acts confessed. This view implies that a perpetrator of apartheid abuses could hypothetically come before the Commission and unrepentantly relate a horrifying tale of murder, torture and misdeeds, which would automatically qualify him or her for amnesty. Truth Commissioners are said to have been brought to tears when informed of this alleged statutory requirement.

But this view vastly understates the creative discretion of the Commission in general. The authority of the Commission, as stated in section 3(2) of the Act, includes a power "to investigate or make recommendations concerning *any matter* with a view to promoting or achieving national unity and reconciliation within the context of this Act" (emphasis added).

This power to make recommendations surely includes recommendations as to the Commission's own internal affairs; its own housekeeping. If the Commission is of the view that a contrition requirement would advance the stated goals of reconciliation and national unity, then its Amnesty Committee, cooperating if necessary with its Reparations Committee (see discussion of section 3(1)(c) below), has ample statutory discretion to impose a contrition requirement in its amnesty procedures. A contrary interpretation would undermine an overriding aim of the Act, which is to restore the human and civil dignity of the victims.

Additionally, the Commission is empowered by section 3(1)(c) of the Act to make recommendations as to reparation measures in respect of human rights abuses. Reparation is defined in section 1(1)(xiv) of the Act as including "any form of compensation, *ex gratia* payment, restitution, rehabilitation or *recognition*" (emphasis added). Apology is the most obvious form of reparation or "recognition" and could surely be imposed by the Commissioners, should they so choose, as a precondition to a grant of amnesty; nothing in the Act precludes such action by the Amnesty Committee. Moreover, the Act's definition of "reparations" is not an exclusive one, as it merely includes the forms stated, but is not limited to them. Thus an apology or contrition requirement would seem an admissible form of reparation in its own right.

Crucial to this suggestion that the Act gives the Commission a discretion, should it so choose, to decline amnesty to an unrepentant perpetrator, is the fact that the statute does not give perpetrators any automatic right of amnesty. Automatic amnesty was in fact demanded during the negotiations in 1993, and was aggressively advocated from certain quarters during the public and parliamentary debate surrounding the Act in 1994 and 1995. Yet the idea of any such automatic amnesty right was unambiguously rejected in the Act: under section 19(4), the Amnesty Committee has a decisive role, based on a plurality of factors, in "granting or refusing amnesty." Should the Commission so choose, the Act leaves it ample room, in practice and should the need arise, to ensure that victims are not subjected to the indignity and new pain of unrepentant perpetrators exploiting the Act's amnesty mechanisms while openly flouting its goals of reconciliation.

A further area of concern is the increasing judicialisation of the Truth and Reconciliation Commission's proceedings. In fact the Commission owes its existence in part to a rejection of the judicial option for dealing with the past, which could have involved holding Nuremberg-style trials of the officials of the old order. There are a number of sound reasons for this decision.

While apartheid South Africa was not formally a military dictatorship, the military had become increasing powerful. The National Security Management System, which the regime set up in the 1980s, was described by parliamentarian Helen Suzman as a "sort of creeping *coup d'état* by consent, in which accountable politicians have abrogated their power to non-accountable members of the security forces."[6]

The generals were thus in an exceptionally powerful position. In the lead-up to the 1994 elections, with the growth of the extreme right and the bombings and other incidents, the political atmosphere became increasingly overheated, veering almost daily from euphoric expectation of change to sombre fears of right-wing intentions. The resistance movement effectively calmed the country, most notably after the assassination of prominent ANC leader Chris Hani. Because of this success, the resistance was able to reject the apartheid regime's attempts to secure a general blanket amnesty for its functionaries prior to the election. The resistance insisted that the apartheid regime could not be allowed to grant amnesty to itself.

Nevertheless, as a product of negotiated revolution, the newly elected democratic government understood that there was no certainty that it could succeed in imposing victors' justice, even had it wished to do so. It faced the risk that to test the limits of the political balance of forces in order to punish individuals would result in what has been called "justice with ashes." Hence the rejection of that approach.

There could be no summary trials and executions of torturers as there were in the German concentration camps; no Nuremberg trials. There have been no purges, no vindictive "lustration laws" on the recent Czech model, which disqualify certain persons, allegedly from the old order, from holding categories of public or private office – without a semblance of judicial process. There has been no blacklisting of collaborators, as in post-war France and Belgium; nor any dismissals of apartheid social engineers or university academics as in today's unified Germany or yesterday's de-Nazification measures. Such approaches were rejected by South African negotiators and legislators for practical as well as principled reasons.

For reasons of principle also, the triumphalist approach of victors' justice, with its inevitable selectiveness and political opportunism, was rejected in favour of ideals of nation-building and reconciliation between the oppressors and the previously oppressed. (The widely misunderstood meaning of reconciliation, its actually onerous demands on the former oppressor, are discussed in detail in chapter 6.)

This rejection was consistent with the longstanding humanist ideals of the anti-apartheid resistance, unmatchably expressed by Chief Albert Luthuli, who was the ANC's President at the time of its banning in 1960. He frequently pointed out that it would have been easy, under apartheid, for a black chauvinism to have arisen as a counterweight to systematic white arrogance and rejection of blacks; and that such a result had been avoided, not by accident, but through the express ANC rejection of all forms of "racial vaingloriousness."

In addition, and most relevantly to the present discussion of the Truth and Reconciliation statute and its procedures, a judicial process would have focused too much on the perpetrators to the exclusion of the victims; it would have overly individualised the horrors of apartheid and provided merely a piecemeal picture of the past, at the expense of necessary attention to its systemic and collective evils.

The Nuremberg trials, after all, reached only a few perpetrators. Many prominent Nazis fled the country, and others remained in positions of authority, escaping any kind of accountability. The Nazi courts continued seamlessly into the post-Nazi era, without having to face any fundamental reorientation of approach. The conduct of criminal trials, in South Africa too, inevitably places the prosecutorial bureaucracies of the old order in a position of enormous influence. This is hardly an ideal way to make a new start.

Moreover, ordinary Germans themselves remained wholly outside the Nuremberg trial process. Rather than taking the measure of their own responsibility for historic and collective events (see further, page 144), they could too easily escape self-probing by simply parroting the world's demonisation of the few in the dock.

Furthermore, over-judicialisation of the South African process would have resulted in a time-consuming and expensive process of facing the past, as we have seen in the abortive inquests of the past and in the well-publicised trials of hit squad commanders in the present. Consequently, the negotiators of the new South African Parliament deliberately decided upon a non-judicial forum that would allow the country to confront and renounce its past without placing unreasonable demands on the resources of the new country.

Additionally, a judicial process would have meant new ordeals for victims, through for example cross-examination, rather than a cathartic experience.

The particular kind of credibility that derives from criminal trials may be inappropriate for historical verdicts. The necessity to prove the minutiae of individual cases beyond a reasonable doubt in an elaborate and formal process can establish an uneven playing-field in favour of the perpetrators; and it can constipate historical debates. Moreover, it is common knowledge that there is often a difference between a criminal verdict of "not guilty" and an affirmative finding of innocence. Thus history suffers if viewed through a judicial lens.

Conversely, processes of criminal justice suffer if made to bear the weight of history. For example, the Charter for the Tokyo Trials, which were to Japan what the Nuremberg Trials were to Germany, provided that "the tribunal shall not be bound by technical rules of evidence . . . and shall admit any evidence that it deems to have probative value." This gave the courts naked discretion to reach politically expedient results, undermining in the eyes of the Japanese public the particular kind of credibility that the rules of evidence generally confer upon judicial proceedings.

Moreover, as one commentator has pointed out, the need to prove the particular facts relevant to narrow and specific criminal guilt can lead prosecutors to over-emphasise those facts or arguments relevant to the technical charge as laid – at the expense of undoubted or valuable historical realities.[7]

For example, the emphasis at Nuremberg on proving the charge of plotting a war of aggression against other states – a charge, incidentally, of geopolitical interest to the allied victors – led to a downplaying of the Nazi war against the Jews. Thus Justice Robert H Jackson, the US Chief Prosecutor, acting as a competent lawyer, was constrained to argue that the Jews were merely used as exemplars of Nazi discipline and that their persecution eliminated an obstacle to aggressive war.

Such an argument placed history on the altar of prosecutorial expediency. It was a clear understatement of the place of virulent anti-semitism as a distinct driving force of Nazism. Thus, building the legal case for the particular narrow charges as laid can lead to a putting of the historical cart before the horse. Jackson's argument was roughly the equivalent of a claim that apartheid's suppression of blacks removed an obstacle in the way of the regime's plans for aggressive war against the front line states – exactly the wrong historical relation of cause to effect.

Yet because the Nuremberg Trials, with their lavish and conveniently organised documentary records, exerted enormous influence over the early historiography of Nazism, the resultant imbalances in the historical record were only corrected after years of research and debate.

Those who would insist on criminal prosecution in South Africa seek to dismiss the fore-going concerns as merely "sociological" as opposed to legal.[8] They claim that international law mandates automatic prosecution of apartheid offences, with no room whatsoever for a diversity of approaches in dealing with the past. As we outline below (chapter 16), apartheid indeed comprised an extensive and diverse practice of international outlawry. But to suggest that the only legally valid response to this conduct is the inflexible prosecution of offenders is to misunderstand the nature and sources of international law.

International law – and this is its strength – is built upon the practice of states and not upon narrow legalisms. Large parts of it express the collective norms of humanity, norms that do not require – for such would be contradictory – an indifference to human consequences. No rule of international law requires the pursuit of perpetrators regardless of the risk of reducing the body politic to ashes. This is a large subject and could in itself form an entire study, which is not our present purpose. In this context, it is enough to note that the practice of states in dealing with atrocious pasts amidst democratic transitions, notably in

Latin America, confirms the view that there is no established practice of pursuing prosecutions at the cost of destroying a country.

In South Africa, the interim constitution, under which the historic 1994 elections were held, contained an explicit coda (known as its post-amble) warning the country against the risks of pursuing strategies of vengeance or victimisation at the expense of the new country's flourishing (captured in the constitution by the African word *ubuntu*, implying both "compassion" and "recognition of the humanity of the other"). Those who insist upon automatic trials as the only legitimate manner in which to mete out justice generally ignore this novel constitutional concept of ubuntu. It is not enough to demand systematic trials as the automatic means of dealing with the past; one must demonstrate also that the trials-only approach would maximise the underlying value of ubuntu.

Moreover, even in those countries where prosecutions have in fact been the chosen route for dealing with the past, the nature and extent of such trials has remained guided by concerns of societal welfare. The very manner of implementation of past war crimes tribunals reflects a guiding concern with sociological consequences; there has never been a trials-at-all-costs fundamentalism.

The Japanese Emperor Hirohito was, as subsequent research has confirmed, an active architect of Japan's wartime atrocities.[9] Nevertheless, based on the military strategic advice of General MacArthur, Hirohito was deliberately excluded from the lists of the accused at the Tokyo Trials. MacArthur feared that to put the revered figure of the Emperor on trial would move the Japanese population from sullen acquiescence in the trials (as in fact occurred) to outright resistance and guerrilla warfare. Thus "sociological" factors drove the scope of the prosecutions. Similarly, Cold War concerns and the need to consolidate the NATO alliance led to a post-war evaporation of interest in prosecuting German collaborators with the Nazis. One can criticise the influence that these extraneous factors exerted on judicial proceedings, but one cannot deny their presence. Thus sociological factors impact upon the implementation of judicial proceedings no less than upon the choice between judicial and non-judicial mechanisms for dealing with the past.

It is ironic that the calls for a prosecution-centred approach to past human rights abuses – and the contemptuous dismissal of "mere" sociological counter-arguments – is presented as a form of progressive politics. For the idea that a bright line divides law and sociology and separates law from politics is itself a recognised reactionary falsehood in legal academia today. Those who assert that a wall separates law and politics urge, in general, that judges should be oblivious to the social consequences of their decisions. It is a view that civilised jurisprudence – all law, not only international law – must reject. A preferable starting point is that law's highest purpose is to serve societal ends.

It is vital for everyone, most of all the Truth Commissioners themselves, to keep such rationales in mind as the work of the Truth and Reconciliation Commission continues in the shadow of two sorts of legal challenges that have been launched against the Commission, as well as certain legal initiatives undertaken by the Commission itself.

First, some victims and relatives of victims have challenged the constitutionality of the amnesty sections of the Act, which remove the possibility of criminal or civil recourse against perpetrators. These legal challenges essentially echo the academic advocates of an automatically prosecution-focused approach to dealing with the past, while additionally rejecting the Truth Commission's ability to extinguish civil liability.

Second, perpetrators themselves have initiated legal actions designed to enforce a judicialisation of the commission's procedures, insisting on rights to notification and discovery of documents if their names are to be mentioned and also suggesting that there ought to be rights of cross-examination of victims.

Finally, far from resisting these moves towards judicialisation, the Truth Commission itself has furthered the process. Where facts have emerged seeming to implicate individuals, the Commission has proposed initiating subpoenas of them rather than waiting for criminal charges to be laid by the responsible attorneys general. The Commission has argued that to wait upon the criminal justice processes would take "forever."

These three categories of legal activity surrounding the Truth and Reconciliation Commission introduce a number of avoidable anomalies and pieces of illogic, each of which will be discussed in turn.

There are, first of all, the victims' constitutional challenges. These are understandable and raise a genuine dilemma worthy of sombre reflection and of a considered response. The anti-apartheid struggle was a collective struggle conducted, as always, by committed organisations and individuals, some of whom fell victim to it on the way. The entire exercise of the Truth and Reconciliation Commission is one of collective homage to these individuals, sung and unsung; and of empathy with the victims of the anti-apartheid resistance's missteps.

By the same token, the goals of the progressive movement in dismantling apartheid today remain collective goals. The same logic of sacrifice that drove our fallen resisters towards collective efforts in the past also suggests that our acknowledgment of their personal grief should not sacrifice their own continuing societal project, their work in progress, of which we remain the living embodiment. To act otherwise would be to dismantle, not fulfil, the working legacies that they left us.

There have in fact been ordinary criminal trials concerning past apartheid abuses; and more such trials may be initiated where the perpetrators of injustice fail to bring their stories to the Truth and Reconciliation Commission, seeking amnesty. Without such amnesty, they leave themselves open to prosecution or the civil law suits of victims. However, it is remarkable how few of the survivors of past injustices today suggest that judicial punishment should be pursued regardless of damage to collective efforts to strengthen democratic institutions.

Moreover, success in the one goal of consolidating democracy actually enhances our ability to pursue the other goal, the punishment of perpetrators.

It is no accident that upon his arrest on a charge of organising hit squads, apartheid's Defence Minister Magnus Malan's first (and unsuccessful) tactic was to warn that his arrest marked a dark day for democracy. Where democracy is weak, his kind is untouchable. What is wonderful about his comments is their lack of effect. Democracy held firm and his trial continues; the polity is unruffled and Malan's sort is isolated. This outcome would not have been certain in the early weeks and months after the 1994 election.

So it is necessary to strike a balance. The confession and renunciation of past violence by its perpetrators can strengthen democracy immeasurably. This means that there must be apology and renunciation of past atrocities as a precondition of amnesty. But once that is done it may well be reasonable to suggest that extinguishing further civil and criminal remedies would be, all things considered, a difficult but necessary price to pay in pursuance of the underlying goals of consolidating democracy. This was the view ultimately reached by the Constitutional Court in adjudicating on this matter in July 1996. In upholding the Act, the Court noted that dealing effectively with the legacy of the past "is an exercise of immense difficulty interacting in a vast network of political, emotional, ethical and logistical considerations."

No one can dictate to the aggrieved survivors that this should be taken as an acceptable state of affairs. It is not a view that can be stated glibly or even with a degree of comfort; and it should be kept under constant review (remembering that the Truth and Reconciliation Commission itself is not automatically required to grant amnesty). But in the final analysis it is a defensible view.

Another, very different, set of legal challenges has been raised by perpetrators who would themselves like to judicialise the proceedings of the Truth Commission. They want to put victims through new ordeals of cross-examination and they want a whole panoply of pseudo-judicial safeguards to blight the Truth and Reconciliation Commission's proceedings. The response to these attacks is straightforward: those perpetrators who would turn the Truth and Reconciliation proceedings into quasi-trials run the risk of finding themselves in the midst of real trials; they revive the logic of the Nuremberg approach and invite systematic trials for political and human rights offences.

The Truth and Reconciliation Commission lacks a prosecutorial function precisely because it lacks the procedural safeguards necessary to determine individual guilt or innocence. If those safeguards are built into the process by judicial *fiat*, then the question arises: why should the Commission not pronounce on individual guilt or innocence, converting itself into a full-blown war crimes tribunal that recommends criminal and civil sanctions, or even – by statute – is empowered to impose them? If judicialised procedures are insisted upon, with all the expense and delay they entail, the arguments in favour of judicialised outcomes (findings by the Truth Commission of individual guilt or of civil liability) are enhanced. Judicialising the procedures inexorably judicialises the substance – or ought to.

But since this approach has already been rejected in the 1995 legislation and ought not, for the reasons discussed above, actually to be revived, there is one ideal way to deal with calls for judicialising the Truth and Reconciliation proceedings: ignore them.

Instructions in favour of a judicialised process are, however, impossible to ignore when they come by way of the court order, as in certain recent instances. Perversely, such judicial instructions – and the manner in which the Commission implemented them – have led to criminal proceedings for contempt of court being laid against Archbishop Tutu and other senior commission officials. We have been subjected to the wholly inappropriate spectacle of Archbishop Tutu entering a plea, through his lawyers, for a fine or a suspended sentence.

A procedure meant to expose and unwind the criminality of the past is being hijacked by the perpetrators in order to criminalise, yet again, some of the most eminent and respected among the anti-apartheid movement. This is in itself a sufficient reason to eschew the overjudicialised direction of some aspects of the proceedings to date. The solution here is for the Truth and Reconciliation Commission to seek advance certification of its procedures from the Constitutional Court. It should do that.

Finally – and oddly – senior Truth and Reconciliation Commission officials have themselves supported reference to the courts. They have recommended the subpoena of perpetrators named during Truth and Reconciliation Commission proceedings and have done so on the express basis that this is a better (because faster) path than that of criminal prosecution by Attorneys General in the ordinary way.

The illogic of this approach is striking, especially when combined with the erroneous view, held by some of these same officials, that the Commission must give amnesty even in the absence of contrition (a view which, as argued above, is incorrect). It would mean that a perpetrator could be brought before the Commission involuntarily, tell all unrepentantly, and leave with amnesty.

This approach discards the core ideas of voluntary confession, the renunciation of bad ways, and of reconciliation within humane norms. Instead it turns the Commission into an unsatisfactory hybrid organ of mild punishment (involuntary subpoena) and wholesale exculpation (amnesty without contrition). It undoes the sound early logic that underlay the idea of a Truth and Reconciliation Commission. According to that logic, a looming threat of criminal prosecution in the ordinary courts would furnish an incentive for perpetrators to approach the Commission on a voluntary basis and seek reconciliation through genuine contrition.

Moreover, every person who testifies by subpoena has an automatic and costly right to legal representation, which itself will increase the length and complexity of the testimony, unnecessarily inflating, again, the overall cost and administrative burdens placed on the Commission – and on the scarce resources of the new country.

None of this need mean that the subpoena and other quasi-judicial powers of the Commission ought simply to be ignored or entirely disused. The search and seizure powers are, for instance, potentially vital in avoiding the problems experienced by previous inquiries, which sat by powerlessly as crucial evidence was concealed and even destroyed. The subpoena power itself may have uses in a range of ancillary ways; but certainly it ought not to be used to dragoon impenitent perpetrators into pretended rituals of reconciliation.

A final heresy that has been in circulation about the operations of the Commission is the claim that the statute "screens out" abuses that were nominally lawful under apartheid: such as detentions, bannings, forced removals. In fact the statute does no such thing. Its functions, set out in section 4 of the Act, include the investigation of "gross violations of human rights, including violations which were part of a systematic pattern of abuse." The latter phrase could be read as a wholesale reference to the entire edifice of apartheid, including the abuses listed above in this paragraph.

Moreover, the term "gross violation of human rights" is broadly (and accurately) defined in the Act to include any violation through "killing, abduction, torture or severe ill-treatment of any person" or "any attempt, conspiracy, incitement, instigation, command or procurement" to commit the foregoing. If the term abduction is not sufficient to include, for example, forced removals at gunpoint, then the phrase "severe ill-treatment" certainly fills that gap, and captures much else besides.

Additionally, the statutory definition of the term "victims" includes those "who, individually or together with one or more persons, suffered harm in the form of physical or mental injury, emotional suffering, pecuniary loss or *substantial impairment of human rights*" (emphasis added). The latter term is usefully broader than "gross" violations of human rights. The term "emotional suffering" is broader still.

Again, the Commission is mandated to "facilitate, and where necessary initiate or coordinate, inquiries into . . . the nature, causes and extent of gross violations of human rights, including the antecedents, circumstances, factors, context, motives and perspectives which led to such violations"; as well as into the "accountability, political or otherwise, for any such violation," among other things.

These responsibilities, particularly of inquiry into "causes" and into political accountability, place crucial questions of moral and political responsibility on the agenda of the Truth and Reconciliation Commission. It must investigate – or "initiate" such investigations by third parties – and reach conclusions as to the primary causes of South Africa's past troubles.

It must make a finding, for instance, as to whether the soldiers of the anti-apartheid resistance were murderous initiators of violence; or whether, rather, the primary violence in the old South Africa was that of apartheid, to which the resistance reacted. Such questions of causation are necessarily moral and political ones. And the statute mandates the Truth and Reconciliation Commission to provide the country with its conclusions on these issues.

In short, the scope of investigation within the Truth and Reconciliation Commission's purview as defined in the Act embraces the entire range of those individual and collective abuses as well as the moral and historical issues that are generally taken to have comprised the system of apartheid and its consequences in their entirety. Absolutely nothing is ruled out by statutory *fiat*; in fact everything is expressly included.

What this potentially creates is a practical problem: how can the Commission hear witnesses and effectively investigate the entire historical anatomy of apartheid as well as millions of individual cases, in only two years? The answer is that it need not. Even in that most fact-specific and sensitive area – the granting of amnesty to individuals – the Amnesty Committee may dispense with a hearing in granting or refusing amnesty and may choose to rely on the written application of the perpetrator.

By analogy, in its large tasks of evaluating and stating conclusions on the historical atrocities of apartheid, the Truth and Reconciliation Commission need not reinvent the wheel. It can rely on and distil the vast amounts of existing historical, sociological, legal and other research. And it may "initiate" and "coordinate" such research or synthesis by third parties, such as universities or nongovernmental organisations. These powers to initiate and coordinate such work should not remain unutilised.

What the Truth and Reconciliation Commission must ensure is that in reaching its overall judgements it touches all the necessary bases. Among other things, the present book is an attempt at such a synthesis, guided by the authors' own collective sense of the defining contours of apartheid.

The Truth and Reconciliation Commission need not attempt original or pathbreaking historical analysis; but nor may it avoid historical evaluation and historical judgement. To do otherwise would be to abandon whole swathes of its explicit statutory mandate. This would amount to a dereliction of duties; not only legal duties, but moral and political ones, too.

The Truth and Reconciliation Commission has an august role, a specific function beyond the ordinary norms and procedures of crime and punishment. It must not become ensnared in the banalities of subpoenas and cross examination, nor in the narrow business of determining individual guilt or innocence. We already have courts that can do that.

Nor must the Truth and Reconciliation Commission convert itself, or some form of itself, into a permanent bureaucracy. An important goal of the commission is to act as a catalyst for swift and thorough disclosures of past horrors, in order to accelerate – and so eventually end – the steady and corrosive drip of past pathologies into the new order. Every week it seems that new tales of violence, corruption, illicit arms trade or other misdeeds emerge piecemeal. The Commission is meant to speed up this slow drip of pathology and ensure that it is dealt with in a comprehensive and decisive fashion, so that the country can afterwards continue on a healthy growth path. To make the Commission a permanent body or to extend its period of operation would undermine this goal.

In any event, the brief span of the Truth and Reconciliation Commission's life need not leave an institutional gap. Institutions like the Human Rights Commission and the Gender Commission already have a permanent existence as human rights watchdogs. For the Truth and Reconciliation Commission to become another such body would be duplicative and would remove the Commission's distinctive and rarefied role. It would let boredom in upon magic, and would deprive the Commission of its best chance to change the nation's paradigm of itself through a short, sharp hammer blow of a new beginning.

Acknowledging the Illegitimacy of Apartheid

"My friends, we are marching to victory. We are marching to the victory of freedom over the oppression of apartheid. We are marching to victory, the victory of justice over the injustice of apartheid. We are marching to victory, the victory of light over the darkness of apartheid. We are marching to victory, the victory of life over the death of apartheid. We are marching to victory, the victory of truth over the lie, the corruption, the deceit of apartheid. We are marching to victory, the victory of goodness over the evil of apartheid. We are marching to victory, the victory of gentleness, of kindness, over the harshness of apartheid. We are marching to victory, the victory of goodness, of compassion, over the cruelty of apartheid. We are marching to victory, the victory of compassion and sharing over the competitiveness, the selfishness of apartheid. We are marching to victory, the victory of peace and reconciliation over the violence and alienation of apartheid."

– Archbishop Desmond Tutu, address at Chris Hani's funeral (April, 1993).

A second reason for facing the past is the need for a sustained awareness of the illegitimacy of apartheid and the need to march resolutely away from it – an exercise that requires stamina and deliberation. It is already fashionable among privileged South Africans to concede apartheid's moral and political weaknesses. Few can be found to admit that they supported apartheid in the past. New generations may well find it difficult to believe that such injustices were ever perpetrated, while even now some of the excesses of apartheid seem so extreme, so absurd and susceptible to mockery, that we can forget the real human pain that individuals suffered.

A prime example of the horror and absurdity of apartheid was its legislation dividing the people of South Africa into four major racial groups, and a variety of sub-groups. These laws led to the break-up of families, suicide and tragedy. Such were the consequences of apartheid's deliberate cradle-to-grave categorisation of each person's status and role in life.

Looking back, it is hard to believe that in the South Africa of 1985, in the sunset of race-classification, by official decree and duly gazetted, the following occurred:

*702 "Coloureds" turned white;
*10 Whites became "Coloured";

*one Indian became white;
*three Chinese became White;
*50 Indians became "Coloured";
*43 "Coloureds" turned into Indians;
*21 Indians became Malay;
*30 Malays went Indian;
*249 Africans became "Coloured";
*20 "Coloureds" became Africans;
*two Africans became "other Asians";
*one African was classified Griqua;
*11 "Coloureds" became Chinese;
*three "Coloureds" went Malay;
*one Chinese became "Coloured";
*eight Malays became "Coloured";
*three Africans were classed as Malay.
No Africans became white, and no whites became Africans.[1]

In a healthy (or merely sane) intellectual climate, there would have been no need for the "long period of deep self-analysis"[2] which, according to former Deputy President de Klerk, led to his party's eventual decision, four decades after apartheid's electoral triumph, to question what the United Nations had for decades recognised as a crime against humanity, a form of genocide, something akin to slavery. So what was it that for so long got in the way? Why was the manifest illegitimacy of the system so hard for people to see? Or was its illegitimacy simply and wantonly ignored? This is the single most important oddity that the Truth and Reconciliation Commission must resolve.

Fortunately, the answer is not hard to find. As the novelist Joseph Conrad observed in his *Heart of Darkness*, "the conquest of the earth, which mostly means the taking it away from those who have a different complexion or slightly flatter noses than ourselves [sic], is not a pretty thing when you look at it too much. What redeems it is the idea only. An idea at the back of it; not a sentimental pretence but an idea; and an unselfish belief in the idea – something you can set up, and bow down before, and offer sacrifices to."

The specifically South African variant of this grand idea is the view that apartheid, according to the Verwoerdian doctrine, had idealistic origins; that it was meant to secure the flourishing of all groups under a well-meaning policy of "separate development"; and that what fell down was its implementation: that it was proven merely unworkable (not evil) in the end. Such views are a final desecration of those who fell victim to apartheid's wilful violence.

And yet, even today, they command a constituency among the South African privileged. "If I steal, I'm guilty. If I kill somebody, I'm guilty. But if I'm living an idea which I think has got merit, then I don't think I'm guilty,'[3] said Gert Engelbrecht, a privileged South African in the town of Potgietersrus, which in early 1996 was at the heart of a bitter controversy over racially integrated schooling. It was an unconscious and virtually verbatim restatement of the classic Conradian imperialist creed.

In reality, apartheid was idealistic only if the self-seeking machinations of a ruling elite can be called idealism. Those who developed the philosophy of apartheid in the 1930s were very clear as to its purpose. "The primary consideration," wrote the Broederbond's chairman, Professor J C van Rooy, in 1934, "is whether Afrikanerdom will reach its ultimate destiny of domination in South Africa."4 This was the familiar hubris – not idealism – of a self-styled master race. It was easily recognisable as such abroad. The international community saw very early that, in the words of the UN General Assembly's Resolution 395 on South Africa in 1950, "a policy of 'racial segregation' (*Apartheid*) is necessarily based on doctrines of racial discrimination."

Only its South African architects attempt to argue that apartheid had idealistic origins. It is part of a strategy to whitewash apartheid and thus blunt the new country's determination to dismantle its legacy.

The National Party of the 1990s, although claiming to have broken with its predecessors, actually hoped, during the political transition, merely to update the old order rather than renounce it. Even after his watershed speech in February 1990, F W de Klerk cautioned the world that it should not expect him "to negotiate himself out of power." He told the Transvaal National Party congress in October 1990 that his party had no intention of being what he called "sellouts." The claim that he favoured black majority rule, he said, was "one of the great untruths" of the time. Instead, clearly, his commitment to power-sharing meant the effective perpetuation of white rule through white vetoes at the legislative and executive levels.5

These attempts to forestall the end of apartheid failed, yet we are insistently told by Mr de Klerk that apartheid "started as idealism in the quest for justice" and had to be abandoned only because it "could not attain justice for all South Africans." In 1993, shortly before receiving the Nobel Peace Prize, Mr de Klerk told *Time* magazine that "separate development was morally justifiable."6

He further stated in 1992 that as a student he had supported apartheid "with great idealism"; that the architects of apartheid were well-intentioned and that "condemnation of people who had good intentions I think should be avoided ... My father was one of them. He wasn't a bad man. He was a good Christian."7

Hitler too had good intentions – towards the Aryan race, which was nevertheless ill-served by his attentions. The world beyond South Africa could see beyond the profane good intentions of the South African Aryans. Their protestations of idealism were rejected. It was hardly by oversight that the Nobel Peace Prize-givers failed to make their 1960 award a joint one to both ANC President Albert Luthuli and apartheid's architect and then prime minister H F Verwoerd. There were not two idealisms at issue between apartheid and its opposite, only one.

While Mr de Klerk has expressed his "deep regret" about apartheid, which he repeated in Parliament in February 1996, he has yet to concede, as leader of the

National Party, that apartheid was rotten at its core and in its inception; that it was a deliberate policy of socio-economic pillage.

Mere "regret" is insufficient. One can "regret" hurricanes or similar acts of God or nature that have bad consequences but lack any connection with one's own acts of will and wrongdoing. More than regret, what is needed is an acknowledgment of the role the National Party played as a deliberate and wilful agent of human suffering. What is necessary is an unambiguous abandonment of the continuing pretence that the wrong that was done was fuelled by some kind of idealism. South Africa needs a gesture from today's leader of the National Party equivalent to the gesture of post-war German leader Willie Brandt, who apologised on his knees in the former Warsaw Ghetto.

It is true that in Chile their Truth Commission's findings were followed by a national apology to the victims tendered by the new democratic President Aylwin. But that would be inadequate, if not grotesque, in South Africa. An apology by President Mandela – apartheid's foremost prisoner – would be less than half a loaf of reconciliation; in fact it would defy comprehension. Apology is a task for the National Party leader.

As Afrikaner ANC MP Melanie Verwoerd, great-granddaughter-in-law of H F Verwoerd, said in Parliament, "we owe it to ourselves, our descendants and our fellow-man [sic] in this country to rid ourselves of the stigma of apartheid, not to attempt any longer to disguise the darkness of our collective past with the tempting light of well-intentioned separate development . . . It is important to realise that apartheid was not simply a policy which failed in the course of time and accidentally insulted some people in the process. It was a life-destroying system which left us with a very sick and poor society – in the social and economic spheres."[8] And the sphere of political morality as well.

It is interesting to note that while the National Party of today presents itself as sharply diverging, on a range of issues, from its far-right Conservative Party fellow-travellers, on the issue of the alleged early idealism of apartheid the two parties speak as one. Indeed, when the National Party embarked on a series of cosmetic changes in the 1980s, such as the formal (but not substantive) abolition of the law requiring blacks to carry passes, they were attacked by Conservative Party MPs for undermining the alleged virtues and idealism of separate development.

In refusing to abandon the claim that apartheid was a God-driven enterprise that collapsed because of human error – or what the nationalist newspaper *Die Burger* in 1972 called "administrative stupidity" – in its implementation, today's Nationalists are at one with the earliest architects of apartheid. Daniel F Malan, National Party Prime Minister of South Africa in 1948, said:

"The last 100 years have witnessed a miracle, behind which must lie a divine plan. Indeed, the history of the Afrikaners reveals a will and a determination which makes one feel that Afrikanerdom is not the work of men but of God."

As far back as 1963 the Rev. Beyers Naudé, who had been a leading member of the Afrikaner religious establishment and who after the Sharpeville massacre in 1960 became an unrelenting foe of apartheid, commented that the ruling elite, the Broederbond, "wants to use the Church of Christ to further its own interest." Sadly, many of the former rulers of South Africa have failed to grasp this fact. They still cling to the illusion that the originators of apartheid were idealists driven by genuine religious zeal.

In November 1992 Mr de Klerk, speaking for the Nationalist Party, tried to shore up a tattered veneer of idealism. He suggested that "for too long we clung to a dream of separated nation-states." It might appear from comments like this that the Nationalists, like US civil rights leader Martin Luther King in his famous "I Have a Dream" speech, longed for racial harmony. But is this really what *baasskap* Prime Minister J G Strijdom had in mind when he said in 1957 that "the white man must remain master" and "must retain his supremacy"?

Again, what does the present-day National Party make of the views of B J Vorster, the Nationalists' leading architect of repressive legislation as Justice Minister, even before he rose to occupy the highest office in the land in 1966? In 1942, at the height of the global anti-Nazi war, Vorster, then a leader of the pro-Nazi terrorist group Ossewa Brandwag, said with refreshing bluntness:

"We stand for Christian Nationalism which is an ally of National Socialism. You can call this anti-democratic principle dictatorship if you wish. In Italy it is called Fascism, in Germany German National Socialism, and in South Africa Christian Nationalism."[9]

Meanwhile, D F Malan, J G Strijdom and H F Verwoerd were equally (if not more) unsavoury, the latter having been found by a Johannesburg court (in a defamation suit he initiated and lost) to have allowed the newspaper he edited to serve as a pro-Nazi propaganda tool.

In 1944 Eric Louw, a key participant in the South African anti-war and Nazi politics of that period, rejected any suggestion that a future Afrikaner Nationalist Republic might remain within the Commonwealth. He felt that remaining within that grouping would hinder the intended "efforts to solve the colour problem and the Jewish question."[10] Louw, who by this stage already had substantial overseas experience in the trade and diplomatic services, was one of the few Nazi-Nationalists in this period who explicitly linked Hitler's war against "World Jewry" to Nationalist intentions for blacks. He went on to become Verwoerd's notorious Foreign Minister and was the incumbent when, in 1961, Verwoerd withdrew South Africa from the Commonwealth.

In *Mein Kampf,* Hitler had matched Louw's double-barrelled racism with his own. "The Jews," he said, "were responsible for bringing negroes into the Rhineland with the ultimate idea of bastardising the white race which they hate and thus lowering its cultural and political level so that the Jew might dominate."[11] Such was the mutually nourishing interplay of profane ideas.

The Third Reich's emphasis on the ideal role of women – to be, above all, healthy mothers of healthy children[12] – also did not escape the Nationalists during the intellectual incubation of the war years, as they laid the conceptual basis for apartheid. Ossewa Brandwag's official organ, *Die O.B.,* proclaimed on 30

September 1942 the organisation's desire to reverse the destructive process of gender emancipation "by issuing a clarion call to all women: Back to your homes! Cease being a caricature of the man, and be a woman and a mother once more. Your task of honour is not to imitate the man, but to mould him and bring him into the world and to build a nation."[13]

In the 1930s the Broederbond, which had started in 1918 with the aim of promoting Afrikaner culture, came under the influence of German Nazism and set out to ensure analogous Afrikaner dominance of South African politics. Several of its leading members, including Verwoerd, actually went to study the ugly art in Germany.

The Broederbond was remodelled on the lines of Hitler's Nazi party, with secret cells and a secret membership. Meanwhile the paramilitary organisation Ossewa Brandwag advanced these ideologies by violent extraparliamentary means – despite the already privileged position enjoyed by whites in the apartheid parliament.

Afrikaner leader General Hertzog, the first "nationalist" Prime Minister to rule under the 1909 Union Constitution, despite exemplifying the white supremacist values of the time, was disturbed by the emphasis on an elite among Afrikaners in the Broederbond's plans for boosting white dominance. He launched a furious attack on the Broederbond (of which his own son was a prominent member), asking: "When will this mad, fatal idea cease to exist, with some people thinking that they are the chosen gods to rule over others?" Shrugging off the dissent of such Afrikaners, the Broederbond consolidated an all-pervasive silent grip on every area of the South African power structure.

The apartheid government actively and openly embraced the muscular language of fascism in implementing its policies. Minister Piet Koornhof told Parliament in June 1968 that "the government believed in white *baasskap* in the White areas [sic] of the Republic and would defend and maintain it with violence if necessary."[14] Decades later in the 1980s, State President P W Botha, nicknamed "Piet Wapen" ("Pete the Gun") by those who admired his authoritarian streak, commented, "I cannot say I am a hardliner or trigger-happy or a hawk, but . . . I detest weaklings in public life."

Apartheid was, in the strict meaning of the word, anathema, a cursed thing in the eyes of the world and most of its churches and religions. South Africa's Truth and Reconciliation Commission must demonstrate this, must expose apartheid's lies, and must finally destroy the façade of sanity and idealism that apartheid maintains in the eyes of its erstwhile active and passive adherents. The truth of apartheid – that it was, *by design*, a tribal exercise in state-sponsored looting – must unambiguously be acknowledged.

In 1963 the then Prime Minister, Dr Verwoerd, put his government's policy in a nutshell. "We want to keep South Africa White," he said. "Keeping it White can only mean one thing, namely, White domination, not 'leadership,' not 'guidance,' but 'control,' 'supremacy' . . . White domination . . . can be achieved by separate development." Separate development, in his eyes, was an instrument for preserving white power by means of subjugating blacks, even when he used the Orwellian phrase "separate freedoms." Separate development was not, as later apologists tried to maintain, a way of fostering the equal development of each so-called nation. The way in which apartheid was implemented, whether in such major spheres as land and education, or elsewhere, provides further proof of this.

For instance, there is no doubt that the so-called Bantu education was deliberately designed to create black serfs. Verwoerd proclaimed when introducing the legislation in 1953 that "if the native in South Africa today in any kind of school in existence is being taught to expect that he will live his adult life under a policy of equal rights, he is making a big mistake . . . There is no place for him in the European community above the level of certain forms of labour." It was openly a racial caste system.

The actual implementation of a policy of deliberate hardship is borne out by the figures. Three decades after Verwoerd's Bantu Education Act, the huge disparity in the financing of black and white education had become entrenched. According to the Institute of Race Relations Survey for 1987–88, expenditure per school student in 1986–87 was R368 for Africans, R887 for Coloureds, R1 714 for Indians, and R2 299 for whites. It is clear that the segregated education system was set up for the benefit of whites.

Of particular relevance in discerning the early motivations of apartheid is the Report of the Tomlinson Commission which was initiated by the Nationalists after the 1948 electoral victory, was appointed before H F Verwoerd became Minister of Native Affairs in 1950, and completed its work in 1955.

The Report outlined the investment and socio-economic demands that would need to be met if an effective process of "separate development," itself based on indefensible discriminatory assumptions, was to be implemented. This plan for Grand Apartheid embraced the goal of racial segregation and recoiled from integration, which it felt would lead to the following horrors: assimilation; "Bantu" political dominance; the disappearance of the "European orientation of our legislation"; "miscegenation" and thereby to a frightening "new biological entity" and the end of the European "national organism" that had successfully survived for 300 years. The Report concluded that the "only solution is the separate development of the European and the Bantu."[15]

The Report recommended a woefully inadequate expenditure of 104 million pounds sterling on the "homelands" over ten years, and suggested that the momentum for implementation of the proposed policy would come from outside the bureaucracy, mainly from the private sector, using so-called white capital.

The Report's stated goal was to ensure a fully diversified and balanced, but racially separate, black economy comprising primary, secondary and tertiary activities. It suggested that this was the only credible basis for effective racial segregation, which it accepted as a legitimate policy goal. "The choice is clear," it concluded. "Either the challenges must be accepted, or the inevitable consequences of the integration of the Bantu and European population into a common society must be *endured*"[16] (emphasis added).

The government's official State Information Office, in its *Fortnightly Digest of South African Affairs* for April 1956, trumpeted the fact that the Tomlinson Report was "South Africa's challenge to the outside world, witness to her bona fides" and evidence of her "Christian approach" to what it called "the problem" of racial diversity. *The Digest* summed up:

> For the watching world the report serves as an answer to the many critics who regard South Africa's race policy as evil, it offers clear evidence of the basically honest and Christian intentions of the European in this country; and it presents, indirectly, a challenge to the observers in many countries to undertake a searching reappraisal of their own past attitudes and opinions on the true state of affairs in this nation of sunshine and contrast.

Verwoerd discarded the racist Report's substantive recommendations and decided to spend only three million sterling on the homelands in the first year. Where the Report recommended racism, Verwoerd opted for ultra-racism, without even a veneer of concern for the material well-being of the South African majority. However he continued to use the Report's allegedly idealistic rhetoric of "separate development." It was a remarkably direct rejection of any pretensions to the cosmetic idealism of the Tomlinson Report.

In 1964, National Party historian G D Scholtz, editor of the influential Nationalist *Die Transvaler* newspaper, commented that to avoid economic and political domination by blacks, the policy of separate development was necessary in order "to get rid of the threatening stranglehold of the Non-White proletariat."[17] Since, in the interim, white labour was intolerably scarce, black labour was pronounced acceptable, but only as a stop-gap measure. Every black's place was in the homelands.

Implementation of separate development got under way in 1959 with the Promotion of Bantu Self-Government Act, embodying a "new vision" of bantustans announced to parliament by Verwoerd. Demarcation of black homeland areas began and plans were drawn up and implemented for consolidating the scattered black areas in a way more rigorous and cruel than anything before.

Dr Verwoerd declared in 1962 that he believed that "these people should be given their own States as they desire . . . I have confidence in the mass of our Bantu, with the exception of a small group of agitators . . . We are trying to establish well-disposed little black neighbouring States."[18]

This rhetoric was not only paternalistic and offensive in expression; it was an outright lie. In several bantustans where elections were held for a parliament, it was the party opposing the so-called independence of the particular bantustan that won the most seats (among even those few voters who countenanced the illegitimate voting exercise). But such majorities were uniformly nullified by the nominated members of bantustan parliaments – chiefs who were appointed with the approval of the apartheid regime.

The territory of each bantustan seldom consisted of contiguous land areas.

The Tomlinson Commission reckoned in the fifties that the bantustans consisted of 264 separate pieces of land; in 1968 the government admitted there were 276. Consolidation, when eventually it did take place, was accompanied by the horrendous violence of forced removals and, even afterwards, only three of the ten bantustans that had been set up by 1977 consisted of undivided territory.

KwaZulu was the most scattered; it consisted of ten disparate chunks of land, the legacy of the "grid iron" system of divide and rule implemented by the British under the "Shepstone Policy," devised by prominent Natal lawyer and administrator Sir Theophilus Shepstone. The whole process was carried out with deadly inhumanity and bureaucratic indifference with a blinkered emphasis, for instance, on producing straight lines on a map, regardless of the natural geography of the area or the human consequences of avoidable forced removals.

The consolidation process included the elimination of so-called black spots, which led to the removals of hundreds of thousands of people. The people themselves were never consulted. The most significant debates were between the apartheid regime and the colonial British, who disappointed Verwoerd by declining to transfer to his government the Protectorates (Swaziland and the territories now known as Lesotho and Botswana). Such a transfer would have increased "bantustan" lands from 13 to 50 per cent of the Verwoerdian land mass, as it would then have been defined.

The land allotted to blacks was itself poor and it was never likely that the bantustans could become economically self-supporting. Originally, they appeared to lack mineral resources. Later, when minerals were found in certain areas, those were cut away for whites, as was for instance the asbestos mine at Penge in the middle of Lebowa, as well as the sand-dune area found to contain titanium in KwaZulu. Interestingly, this was an echo of British practices, such as their excision of Kimberley from the Free State.

In rare cases where mineral strikes did not trigger a redrawing of boundaries in favour of whites, mining licences were granted by the central government and its agencies, without any reference to the bantustan authorities, and taxes were paid to the central government. Thus the tax earnings of mineral wealth were controlled and expropriated for the public purse of the white Republic, without even the formal nicety of redrawing the boundaries. These circumstances made it impossible for the bantustans to flourish, or even to exercise the rudimentary functions of self-government.

When the Transkei and Bophuthatswana became nominally independent, in 1976 and 1977 respectively, all Xhosa-speaking and Tswana-speaking Africans in the whole of South Africa automatically lost their South African citizenship, and with it what few remaining rights they had in the urban areas of their country. Bantustan citizenship ironically imposed only disabilities on its supposed beneficiaries.

The whole independence process was a wicked farce, rejected by the entire international community, which refused to recognise the "independent bantustans." It was a device for getting rid of the "surplus" African population, surplus that is to the requirements of the white economy, and it led to the most appalling abuses of human rights and to corrupt administrations for which the new South Africa is still today paying the price.

There is a direct parallel between such policies and those imposed on German Jews by the Nazis between 1933 and the early stages of the war. This was a period when most European Jews were beyond their reach (Poland and France were yet to fall) and when a relatively weak Germany was pursuing dangerous foreign policy goals and consolidating its military strength. The Nazi policy of these years was to deprive Jewish people of civil and legal protections and rights, exclude them from virtually all spheres of social, economic and cultural life and secure their physical removal from Germany.[19]

The 1935 Nuremberg Laws deprived the Jews of citizenship and confined them to the status of "subjects." In 1933, Jews were excluded from public office, the civil service, journalism, radio, farming, teaching, the theatre, and film; in 1934 they were expelled from stock exchanges. Simultaneously, they were, in practice, excluded from the professions of law and medicine and from business generally – an exclusion that was turned into a formal ban in 1938.[20]

By 1936 half the German Jews were without a livelihood. This situation was created even as, between 1933 and 1937, the overall number of registered (predominantly Aryan) unemployed had fallen from six million to one million. The disparity in employment levels between black and white South Africa is equally striking.

From the early 1960s in South Africa, regulations were extended to tighten up control of black access to urban areas, and to get rid of all those who were deemed superfluous, such as women, children, the old and the sick. There were already very restrictive qualifications for Africans wishing to take up permanent residence in urban white areas, but whereas prior to 1964 those who qualified could have wives and children living with them, this was repealed by Act 42 of that year. Subsequently, women were only allowed entry if they qualified independently from their husbands. As a National Party MP, F S Steyn, put it, "We do not want the Bantu women here simply as an adjunct to the procreative capacity of the Bantu population."[21] It was an almost overt anti-black death wish.

The Bantu Laws Amendment Act of 1964 widened the definition of Africans who were labelled "idle and undesirable," and if they were found in a restricted area their residential and economic fates were at the whim of the local bureaucrats. They were liable to be removed from the area and sent to a so-called homeland which they might never have seen before, or else detained in a variety of institutions or sent to work in a farm colony.

This entire system was controlled by the pass laws, a convenient inheritance from the pre-apartheid period. The effect of the intensification and systematisation of the pass law regime was summed up by a Cape Town worker:

"When you are out of a job, you realise that the boss and the government have the power to condemn you to death. If they send you back home (and back home now there's a drought) . . . it's a death sentence. The countryside is pushing you into the cities to survive, and the cities are pushing you into the countryside to die."[22]

This policy, with its overtly genocidal undertones, is a far cry from the more benign gloss of idealism often superimposed on the programme of separate development. (The insufficiently recognised moral and legal reality that apartheid was actually a form of genocide is argued in further detail in pages 209–13.)

The only rationale for tolerating blacks was that they were a source of cheap labour. Blacks who did not specifically fulfil this function were discardable, as a resolution of the 1973 pro-National Party Afrikaanse Studentebond confirmed: "All the black women and children in the white area must be shipped [*sic*] back to the homelands and only the men should be left in the white areas for as long as we need them."

Separate development was the practical expression of apartheid's assumption of God-given white superiority, as Prime Minister D F Malan demonstrated when he said in 1953 that "the difference in colour is merely the physical manifestation of the contrast between two irreconcilable ways of life, between barbarism and civilisation, between heathenism and Christianity, and finally between overwhelming numerical odds on the one hand and insignificant numbers on the other."[23] Such language borders on ideas of extermination, not idealism.

In 1972, one of Verwoerd's chief civil servants and co-architect of apartheid, Dr W W M Eiselen, frankly admitted that the policy of separate development offered no solution to the needs of the urban African people within the borders (themselves illegitimate) of the old South Africa. Nationalist electoral strategists cynically took the view that "the more apartheid fails, the more it succeeds," since each new failure would heighten the appeal of the Nationalist clarion call, at successive elections, to make apartheid work.[24] The National Party knowingly propagated an unworkable and atrocious policy in the narrow pursuit of an ugly ideology and (all-white) electoral gain.

Of Morsgat, one of three major resettlement schemes in the western Transvaal centred round Rustenburg near Pretoria, the *Rand Daily Mail* reported on 25 October 1969 that:

> For ten months more than 100 families have been living in tents at the side of a dirt road . . . They have camped through most of one summer and all of one winter . . . There are well over 300 families at present camping on the makeshift site. They have no prepared sanitary facilities. There is no health clinic. The single water tank supplying the entire community has a layer of green slime floating on the surface; the families have complained of severe stomach disorders . . . No sanitary pits had been dug before the families arrived last December. There are still none. "We started to dig pits," says a resident, "but they told us to stop. They promised us lavatories, but we haven't seen them yet. Now we use the veld!" Families living on the perimeter of the settlement obviously suffer most from this practice. "The stink is

terrible after the rains," says an elderly woman. Until two months ago there was some sanitary relief in the form of a dozen black pigs who kept human waste under some control. But their presence was illegal and so they were slaughtered on official instructions . . . Families complain of starvation, malnutrition, skin diseases, and stomach troubles . . . Many people have terrible sores, especially the children . . . The removals have forced a new social pattern on the families. Where before they had something approximating an integrated family life, they are now separated. Morsgat is in fact mostly a settlement of women and children, who receive short visits – at weekends – from their menfolk. Poor, often non-existent facilities; unhealthy and degrading living conditions; additional costs eroding wages that are already far too low; the enforced break-up of families. These are the morale shattering hardships responsible for a comment that is heard again and again in Morsgat: "We have been thrown away."

There were scores of Morsgats throughout South Africa. They were part of a policy of "ethnic cleansing."

In 1963, in the bleak early years of the armed struggle of the anti-apartheid resistance, the United Nations Declaration on the Elimination of All Forms of Racial Discrimination contradicted those who would, even today, argue that apartheid was driven by idealism. The Declaration, which was further formalised in the 1965 International Convention on the Elimination of all Forms of Racial Discrimination, codified the civilised international consensus that "any doctrine of differentiation or superiority is scientifically false, morally condemnable, socially unjust and dangerous, and that *there is no justification for racial discrimination, in theory or in practice, anywhere*" (emphasis added).

The international community was not detained by the debates in which some in South Africa remain mired as they still cling to the untenable thesis that apartheid had idealistic beginnings.

When President Mandela travelled to Oslo in 1993 to receive the Nobel Prize, he pointed out in an interview that it was vital to engage in constructive dialogue with the incumbent apartheid government even though they are "political criminals" because "we cannot avoid working with them."

This is a strikingly different vision of the old South African government from the one claimed by Mr de Klerk when he told the National Party faithful in Bloemfontein in 1991 that their party stood for "a proven and civilised value system."

The non-violent birth of a new South Africa required a careful and complex balancing of strategy and idealism; it was an historical tightrope. But now, as the new democracy gathers momentum, it is crucial to recognise that the ground has become firmer underfoot. Milan Kundera tells of an English lord who said to his lady the morning after their wedding night, "I do hope you're pregnant my dear. I shouldn't want to go through all those ridiculous motions again."[25] As the newborn South Africa examines the wreckage of its past, we must put ridiculous motions – all of apartheid's revisionist gyrations – behind us once and for all.

This kind of revisionism, attempting to preserve a semblance of morality underneath the atrocities of apartheid, is our own South African brand of holocaust denial.

Such claims amount to a "disparagement of the memory of the dead," which is an offence under many criminal codes in European countries. Germany, Belgium, France, Austria, Sweden, the Netherlands and Canada have, in the interests of collective memory, specific statutes criminalising Holocaust denial. Whether or not South Africa decides to follow this practice, well-established in the Western democracies, of criminalising historical profanities, the criminal nature of such revisionism should not pass unremarked. These overseas laws also have relevance to proposals for South African legislation to deal with hate speech and racist insults, the verbal embodiment, in the new South Africa, of the apartheid past.

Some suggest that the most appropriate way to deal with the past is to put it behind us and forget it because, this view asserts, none of us are blameless. But this approach confuses truism (to err is human) with sobering historical truth (some errors, like apartheid, are sub-human). Constantly to repeat an error, to sustain it for more than four decades, is something more than just a mistake; its aftermath cannot safely be overlooked; and its origins cannot, without obscenity, be found in idealism.

Stark Opposites: Apartheid and the Resistance to It

"The struggle in South Africa is not a struggle between two races for domination; it is a struggle between the protagonists of racial domination and the advocates of racial equality . . ."
– Report of the UN Expert Group on South Africa, April 1964.

The scale and nature of human suffering associated with the armed struggle against apartheid can never be equated with the scale and nature of the pain inflicted by apartheid. On a purely numerical basis, the deaths or injuries inflicted by the ANC in the course of the struggle simply cannot be compared with the numbers of those killed in the defence of apartheid. Precise figures may never be ascertained. Yet, in putting what was presumably his strongest case in a submission to the Justice Department opposing the Truth and Reconciliation Commission, former Commissioner of Police, General Johann van der Merwe, attributed 153 deaths to alleged ANC "acts of terror." This hardly matches the thousands who directly died at the hands of the apartheid regime and its South African surrogates, nor the larger number who fell victim to the systematic abuses of that system, nor the hundreds of thousands killed, maimed and injured by apartheid in southern Africa.

The suffering of each individual who died, the suffering of that person's innocent family, may be comparable. But this cannot obscure the fundamentally different moralities of the causes in which individuals died. The primary root of the whole conflict lies in the very existence of apartheid, which must be held responsible for the consequences of the resistance to it.

Apartheid, in its essence and in its most everyday manifestations, amounted, as the United Nations repeatedly confirmed, to violence and genocide against blacks. It was a crime against humanity and a crime against peace. It fostered the commission of war crimes. Over time the fundamentally evil and flawed nature of apartheid warped the workaday morality of the administrative corps that imposed it on the country. Apartheid deprived the state's bureaucratic machinery in its entirety of any hint of moral or political legitimacy.

Another major stumbling block which prevents us from putting infringements committed by the resistance on the same plane as the systematic atrocity that was apartheid is, of course, its voting system. Apart from tokenistic and short-lived exceptions, only non-blacks had votes under apartheid, so that blacks had no democratic means of altering the apartheid system. The voteless spent fifty years – half a century! – pleading for justice by peaceful means, and only turned to force in the 1960s after their calls for conversation had been consistently and contemptuously ignored and when passive resistance and unarmed demonstrations were met with violence and gunfire and were, later, effectively made illegal.

Thus the ANC's culpability in causing suffering is not only quantitatively but also qualitatively different from that of the apartheid regime. Those who accuse the anti-apartheid resistance of employing a double standard in making this point are mistaken. There are no double standards, but rather two wholly separate and legitimately different standards. A Nationalist spokesperson claimed in March 1995 that his party is determined to "make the playing field more even"[1] as the process of evaluating the past unfolds. But this sporting metaphor, falsely resonating with ideas of fair play, arrives several decades late. When the question is who bullied whom in the past and how, the bully and the bullied can hardly occupy the same moral plane.

Subtract illegitimate violence from apartheid and zero remains. Conversely, the use of force as part of the resistance to apartheid was a legitimate exercise of the right to self-determination and an expression of constitutionalism; illegitimate violence arose only as a marginal excess. These legal distinctions are developed elsewhere in this book (see chapter 16 below). For now, the main point is this: *there is a helpful difference between a bad apple and a bad apple tree.*

Apartheid has been accurately described, in its every warp and weft, as an edifice of "structured sinfulness." The apartheid state stood outside any possibility of beauty or of simple decency. To act in defence of apartheid was to choose a path of immorality and international outlawry, with no possibility of ever approaching the good. To act against apartheid was to embark on a fundamentally legitimate exercise, blessed by international law. Certainly, the risk of committing individual acts of ill-judgement, immorality or illegality remained. So it did in all resistance struggles against evil and illegitimate regimes. There could be – and were – isolated bad apples. But these genuine mistakes, including serious human rights abuses, are not equivalent to the systematic atrocity – the bad apple tree – on the other side.

Despite these important moral and political distinctions between apartheid and its opposite (the resistance), some have sought to reduce the truth and reconciliation process to a banal exercise of isolating "bad apples" on both sides of the conflict. This approach is flawed because all apples on one side were congenitally bad. *There is and was no such thing as a morally defensible act undertaken in defence of the crime of apartheid.* So to overcentralise blame for apartheid on a few chosen culpable devotees (the supposed "bad apples") is to acquiesce in the old regime's trick of massive self-exculpation. As Archbishop Tutu said in 1989:

"Apartheid is in and of itself violent. Apartheid is in and of itself evil, totally and completely. There is no way in which you can use nice methods. It has, *ipso facto*, to use methods that are consistent with its nature."[2]

There is an instructive analogy in the post-war German debates on the question whether anything of value could be salvaged from the military tradition of Hitler's army, the Wehrmacht. Some argued that a continuity of military tradition was impossible; that it was impossible to honour even ordinary soldiers, innocent of atrocities, who had offered compliant and disciplined service to the Nazi state in aggressive wars; that the new "tradition decree" then under discussion should rather celebrate as heroes those who plotted to assassinate Hitler.

Conservatives argued that this latter suggestion in particular was too anarchic to be workable in a military setting and that there should be an acknowledgment of that category of innocent personnel who took the "path of obedience out of honest conviction."[3]

In 1965, after years of debate and a progression through several drafts, a decree was agreed upon which condemned the institution and leadership of the Wehrmacht, but exonerated and praised the rank and file, including middle-level officers. This artificial distinction was, however, washed away by the tide of historical research that increasingly implicated all levels of the military in the slaughter of Jewish people. The upshot was a new decree in 1982 containing an unequivocal condemnation of the conduct of German soldiers in the war.[4]

The doctrine of evenhandedness – with its idea of isolated bad apples on the side of apartheid – will doubtless equally become a laughing stock of history. But South Africa cannot wait forty years for this acknowledgment. A new military for the new South Africa must renounce its past now, rather than seeking to defend it.

It is instructive to note that it was apartheid Defence Minister Magnus Malan who first complained, when under attack in late February 1990 for the state terrorism over which he presided, that too much attention was being paid to the SADF misdeeds and none to the allegedly monstrous deeds of the ANC. The idea that there were equivalent abuses on both sides of the anti-apartheid conflict, an idea that is taken seriously by some who ought to know better, is a rare and notable propaganda triumph of the old apartheid military machine.

This false doctrine of evenhandedness is the sort of thing that the egregious Jimmy Kruger, Minister of Justice in the mid-seventies, the era of the Steve Biko killing, could only invoke sarcastically: "I am not glad and I am not sorry about Mr Biko. It leaves me cold . . . Incidentally, I can just tell the [National Party] congress, the day before yesterday one of my own lieutenants in the prison services also committed suicide and we have not yet accused a single prisoner" (laughter).

In Kruger's day, the doctrine of evenhandedness – the idea that the jailer and the jailed could be regarded as having equal resources of violence and so as bearing equal responsibility when harm occurred – was a pretext for sadistic humour, at best. But in 1996, this idea – that blacks, a wrongly jailed population under apartheid, can somehow bear equivalent moral responsibility for acts committed in self-defence and *in extremis* – is advanced with a straight face by the erstwhile jailers. More alarmingly, this claim is taken seriously by usually responsible observers, who speak solemnly of the need to avoid "moral favouritism," as though apartheid and its opposite were two upright chaps, each equally deserving a fair break in life.

In reality, the "good apple" category is simply non-operative on the apartheid side. The only meaningful distinction among those who sought to uphold apartheid is between bad apples and worse ones – with some of the latter being denied all possibility of amnesty and indemnity. Only on the side of the resistance can it be said that the overwhelming mass of participants fell into the "good apple" category.

As Cosmas Desmond has put the point, "it is the excesses of the liberation movement that need to be exposed by the truth commission, as opposed to even the everyday activities of the apartheid regime . . . The principle of proportionality applies only to the liberation movement, not to the forces of apartheid."5

There is no humane or patriotic way to commit a crime against humanity, which is what apartheid, in its every everyday manifestation, was.

The ethical effect of apartheid was like the Midas touch in reverse. Everything it handled turned not to gold but to an immoral swill. In the traditional analogy, a few bad apples will spoil the whole bunch; if those bad few are removed in time, then the bunch may be saved from corruption. But apartheid never had this possibility of redemption. Like a Tree of Death in a netherworld Garden of Eden, all its fruit was congenitally tainted.

Mark Behr's debut novel *The Smell of Apples*, a nuanced cultural artifact of reconciliation clawing its way from the old to the new South Africa, tells the story of the Erasmus family, a veritable model of familial bliss in the old South Africa. The Erasmus clan superficially resembles the Partridge Family or the Brady Bunch (from the US television serials formerly popular in South Africa) in the suburban wholesomeness of their existence under apartheid. Daddy is at the pinnacle of the SADF. Young Ilse dominates her school's prize-giving and is anointed head girl. Young Marnus (the narrator) is a maths whizz whose worst sin is that he helped his "blood brother" Frikkie cheat on a test. Picnics abound and the idyllic scenery of the Cape's False Bay is prominent.

Yet gradually truth erupts as Marnus (in flashforwards) fights hidden wars in Angola and as (in real time) his family hosts a mysterious Chilean general. Things finally fall apart as Marnus, finding truth by stealing glimpses through knots in the family home's timber flooring, sees his father, pillar of the community, buggering Frikkie after making Frikkie fondle him. When, immediately afterwards, a shaken Marnus joins his chum for breakfast:

> Neither of us are really hungry so we take apples from the fruit-bowl on the table. "These apples are rotten or something," says Frikkie, and he turns his apple around in his hand after sniffing it. "They stink. Smell this," and he holds the apple to my nose. I smell the apple in his hand. It smells sour.
>
> "Ja," I say. There's something wrong with it. Take another one." I sniff at my own apple to make sure it's OK.

Frikkie brings the new apple to his mouth, but he pulls a face, and says: "This one, too."

"Let me smell," I say, and take it from his hand. It smells like an ordinary apple.

"No, this one's fine," I say. '*It's not the apple, man. It's your hand,*' and I take his hand and sniff the inside of his palm. It smells sour. He pulls his hand back.

"What smells like that?" I ask. But he shakes his head and pushes his hand under the open tap.

He takes some Sunlight liquid from the window-sill, and pours it into his palm. Then he wipes his hand against his PT shorts. He sniffs again, but shakes his head and says it's still not gone. We stand in front of the sink, staring at each other.

"What did you touch?" I ask, but he only shakes his head and says he doesn't know." (Emphasis added.)

Attempting to cleanse ourselves of apartheid by narrowly seeking its bad apples will lead us to overlook the thing's spilt seed all around us. It would foster a false purification, a continuing stench, even a mutant rebirth. And as Breyten Breytenbach has put it, in that Big Rot and seeming sunshine of an uncleansed South Africa, amidst "glistening valleys and a silver wind," the crocodiles would still feast among the children.

Achieving Genuine Reconciliation

"I have always said I don't know what this conciliation means"
– Gen. J B M Hertzog (1912), two years before he founded the National Party, speaking of relations between Afrikaners and other whites.

Finding the truth about the South African past is less about locating bad apples than about choosing between incompatible apple trees, and in the process keeping dirty hands out of the way. It inevitably means defining properly what dirtiness means. That task – paring the clean from the unclean parts of the past – is in fact at the heart of that much misused concept, "reconciliation."

Much public debate, over the Truth and Reconciliation Commission and elsewhere, has falsely pitted truth against reconciliation. Right-wing objectors have spoken as though the search for a morally accepted view of our history conflicts with, rather than advances, the several goals of reconciliation. They think reconciliation means a painless forgetting.

This is a fundamental misunderstanding of the entire concept of reconciliation. If this false view of reconciliation prevails, the South African majority will once more be required to swallow their anguish and defer to false history. Like the battered wife who blames herself for her husband's violence, the oppressed would be expected just to grin and bear it, while historical falsehoods continue unchecked.

But the real meaning of reconciliation is something else. To reconcile is, according to the *Oxford Paperback Dictionary*, to:

"1. restore friendship between (people) after an estrangement or quarrel. 2. induce (a person or oneself) to accept an unwelcome fact or situation; *this reconciled him to living far from home*. 3. bring (facts or statements etc) into harmony or compatibility when they appear to conflict."

The heart of reconciliation, as this definition makes clear, is not the manufacture of a cheap and easy *bonhomie*. Nor is it an escapist flight from the facts, or an arrival at jerry-built consensus through the avoidance of debate and accountability. Rather, it is the facing of unwelcome truths in order to harmonise incommensurable world views so that inevitable and continuing conflicts and differences stand at least within a single universe of comprehensibility. It is part of what the Chileans call *reconvivencia*, a period of getting used to living with each other again. In the political context, reconciliation is a shared and painful ethical voyage from wrong to right, and also a symbolic settling of moral and political indebtedness. It is, as André du Toit puts it, "a conscious and justified settling of accounts with the past."

Reconciliation, in this its rich and meaningful sense, is thus a real closing of the ledger book of the past. A crucial element in that closing is an ending of the divisive cycle of accusation, denial and counter-accusation; not a forgetting of these accusations and counter-accusations, but more a settling of them through a process of evaluation – like the accountant's job of reconciling conflicting claims before closing a ledger book.

Reconciliation is part of a revival of the South African conscience, a word rooted in the Latin *conscientia*, which means joint knowledge. It carries also the sense of "oughtness," or "a comparative evaluation of ways of conduct and a censuring of the self for choosing the wrong way."[1] The necessity for ethical grounding and thus for censuring is central both to conscience and to reconciliation and cannot be evaded; it is the moral flipside of forgiveness.

Moreover, thorough reconciliation must reach all institutions. No political party or organisation must be seen as above the need to accept its culpability as author and implementer of apartheid. As Professor Charles Villa-Vicencio, the Truth Commission's Director of Research, has cautioned: "the inherent link between memory, history, interpretation and political point-scoring" must be acknowledged. In a democracy, the political process draws the country into orderly conversation with itself about itself and about the real nature of competing parts of the polity. After a period of atrocity, genuine reconciliation cannot leave the institutional architects of past atrocity unscathed. Or else a dirty hand with an invisible stench would survive in our seemingly renewed midst. And the very nature of that renewal would be compromised.

Genuine reconciliation involves moral and political restitution in the sense of the German term *wiedergutmachung,* which means to "make good again." We cannot really enter upon the process of making good the history of South Africa unless we acknowledge precisely what bad there is to undo. We cannot enter upon the rich and nuanced process of reconciliation armed only with mumbled banalities about the past being an "innocent mistake."

It is one of the most vital tasks of the Truth and Reconciliation Commission not only to restore friendship between the pro- and anti-apartheid sides to the past in South Africa, but also to bring them to a shared debate about that past. Some, like former Minister of Defence Magnus Malan, who presided over apartheid's desperate violence of the 1980s and yet can say "my conscience is clear," still fail to see their role in the past in any defensible light. They are beyond the parameters of meaningful post-apartheid debate. The faculty of remorse, as anti-apartheid stalwart and now South African Minister of Finance Trevor Manuel has said, is vital for genuine reconciliation. And it is scarce among the erstwhile defenders of apartheid.

Reconciliation requires an acknowledgment of wrongs committed and a re-evaluation by their perpetrators of the morality which lay behind them. Only

47

then can reconciliation trigger real catharsis, a word which, in its original Greek meaning, contains the ideas of purification and spiritual renewal. Reconciliation, accurately conceived, must bring about a rupture with the skewed ethics [*sic*] of apartheid, and so upset any possibility of smooth sailing on a previously immoral course.

This is why it is fundamentally wrong to approach the sins of the past from the perspective that the National Party adopted during the political transition and still stands by today. In November 1992, the then State President, F W de Klerk, explaining his reluctance to face the past, said that the country "dare not be forced off course by new shocks about old things."[2] This is similar to Magnus Malan's "concern," upon his arrest in 1995, that his prosecution "and the Truth Commission have all the elements of antagonising the moderate mainstream of citizens of the country" and that "polarisation is the last thing I would like to see."[3]

Apart from the curious suggestion that the moderate mainstream of South Africa would prefer that accused murderers evade a fair trial, Malan's remarks, like De Klerk's, reflect a desire for cheap and painless reconciliation amounting in fact to an acceptance of the past as normal rather than a renunciation of it.

Reconciliation cannot mean a seamless recycling; it means changing course and discarding what is morally irredeemable. Even in Argentina, where the old repressive military remained intact and extremely influential in the new democracy, where the Punto Final legislation put an end in February 1987 to attempts at prosecuting them, and where active attempts were made by the new democrats to downplay the criminality of the prior regime, there has been a discernible process of ethical forward movement. Eminent historian Tulio Halperin Ponti points out that General Videla, Magnus Malan's Argentine counterpart, inspires today such "horror" that his neighbours – essentially apolitical suburbanites, apathetic under the prior regime – cross the street to avoid sharing the sidewalk with him.[4] Such has been the transformation of the political morality of the moderate and apathetic mainstream, even in the unlikely circumstances of the Argentine transition.

So the old South African Police, through their former representatives, were wrong when they suggested, in seeking automatic exculpation from past crimes, that "the morality of the actions then taken could not and should not be judged according to standards now prevailing."[5] This is an overt call for yesterday's immorality to govern today's processes of moral repair. The absurdity of such calls for moral indifferentism is obvious. To heed them would be to embrace amorality.

At the same time, to allege that the Truth and Reconciliation Commission is an intended instrument of anti-apartheid vengeance, as some journalists and politicians have done, is untenable. During the transitional negotiations between the ANC and the National Party in the early 1990s, the ANC emphasised again and again, both to its political opponents and to its own supporters, that no narrow factional "victory" was being claimed, and that no defeat, except of apartheid itself, had been inflicted. The outcome of negotiations was meant to be a victory for all the people of the country.

In the same way, the purpose of the Truth and Reconciliation Commission is not to seek revenge against the individual perpetrators of apartheid, but rather to expose and renounce the evil of the system and the profane acts that were committed in its name. Only when all sides recognise such truths about the past can real reconciliation begin.

Thus by definition, reconciliation cannot be a symmetrical process of mutual absolution. As early as 1963 one commentator, characterising apartheid as "the most vicious regime the world has known since the death of Hitler," remarked that "when the time comes for the settling of accounts, White South Africa will have to bear its full burden of guilt and atonement."[6] The gist of genuine reconciliation is that apartheid's beneficiaries must be persuaded to accept unwelcome facts about their past.

The dispossessed may have lost a great deal but they have not as yet been divested of what human rights jurist Albie Sachs, now a Judge on the new South African Constitutional Court, has called their "right to forgive." The process of reconciliation hinges entirely on "the African comrade's power or prerogative to be the forgiving one. The right to be magnanimous cannot be exercised if all the wrongs are excused or justified or blamed on history."[7] The Truth and Reconciliation Commission is nothing less than the new South Africa's facility for the oppressed. It will enable them, should they so choose, to fulfil a civic sacrament of forgiving.

The fact that this right or prerogative to forgive vests in one side (the historically oppressed) and not the other (the historical oppressors), is not an arbitrary or partisan position. It is not a product of favouritism. Rather, it arises from the truly one-sided immorality of apartheid. And it arises from the prior one-sidedness of apartheid South Africa's view of itself. As Desmond Tutu said in 1985 when resisting apartheid's reformist machinations, "it is the victims, not the perpetrators, who must say whether things are better or not. When you are throttling me you can't really tell me that things are better, that you are not choking me quite so badly . . . When will the world listen to the victim rather than the perpetrator?"[8] That time is now.

The apartheid state's all-pervasive thought control may have seemed ineffectual to sane outsiders, but it has taken a toll within South Africa. Some people really believe that the country's history was a clash of two legitimate patriotisms or of equally well-grounded political moralities.

Beyond censorship and the overt repression of ideas, apartheid actively imposed hallucinatory history on its privileged citizens. Apartheid's architects treated history as a matter of legislative whim. In March 1968 the Minister of National Education and father of F W de Klerk, Senator Jan de Klerk, said in defence of the tailor-made National Party history syllabus that was then being forced into South African schools: "the policy of the Government since 1948 has been laid down in Acts, and the Acts have been implemented. It is therefore history."⁹ Amen.

It is no exaggeration.to say that apartheid policy-makers attempted to legislate fake truths to the world both within and beyond the country's borders. Speaking at a political rally in 1968, John Vorster proclaimed that "as an Afrikaner I am not prepared to cooperate with the world if that means I have to sacrifice my Afrikaner identity."¹⁰ This belief – that global and domestic reality would bow down before apartheid's sovereign parliament – would be comical except that it was firmly held and savagely acted upon. It was based on the idea, expressed by D F Malan, that apartheid "is not the work of man but a creation of God ... Our history is the highest work of the architect of the centuries." Amen.

So, unsurprisingly, much of privileged South Africa grew up like young Marnus in Mark Behr's *The Smell of Apples*, perplexed, but not much caring that the whole world "just won't listen when Uncle John Vorster explains to them that they really don't understand the problems we face in this country. Dad says it doesn't matter that much what the rest of the world says anyway."

In July 1996 Behr himself confessed that, intoxicated by the false values of the privileged milieu he enjoyed as a student at Stellenbosch University in the mid-eighties, he had served as a spy for the apartheid regime. His journey from confessed treachery to apparent contrition gives his novel an extraordinary resonance today.

Many privileged South Africans, having blinked awake to the fact that Nelson Mandela is not a bloodthirsty terrorist, need still to learn that he never was. They need to realise, for instance, that Joe Slovo did not, with the arrival of the new South Africa, abruptly transform from Stalinist child-eater to humanist Housing Minister. They need to understand, rather, that humanism travelled always with the resistance; and that barbarism walked with apartheid.

Many privileged South Africans, reconciling themselves to these long-lost realities, are now entering a whole new ethical universe, discarding a previous moral illiteracy, and learning a new vocabulary of right and wrong. For them, as for Colonel Aureliano Buendia in Gabriel Garcia Marquez's *One Hundred Years of Solitude*, the world is so recent that many things lack names, and in order to indicate them it is necessary to point.

In the historical process of giving voice to the unspeakable, privileged South Africans have much to learn. The primary task for privileged South Africans in forging national unity is to reconcile themselves to the anti-apartheid foundations of the new order, the truth that human dignity was entirely absent from the prevalent politics of the old and from its state machinery through which they profited, materially anyway. The epigram from W B Yeats, significantly chosen by Nadine Gordimer in opening her very first novel, *The Lying Days* (published in 1953), presciently made this point:

Through all the lying days of my youth
I swayed my leaves and flowers in the sun;
Now may I wither into the truth.

Some may still hanker nostalgically for what they see as past splendours, the myths of security and standards evoked even in 1996 election campaigns. But as the days of lies give way to the beginnings of debates over truth, even the erstwhile privileged opponents of apartheid face, inevitably, a time of some withering. The country is no longer a stage bestrode by them alone. Reconciliation contains this kind of existential rebalancing, too.

And yet the overweening arrogance of the apartheid legislators in parliament, their belief that they could alone legislate domestic and world history, continued even in the final days of the transition. They continued to believe that "reconciliation" could be a unilateral act piloted by themselves.

So in October 1992, the resistance stated that it would not be bound by the apartheid government's attempts at forcible reconciliation which would have meant granting blanket self-indemnity to its own state officials. Mr de Klerk, the State President, responded that he would not accept a constitution that would allow a future government "to randomly alter or undo what we have done in the spirit of reconciliation and the maintaining of security and stability in South Africa."[11] This idea – that unilateral action by an apartheid government could constitute "reconciliation" – is a dizzying contradiction.

The essence of reconciliation is a renunciation of the past and an inducing of the South African privileged to accept unwelcome facts about their past. The 1992 apartheid government was the last-gasp embodiment, not yet the renunciation, of that past. The apartheid state could no more function as reconciler than a corpse can function as its own coroner. The idea is inherently contradictory. More so where the particular legislation in question, the Further Indemnity Bill of October 1992, sought to confer upon the apartheid State President enormous, practically personal, discretionary powers of forgiveness. It was as though reconciliation could be force-fed.

Apartheid (which means "apartness") was fundamentally built on an idea of the irreconcilability of peoples. As the 1982 Belhar Declaration of the Dutch Reformed Mission Church (the Coloured branch of the Dutch Reformed Church) acknowledged: "as opposed to the Gospel of Christ's stress on the reconciliation of human beings with God and their fellow humans, the forced separation of peoples on the grounds of race and colour is based at heart on a belief in the *fundamental irreconcilability* of the people so separated" (emphasis added). Apartheid's architects, like the party's founder General Hertzog, never comprehended – and still do not – the concept of nonracial reconciliation.

There is a risk that privileged South Africans, if they forgo the opportunity to reconcile themselves with uncomfortable historical facts, will find themselves in a kind of psychological exile, or an escapist historical dungeon. In Romania, where the repressive Ceausescu policing apparatus evaded investigation in the new order, the very identity and political substance, the simple reality, of the political transition was cast into doubt.

The drama and sated bloodlust surrounding Ceausescu's summary execution in late 1989, while seemingly an archetype of popular revenge swiftly attained, actually diverted attention from the need for a systematic dismantling of his legacy. According to one observer, average Romanians remain uncertain about the elementary nature of their body politic: "Did their nation undergo a revolution or a *coup d'état*?" they ask.

In this vacuum of truth, "to reconcile their self-image with the historical past, so vital for a national conscience, the peoples of Eastern Europe are trying to embellish pre-communist symbols, heroes, places and events. The Russians have gone back to the glamour of St Petersburg, the Czechs are revering the noble figure of pre-war president Thomas Masaryk and the Romanians are being presented with an idyllic picture of the Hohenzollern kings who reigned during the first half of this century."[12] They are paradoxically imprisoned by an escapist phantasmagoria.

In South Africa, which began to grapple with change forty-three years after the 1948 victory of venomous policies, one recalls the protagonist of Faulkner's novel *Absalom, Absalom!*. He was a young white southerner who, forty-three years after the defeat of venomous policies in the US Civil War, found that

> his very body was an empty hall echoing with sonorous defeated names; he was not a being, an entity, he was a commonwealth. He was a barracks filled with stubborn backward-looking ghosts still recovering, even forty-three years afterward, from the fever which had cured the disease, waking from the fever without even knowing that it had been the fever itself which they had fought against and not the disease, looking with stubborn recalcitrance backward beyond the fever and into the disease with actual regret . . .[13]

In South Africa there is no real scope for a whole subculture of historical oblivion, for few citizens can be in any doubt that political transition has been palpable and dramatic. Whereas the failure to purge past lies has led in Eastern Europe to a kind of circus historicism, or led in Faulkner's American South to a stubborn, insular and defeated inner commonwealth, there will certainly be no such vacuum in South Africa. A rich and nuanced cultural transformation is well under way. White South African literature itself is a major creative beneficiary of, and contributor to, the new order.

Less clear is to what extent large numbers of individual privileged citizens may have locked themselves out of this reality and into the status of ahistorical hermits. In December 1967, a time when books were being banned by the South African Publications Control Board at a rate of at least two every week, the Afrikaans writer, W A de Klerk, was driven to comment that the most subtle and damaging censorship was self-censorship, where the Afrikaner author "has been so conditioned by things around him that he, too, must hesitate, look warily around him and then over his shoulder."[14] How many are still like this, looking backwards at ghosts, unaware of the exorcism so decisively under way?

Today the exhausted orthodoxies of apartheid have lost their statutory oxygen tents. The successful new students of Afrikanerdom realise, indeed affirm, that for those irrevocably wedded to nostalgias, "death brings its own freedom, and it is for the living that the dead should mourn, for in life there is no escape from history."[15]

To put the point bluntly, a reconciled South Africa must renounce either apartheid or nonracial democracy. The two cannot ethically be reconciled. The only question is: which moral order to renounce? Which side is it that must be induced to accept unwelcome realities fundamental to its perception (or pretended perception) of its own past? Certainly, the resistance will need to remain relentlessly self-critical in its new role of governance and in viewing its own past. But a revisionist view that apartheid was not so bad after all is an unlikely candidate for admission to the lists of the new democracy's meaningful self-probing.

At the 1987 Dakar talks, designed to bring together the ANC and leading Afrikaners as a precursor to political negotiations, Theuns Eloff, voicing a perspective shared by many in the old order, insisted that one cannot just confine oneself to questioning the "political effectiveness" of the resistance's armed struggle, but "we must also question the moral legitimacy of that action."[16]

This question is indeed central to the entire process of genuine reconciliation, the essence of which lies in inducing one side in an estrangement or quarrel to accept unwelcome facts or perspectives, so harmonising seemingly incompatible visions. That question – the relative merits or comparative legitimacy of apartheid and of its opposite, the resistance – cannot be left dangling. It is one of the vital questions that the Truth and Reconciliation Commission must consider and on which it must pronounce.

Under apartheid, culture, language, morality, politics and law, all lost a certain consonance. A country's common public language came undone, while its institutions strove mightily to pretend otherwise. Fine-grained rationalisations arose which survive today, in increasingly rarefied variants, as shifting obstacles in the path of reconciliation. For, as Wordsworth has said, "to be mistaught is worse than to be untaught; and no perverseness equals that which is supported by systems, no errors are so difficult to root out as those which the understanding has pledged its credit to uphold."[17]

Undoing the vast areas of historical misteaching that still abound in South Africa is the hard work at the heart of reconciliation. Properly done, it will enable individual South African citizens and the entire society alike to arrive, for the first time, at that elusive "mutual attunement" – a fractious and contested but profoundly shared interaction – that is the true mark of mutual and genuine communication.[18]

"Oh for a good *row* in close proximity," wrote Ruth First to her husband Joe Slovo during one of their unavoidable separations. This yearning for constructive provocation is the emotional footprint of that educational process, that healthy recrimination, that is surely the real core of reconciliation in post-apartheid South Africa.

The Need to Decriminalise the Resistance

"I would say that the whole life of any thinking African in this country drives continuously to a conflict between his conscience on the one hand and the law on the other . . . The law as it is applied, the law as it has been developed over a long period of history, and especially the law as it is written by the Nationalist Government is a law which, in our view is immoral, unjust and intolerable. Our consciences dictate that we must protest against it, that we must oppose it and that we must attempt to alter it."

– Nelson Mandela, speech to court (1962).

If the new South Africa as a whole acknowledges, as it must, the profound and rotten-core illegitimacy of every defining aspect of the old country, this shared realisation must necessarily throw into sharp relief the need for a decriminalising of the resistance. After all, only under the criminal apartheid system that it was attempting to end were its acts automatically condemned as crimes.

It is one of those rare strokes of brilliant propaganda that the apartheid regime so pervasively used the legal system to give a semblance of order to cruelty and oppression; unsurprisingly, what the regime created was little more than a well-resourced system of kangaroo courts.

No matter how many laws were purportedly passed, the defining aspects of apartheid remained outside the bounds of accepted legal norms and practice. This was early and easily recognised by the international community, whose collective verdict is clearly relevant to the new South Africa's domestic processes of facing the past.

As Nelson Mandela faced the Rivonia show trial in October 1963, the United Nations General Assembly, by Resolution 1881 (XVIII), formally called upon the apartheid regime to "abandon the arbitrary trial now in progress and forthwith to grant unconditional release to all political prisoners and to all persons imprisoned, interned or subjected to other restrictions for having opposed the policy of apartheid." Introducing this resolution, Mr Diallo Telli, the chairperson of the UN Special Committee on the Policies of Apartheid referred to the accused as the likely future government of South Africa, described the proceedings as a "bogus trial" and characterised the then government as "bloodthirsty executioners."[1]

Such was the international community's contemporaneous verdict on the criminalisation of dissenters against apartheid – and on the nature of the government that sought such criminalisation. The question for South Africa today is what action the new country should take in dealing with this part of the past. President Mandela himself expressed views on this question. He bluntly told the court at the time that "I have done my duty to my people and to Africa. I have no doubt that posterity will pronounce that I was innocent and that the criminals . . . are the members of the Verwoerd Government."

That posterity is us. As part of dealing effectively with the past, there must be a formal – probably statutory – doing away with the kangaroo convictions of the past. The new South Africa needs a law of nullity, rescinding the previous illegitimate convictions that the apartheid regime sought to impose on the Mandela government, then in exile in its own country, as part of its strategies of state violence. Such legislation would enjoy the full sanction of international law, according to which any treaty, act or legislation that violates the "peremptory norms" of international law is void in its inception (*ab initio*, in the lawyer's phrase).[2]

Moreover, such a law would be consistent with actual processes of reform already under way in the new South Africa. An appreciation of the actual voidness of apartheid's laws already underpins, for instance, present land reform and restitution initiatives. Such initiatives – the undoing of what was illegally done through past compliance with apartheid's alleged laws – can make no sense without an assumption that past legislation lacked substantive validity, whatever its narrow or formal legality under apartheid.

Apartheid, itself a lawless system, could confer no genuine legality upon acts done in its furtherance. While this is widely realised in the civil sphere (as the land reform example attests), the implications for apartheid's criminalisation of dissent have not been pursued with the same rigour.

Today's Deputy President Thabo Mbeki was at the time of the Rivonia showtrial a second-year student at Sussex University. Facing the ghastly prospect of his own father's imminent execution, he addressed the UN Special Committee on the Policies of Apartheid in London in April 1964. Mr Mbeki emphasised the calibre of the accused and the irony of their facing accusers who "only yesterday found glory in Nazi Germany." He went on to summarise the problems at the heart of apartheid's violent misuse of the criminal justice system. Apartheid had, said the future Deputy President, "declared freedom from poverty, from suffering and from degradation, and human equality without discrimination on grounds of colour or race, to be illegal and criminal in its eyes. And by the Rivonia trial, the Government intends to make ten times more its case that freedom is illegal."[3]

Alongside these perverse criminalisations, the apartheid regime had in fact itself criminally taken up arms against the South African people – through means including the use of the courts and legislative process. Apartheid's implementers made generous use of legislation like the South African Defence Act, section 103 of which provided automatic exculpation of its footsoldiers for acts committed in "good faith." This law placed a good deal of lawless discretion in the hands of individuals, including the State President himself.

In July 1986 for example, P W Botha personally invoked this law to block the trial of four South African soldiers charged with murder. Again, when two former members of Koevoet, a notorious police counter-insurgency unit, were accused of murdering two civilian survivors of the Kassinga massacre in Angola, whom they had detained, they claimed they had shot two "terrorists" and that they were unaware that the victims were civilians. The Administrator-General – Pretoria's representative running Namibia – granted them amnesty on Botha's instruction, claiming that they had "acted in the heat of the armed struggle." But even if it were true that the captured victims were combatants, murdering them in detention would nonetheless have been a serious war crime.

The apartheid bureaucracy was gripped by a surreal oblivion to binding norms of trials, of criminality and of punishment. In what may serve as a striking metaphor for the topsy-turvy nature of the whole system, Afrikaner legal academic Barend van Niekerk was convicted – his appeal failing in the highest court of the land – for suggesting, in a rigorously argued and empirically based law journal article, that, under apartheid's criminal sentencing practices, whites tended to escape the gallows and blacks did not. So the bringers of news about the criminality of the system were themselves criminalised – and their message ignored.

Such past realities led Norwegian Prime Minister Mrs Gro Harlem Bruntland, in her 13 February 1996 address to the South African Parliament, to note that the new South Africa has "risen above a situation where normality was criminalised and criminality normalised" and that "the rejection of this past abnormalcy will forever rank as a constitutional founding principle for this new beginning." But while the constitutional rejection has been made, the formal undoing of the false criminalisations of the past is yet to be implemented. In the seventy years of their operation, 16.5 million people were criminalised and harassed under the pass laws.4 A statute nullifying the false criminal convictions of the past is an important piece of the new country's housekeeping that must be attended to in dealing with the past.

In partial furtherance of these goals of decriminalisation, section 20 (10) of the Act establishing the Truth and Reconciliation Commission provides that "where any person has been convicted of any offence constituted by an act or omission associated with a political objective in respect of which amnesty has been granted in terms of this Act, any entry or record of the conviction shall be deemed to be expunged from all official documents or records and the conviction shall for all purposes, including the application of any Act of Parliament or any other law, be deemed not to have taken place . . ."

So decriminalisation will follow a grant of amnesty. However, the notions of amnesty or indemnity are inadequate to capture the nature of the reparation necessary for the categories of offences of gravest concern here.

This is because when a new society grants amnesty or indemnity to members of a liberation movement, there may be unintended connotations of guilt and absolution, or it may be inferred that some real crime was committed and is being pardoned. Ultimately, grants of amnesty or indemnity in these circumstances represent a kind of accountability, even homage, to the previous apartheid order that had branded the particular deeds a crime.

There may be some individual instances where such limited acknowledgment of the apartheid criminal justice system is appropriate (for example where crimes of dishonesty were committed for personal gain outside of any intention to advance the political goals of the resistance). But in general, almost by definition, to have broken apartheid's criminal and civil laws in pursuit of the political goals of the resistance was to have done something right, not wrong; it was to have done something that was perfectly legal and acceptable under international law. In such cases, the concept of indemnity or amnesty is wholly misplaced. What was wrong was not the deed itself, but the branding of it as a crime.

This kind of alleged offence must be decriminalised in order to restore the historical integrity of the criminal justice system, as well as for the practical convenience of yesterday's falsely convicted: the stigma of criminal convictions must be removed. There should be a general law of nullity pronouncing whole categories of offences – generally those detailed in chapter 9, especially pages 77–86 – void *ab initio*.

An example worth specific mention here is that of "offences of opinion" under apartheid's oppressive regime of censorship. People previously found guilty or subjected to legal or administrative sanctions under apartheid laws like the Suppression of Communism Act deserve apologies and societal reparation. At a minimum, they deserve to be unbranded as criminals.

Apartheid's grotesque annals of criminality must be reopened and their contents discarded; it is the legitimate iconoclasm of the human rights culture, the justified irreverence, even contempt, with which virtue treats vice. And it is a vital part of the reconciliation of the old legal system with the new society. We must recognise that it was generally the penalisers, rather than the penalised, who committed offences, sometimes in the very act of announcing ostensible "criminal convictions." We must rob past evil of its grandiosity.

Far from advancing these objectives, the apartheid regime in the 1990s demanded that all returning exiles and members of the resistance identified or confessed to crimes committed, before they could be granted immunity or indemnity from prosecution. Father Michael Lapsley, survivor of an apartheid letter bomb, was one of those required to obtain indemnity upon his return from exile in 1992. He commented on this curious situation: "I am a priest not a lawyer. I understood that they were forgiving me for their sins."[5] In fact, those who worked to overthrow the apartheid state, by word or deed, were all considered criminals up to 1994; now they must rightly be acknowledged as heroines and heroes.

The key question in all this is: which society is to make these judgments, the old or the new? It is a question that cannot safely, even sensibly, be avoided. Avoiding it would make a nonsense of reconciliation in its genuine sense of closing the ledger book of the past. We cannot possibly close the ledger book while credits and liabilities still masquerade as each other, unreconciled.

The idea of indiscriminate repentance – that the major figures of the resistance must atone for that resistance – would transport South Africa's political culture from the old depravity to a new chaos, rather than repairing it. Morally rudderless repentance by resisters and oppressors alike would further undermine, not reconstruct, the rule of law. The proper guiding principle is this: *The resistance fighters should repent and acknowledge wrongdoing wherever they overstepped the bounds of international law or norms; but where they merely contravened unjust laws or attacked apartheid in any of its manifestations, no such acknowledgment is required.*

The defence of apartheid simply was not a patriotic act. It had nothing in common with the shared nonracial patriotism that flourished in the anti-apartheid resistance. Take for example the occasion on which President Mandela led sports enthusiasts in an expression of national unity surrounding the June 1995 Rugby Cup final. Contrast it with a different occasion, in 1963, when apartheid's prominent torturer for two decades, Theunis ("Rooi Rus") Swanepoel, told one of his victims, Indres Naidoo, that the two would "play South Africa's national sport" – and that Naidoo was the ball. Naidoo was kicked, beaten, thrown to the ground and, when he survived, was called a "lucky coolie."[6] Patriotism itself was disfigured by criminality.

In 1981, an SABC commentator celebrated a rugby victory in these words: "Just as, over the weekend, South Africans rejoiced at the splendid victory of the Springboks in New Zealand, others of the country's representatives were returning from the battlefield in Angola. Their mission there, too, was splendidly accomplished."[7] Disfigured criminal patriotism was carried across southern African borders.

This sort of thing was evident as late as mid-1996, when elements within the South African Defence Force held their traditional Kassinga Day parade, perversely commemorating a 1978 attack on a refugee camp in Angola. The old patriotisms and symbols, however genuinely they were revered, were only ever celebrated by the minority.

Conversely, the resistance was participating in a struggle that was fundamentally *legal and legitimate*, in defiance of apartheid's unjust civil and criminal laws. The only novelty relating to President Mandela's "new patriotism" in South Africa, a patriotism of nonracial collective effort, is the extent to which it is shared by the whole country, whereas previously it was confined to the anti-apartheid resistance.

The decades-long struggle to broaden the hold of this previously marginalised patriotism is not something for which the resistance owes an apology. As ANC National Chairman Jacob Zuma has said, "if people think I have to make a confession about liberating myself then they are mistaken."[8]

Throughout the apartheid years, the courts continued to go through the motions of trying people for crimes, even where they must have known confessions were extracted by torture or based on false evidence. President Nelson Mandela himself, the single most morally respected statesperson in the world today, remains nominally a convicted criminal in the state that he governs so well. This is intolerable.

Whole categories of resisters still carry the taint of convictions, obtained under immoral and vicious laws, against their names. Exemplary legal dissenters like Bram Fischer, excommunicated by the apartheid legal profession, remain nominal outcasts even today. While some living individuals who were previously struck off professional rolls for their convictions have been reinstated, no systematic restoration, no systematic acknowledgment of wrongdoing, has been made. Professional legal bodies such as the Bar Council of South Africa have yet to renounce the systemic complicity of their pasts and to face the uncomfortable facts of that past.

For instance, in 1992 the then chairperson of the Bar Council, Brian Southwood, managed somehow to equate serial killer Barend Strydom with resistance fighter Robert McBride. Strydom, goaded only by an inward racist demon, deliberately attempted to shoot as many black civilians as possible and at random. Conversely, McBride was a member of the armed wing of the African National Congress and acted at all times under the direction and control of his superiors and in pursuance of the strategic and political objectives of the organisation.

At the time of the bombing of the Magoo Bar in Durban, the resistance faced intensified violence from the apartheid bureaucracy. Attacks had been stepped up on "soft targets," such as that in 1985 on a Botswana refugee camp. The ANC's 1985 National Consultative Conference in Zambia, which took the form of a Council of War attended by the top leadership including President Oliver Tambo, expressly addressed this issue. It decided that the situation required a measured and proportional response.

It took a decision to intensify the liberation movement's armed struggle. There would be more attacks on security personnel to show that MK would not allow killings in townships to carry on with impunity. MK actions would no longer be constrained by the absolute requirement to attack only "hard" military targets. In future, it was decided that a wider set of targets, including military personnel, would also be permissible. As Oliver Tambo said in a November 1985 interview, "we will move into military personnel, police and so on . . . we will not go for civilians as such."[9]

It was in pursuit of this policy and under express instructions that McBride targeted the Magoo venue in Durban, known to be frequented by off-duty members of the security forces and which was in fact so frequented on the night in question. To the extent that non-military personnel were, regrettably, harmed in the blast, McBride is entitled to the benefit of the principle of "collateral damage" – that foreseeable but unintended civilian deaths may arise in the course of legitimate military strategies.

He has, in any event, repeatedly expressed profound, even abject, regret and penitence for the loss of civilian life in the blast. He was detained without trial and, additionally, served six full years in jail. Four of those years were spent on death row, in daily anguish as to whether and when he was to be executed.

Like so many others in the resistance, McBride has paid a price. The resisters have been defamed, detained, tortured, banished, exiled, imprisoned, even executed. In addition, they have suffered the systematic oppression and lost opportunities of apartheid. From the point of view of accumulated penance – often unjustly imposed – the scales are heavily weighted in favour of the resistance. Those who defended apartheid celebrated their misdeeds and were lionised and rewarded for them. Simple equity, let alone anything else, precludes us now from placing the resisters, who suffered severely for their efforts, on the same footing as those who gainfully upheld apartheid.

In no event can McBride be classed a "bad apple." His actions, under the direction and control of his superiors, were unambiguously the product of the apple tree as a whole, of the anti-apartheid resistance struggle sanctioned by international law. He was motivated by hatred of the system, not by hatred of all those of the same skin colour as the apartheid rulers. He must therefore be judged by the standards of international law and of the ANC's rights as a liberation movement under international law. In this regard, the 1985 Zambia conference prior to McBride's mission noted: "The question of intensifying the armed struggle poses new challenges and responsibilities on the ANC and on the international community which – by the look of things and the nature of the violence of the enemy – is going to become more involved in that struggle for our liberation."[10]

Robert John McBride undertook his Durban mission literally within days of the apartheid bureaucracy's declaration of its repressive state of emergency on 12 June 1986. The state of emergency granted unlimited powers to the apartheid Security Forces, as well as unilateral self-indemnity from prosecution for any abuses.

In these painful circumstances, the oppressed majority population of the country chose to exercise its right to self-determination under international law, its right to revolt in the overthrow of a genocidal system and its right to resist a crime against humanity. It was in this context that Mr McBride, as a member of Umkhonto weSizwe, joined an organised political uprising against a repressive international outlaw. His victims were victims of the situation of political violence and widespread conflict initiated by the repressive bureaucracy.

At the landmark Dakar talks in 1987, the year after the McBride mission, South African liberal Dr van Zyl Slabbert commented, after listening to ANC participants, that one thing stood beyond any shadow of a doubt, "the only entity that has a choice in resolving the problem of the armed struggle is not the ANC, it's the South African government. They have got to take the initiative. They can decide whether violence is going to escalate or not."[11]

Even South Africa's liberal constituencies have long acknowledged that the apartheid bureaucracy bears *causal* responsibility for triggering the armed response of the struggle for liberation. Helen Suzman commented in 1963 parliamentary debates, as apartheid's repressive manipulation of its legal system intensified, that "long before the final chapter of the struggle ... is written, a great number of people who were formerly peace-loving ... will be driven to desperate acts of recklessness."[12]

But the collective response of the ANC remained methodical; it disavowed recklessness. "We hope that we will bring the government and its supporters to their senses ... before matters reach the desperate stage of civil war," announced Umkhonto we Sizwe, the ANC's newly formed armed wing, in its December 1961 Manifesto. Even in the very hour of its turning to armed struggle, the anti-apartheid resistance left open a possibility of conversation in the face of state recklessness and rejection.

At the 1987 Dakar talks, the anti-apartheid Afrikaner the Rev. Beyers Naudé put the full weight of his spiritual authority behind the view that there was a "grave responsibility to continue to challenge the white community in South Africa to think about the root causes of violence. We must consistently challenge the white community and say that the source of the violence is the systems, the laws, the police actions."[13]

Robert McBride correctly insisted in 1992 that "I am not a criminal, never have been and never will be. Thousands of criminals sit in government and wear its uniform." Similarly, lawyer Albie Sachs commented in 1994 that the members of the anti-apartheid resistance "belonged to a weird generation: we got into trouble not for being bad, but for being good, and that was wrong."

A striking illustration of Sachs's observation is to be found in the remarks passed by the prosecutor Louise van der Walt following activist David Bruce's criminal conviction and sentencing to the maximum six years for resisting compulsory conscription laws. Defensively, she said: "I had no option. He is guilty in terms of the law. Yes, he is not like the criminals I see in this court. His mother is a very intelligent woman."

His mother, who had fled Germany at the age of 10 and lost relatives to the Nazi holocaust, commented after her son's conviction that "we are proud of him, although we are terribly appalled at the severity of the sentence and also at the lack there seems to be for anybody with strong moral convictions to have an alternative choice."[14] An upstanding citizen, she was truly and rightly proud of her son, a criminal convict. Such criminal laws bore no relation to morality.

"Sentence or no sentence, we stand by our leaders," said one placard among two thousand people outside the court on the day that the Rivonia accused were jailed. "We are proud of our leaders," read another as people stood amidst the hostile jeers of privileged students in Pretoria University blazers. Hostile police set dogs on them. When women protesters fell, hostile onlookers laughed. Policemen took banners and threw them in gutters. From the window of a building, hostile occupants threw water on the protesters. Yet they were proud. Proud and unbowed. As Joel Joffe, attorney to the Rivonia accused, wrote at the time, these sturdy sentiments "proclaimed the failure of the prosecution." Dare we now proclaim its success instead?[15]

At one point in his testimony at the Rivonia show trial, Govan Mbeki made it clear that he did not dispute the factual gist of the four charges against him in spite of the fact that he, like his co-accused including Nelson Mandela, had pleaded not guilty. Why? "For the simple reason," he told his pro-apartheid interlocutor, prosecutor Percy Yutar, "that to plead guilty would to my mind indicate a sense of moral guilt to it. I do not accept that there is any moral guilt attached to my actions." Obviously Mr Yutar did not feel himself equipped to enter into such arguments about morality. He simply responded, "All right, let us forget about moral guilt." Mr Mbeki repeated his not-guilty plea.

Today, we cannot afford to forget about moral guilt. We must vigorously refute past mud-slinging, such as that perpetrated by the same prosecutor, Yutar, when he went out of his way to call Joe Slovo (who was not even an accused in the case) "one of the worst traitors to infest South African soil." We dare not leave intact the false slurs on the integrity of those who sacrificed so much to bring down apartheid.

It can never be a justification for a state to say of its opponents – as Vorster associate and head of the Bureau of State Security, Hendrik van den Bergh, said in the 1960s – that "they kill our chaps, so why shouldn't we kill theirs?"[16] A special horror arises when a state turns to criminality, since it is a fundamental task of a legitimate state to promote human development through, among other things, setting itself decisively against criminal behaviour; and, in so doing, taking only such action as is proportional to the evil that is being combated.

More than that, it is the state's task to perform what amounts to a secular sacrament: defining what should count as criminal and what should not. The state has an inevitable role in the generation and sustenance of civic values. It has a monopoly on the powerful process of articulating these values through legislation and, where necessary and justifiable, enforcing them through coercion. So for the state to break its own laws; for state officials to commit what they know the state has set itself against; for this to happen is especially horrifying. It amounts to the state disinventing itself and abdicating its very role as a state. It means the state descends to warlordism and lawlessness. It means the time is out of joint and that the unfortunate citizens, caught up in a predicament not of their making, must act to set it right.

And that is what the anti-apartheid resistance did. It strove to create law out of a lawless and violent morass. In doing this it was guilty, at most, only of sinning against the embodiment of guilt itself. One cannot sin against a system that is sin itself. One cannot meaningfully speak of sinning against hell's norms. In breaching hell's by-laws and regulations – as in breaching the cruel 1935 Nuremberg Decrees of Nazism – one is, in reality, acting out the good, not the bad. One is breaching ostensible laws that are so evil – quite apart from having been passed by authoritarian *diktat* rather than democratic representatives – as to be incapable ever of approaching the elevated status of law.

When Anja Rosmus, a young German girl in the town of Passau, began research for a post-war essay contest on the theme "Everyday life in your home-town during the Third Reich," she began to discover as Nazi sympathisers people whom previously she had grown up to know as resistance fighters. When later she turned her findings into a book, she was ostracised and received hate mail describing her, for instance, as a "Jewish whore" – a phrase that resonates like that apartheid *bête noire*, the "Kaffir lover."

But more interesting than this was the reaction, during her research in the six-ties, seventies and eighties, of people who had genuinely, quietly, been helpful to refugees (her mother who offered food, a town clerk who issued passports to assist escapes). These people, she found, were strangely reticent about the good things they had done. Ms Rosmus, even today in the 1990s, remains hated by the townsfolk for her work in shedding light on past realities. To them she was, as the title of a film about her life put it, a "Dirty Girl." She elaborated:

> Most people don't want to be criticised for breaking the law. People here feel very ambivalent about resistance. They confuse such things as patriotism and law. That is why resistance, even to the Nazis, was never condoned . . . A priest was killed for defending the Jews in Church. Another priest refused to swear an oath of loyalty to Hitler. He was killed too. But nobody ever spoke about these men with any respect. They had broken the rules. They were dis-obedient. And civil disobedience is thought to be a bad thing. My own grandmother still feels guilty about breaking the laws to help people.[17]

The Truth and Reconciliation Commission must speak clearly on this issue. It must make clear, not only to the beneficiaries of apartheid, but also to the families of resisters, that sinning against apartheid was a blessed thing to do. So an evenhanded approach to the past requires a decriminalisation, a statutory de-stigmatisation, of the South African resistance. Only this can ensure that future generations avoid misplaced shame such as that of the Passau anti-Nazi resis-tance.

Acknowledging the Need for Corrective Action

During the transitional negotiations towards South African democracy, ANC President Nelson Mandela reminded those seated across the negotiating table that the "grievous wrongs, distortions, and inequality established and maintained by apartheid have to be addressed, redressed and removed in an orderly fashion."[1]

This approach is rooted in the idea that policymakers of today cannot undo the long history of apartheid, but can work to dismantle the different parts of its ugly legacy. If the new governance fails, apartheid's legacy will re-emerge by default. Hence it is essential to face the past, identify our inheritance, and undo it. So those whose favoured refrain is to accuse the new country of blaming all its ills on the old are engaged in an effort to obfuscate how much the past remains, actually, the present – and how easily it could become our future. Their favoured approach of benign neglect in relation to the legacy of apartheid is certain to guarantee the survival of the past as an intruder in what ought to be a brighter future.

Too often, the President's careful formulation of the imperatives of corrective action across the length and breadth of society have been reduced to narrower notions, analogous to foreign concepts of "affirmative action" in the job market. Increased access to jobs and to all forms of economic opportunity is indeed an important aspect of the broader processes of corrective action in South Africa, but it is nevertheless only one aspect.

Unlike certain versions of the US affirmative action concept, the scope of corrective action in South Africa goes well beyond the job and business markets. South African corrective action is an avowedly wide-ranging process designed to remake a whole society in an orderly and gradual fashion.

Apartheid entrenched racially skewed systems for the provision of basic needs such as water, electricity, education, housing and medical care. Environmentally hazardous power generation facilities were, for instance, deliberately sited in black townships, which thus absorbed the environmental costs of production but were nevertheless generally denied the benefits, since output was often largely transmitted to white areas.

Blacks subsidised whites with their very bodily health; black infants died at rates per thousand that would have seemed a holocaust had they occurred among whites. Black suffering was the price of white wealth. Even the separation of beaches reflected these grotesque bodily cross-subsidies: designated black beaches were invariably the most dangerous, with the highest incidence of drowning, in order that safe beaches could be reserved for whites.

Apartheid society and its organs of policymaking did not even systematically record the African infant mortality rate; in fact they deliberately ignored it while at the same time increasing its incidence through their actions. As Nelson Mandela mentioned in his statement from the dock in the Rivonia show trial, one of the first acts of the apartheid government upon coming to power was to stop subsidies for African school feeding, knowingly worsening starvation and malnutrition among black children; one of his own first acts as President in 1994 was to institute a school-feeding programme as one of several Presidential Projects symbolising, as well as practically implementing, the country's new values.

So this orderly process of correction to which President Mandela refers is one of profound change at all levels of society. It is based on the introduction of real substantive equality, not the fraudulent, formal and empty equality that features in much constitutional jurisprudence elsewhere. South Africa's final constitution, adopted by the Constitutional Assembly in May 1996, provides not only that "everyone is equal before the law and has the right to equal protection and benefit of the law" but also that "equality includes the full and equal enjoyment of all rights and freedoms." Additionally, the constution allows steps to be taken "to promote the achievement of equality, legislative and other measures designed to protect or advance persons, or categories of persons, who are disadvantaged by unfair discrimination."

Apart from its broad scope in reaching all discriminatory aspects of society, the new constitution and its equality clause amount to an explicit rejection of the false concept of "reverse discrimination" that has plagued US constitutional jurisprudence in this area. This false concept suggests that blacks get special treatment of some sort, to the detriment of whites, where corrective action policies are adopted. It suggests that whites are somehow denied an entitlement and done an injustice.

But in fact race-conscious corrective action does not give disadvantaged communities "special treatment" whether in the US, South Africa, or elsewhere. It rather undoes historical injustices that were perpetrated on disadvantaged communities and not on privileged ones. Those who detect "special treatment" here might just as well complain, as a fire engine speeds to a burning house, that this frantic attention privileges the charred abode, compared to those that are not ablaze.

Those who warn of reverse discrimination and insist on formal equality rely on a vulgar and geometrical idea of equality that is blind to the wisdom of history and to the story that the Truth and Reconciliation Commission must tell; it must give them eyes to see. If this job of historical clear-sightedness is properly done, their false moral geometry will be banished from our ethics, policymaking, governance and business practices.

But this is a large job, given the ways of seeing that are still entrenched among apartheid's privileged, whose thinking has been blunted by decades of false policy during which language was used to obscure and mislead. Fine-sounding pieces of legislation such as the Abolition of Passes Act, or the Extension of Universities Act, in fact meant the opposite of what they seemed to promise blacks; they were saturated with the illogic of white supremacy.

These abuses of language functioned as alibis for the racism of the past, though they failed to conceal it. Such distortions thrived in a mindset that still exerts vestigial influence today, one in which the concept of reverse discrimination slips as easily off the tongue as all the dishonest moral and statutory concepts that preceded it under apartheid.

An extraordinary recent example of this corrupt language is the former Deputy President de Klerk's suggestion, in June 1996, that "the ANC sounds more and more like an apartheid party because they talk of race all the time and not sensible policies."[2] Not only does this deliberately ignore the orderliness and good sense at the heart of Mandela governance, it actually seeks to evade present-day society's accountability for apartheid's legacy by inviting the apartheid privileged to dismiss the dismantling of apartheid as a form of apartheid itself. Even Orwell would surely gasp at this.

At the heart of the corrective action debate is a need to revise the very language and cognitive currency of public life. Corrective action must extend to the basic building blocks of our collective self-awareness. Corrective action includes the undoing of the whole range of falsehoods, all the fake language and dishonest policy, upon which past public consciousness rested and still rests. Where false language has credence, incorrect action is inevitable.

This corruption of language under apartheid was at its most striking when words wrapped themselves like velvet around violence. In a 1988 police commemorative album for example, the egregious Adriaan Vlok, the Minister of Law and Order, alleged that the South African police force has "always maintained Christian norms and civilised standards." This was the same Minister who spoke in 1987 of a need to "annihilate" political opponents[3] and who was responsible for police practices during the three years between January 1985 and December 1987 when 50,000 people were held without trial[4] – the vast majority, as several studies confirm, subjected to some form of torture. This number was roughly equal to the total number of detentions in the preceding quarter century. Between 1960 and 1990 – including the 1985 to 1987 period – a total of 100,000 people were detained.

The apartheid bureaucracy could even transform its murderous behaviour as an international outlaw, an aggressor towards its neighbours, into something seemingly very different. Thus the apartheid bureaucrats openly sought to confer upon themselves the dignified title of "regional power" which, according to apartheid Foreign Minister Pik Botha, meant that "no problems in southern Africa can be resolved unless the legitimate interests of this regional power, [apartheid] South Africa, are taken into account."[5] President Mandela's decision in 1995 to write off significant amounts of Namibia's debt to South Africa must be seen in part as a corrective action initiative on a regional scale.

But the corruption of language under apartheid was more subtle than the foregoing examples would suggest. Similar distortions – respectable excuses for indefensible politics – underlie, for instance, the debate over "federalism" in the new South Africa. In its respectable forms, federalism is a doctrine that harmonises the self-determination of a national unit with that of its various sub-parts; but in its South African usage, federalism is intended to disperse governance, entrench racism, and paralyse efforts at corrective action.

So it is simply wrong to separate, as some still try to do, support for federalism from the moral and political agenda of its advocates. In South Africa, federalism has been the war cry of those who seek an immobilised state, deprived of all ability to implement corrective action.

Another prominent excuse for the preservation of illegitimate privilege is the idea that corrective action threatens existing high "standards," whether of "merit" or of "civilisation," or other such sophorisms – sleep-inducing banalities. In making such claims, the historical realities of job reservation (to the exclusion of blacks) and of barbarity (in defence of apartheid) are conveniently ignored.

Thus National Party leader F W de Klerk said in March 1990, during the early days of the transition, that "anyone who believes that we will accept a dispensation in which the *quality* of existing freedoms and rights is *negatively* affected is making a mistake" (emphasis added). This language turns political morality on its head. Apartheid booty suddenly seems an upright product, almost like full shopping bags after a respectable, high-quality, spending spree.

Nor is this a new gambit for adherents of the old order. "Our tradition-rich school is our pride"[6] boasts the decades-old slogan in the prospectus for white supremacist Potgietersrus Primary School – which gained world-wide notoriety for the racism displayed in 1996 when it resisted the admission of three black children.

Under apartheid there were no discernible limits to the atrocities that could be garbed in soothing civilised rhetoric and talk of standards. For instance, in its 1989 Working Paper on a Bill of Rights, the South African Law Commission, advocating a Bill of Rights, found useful precedent in the nineteenth-century Orange Free State *Grondwet*, a basic law that set out nice-sounding civil liberties but wholly excluded blacks from them and established the basis for inequality between black and white in church and state. Yet the Law Commission ignored the ANC's 1923 Bill of Rights and its more comprehensive 1943 Bill of Rights as useful precedents. There was no shared past for the then Law Commission.

It should give us pause that as late as 1989 a relatively reputable South African legal body could either fall into such manifest forgetfulness, or still be so ignorant of relevant South African human rights traditions, or even, worst of all, be so cravenly compliant with the apartheid legislation that rendered the ANC a banned organisation.

There is profound irony in this last possibility: that apartheid's bannings reduced the Law Commission's deliberations in 1989 on a new bill of rights for South Africa to a form of amoral constitutional nostalgia. Under the lash of apartheid's banning laws, references to state-sanctioned – and avowedly racist – constitutional precedents necessarily displaced humanist and nonracial ANC constitutional materials, exactly because apartheid law at the time so decreed. This illustrates the extent to which apartheid legal practice, even at its most creative and reformist, was a creature of the criminal state that hosted it.

There is a need for a critical and corrective legal practice to undo the apartheid legal profession's seamless entry into the new order. It must abandon the romantic idea that, despite its own past, it is somehow part of a global tradition of common law genius (which is itself heavily dosed with nostalgia). In fact, the apartheid common law system and its lawyers were generally, with some notable and previously demonised exceptions, the bureaucratic face of atrocity.

Outside the common law, in the context of statutory corrective action, the then Minister of Planning Hernus Kriel (now Western Cape Premier) in 1991 flatly rejected the idea of anti-discrimination legislation because, he said, "we believe in free association."[7] Kriel failed to explain how "free" association could be built by pulling up the drawbridge at the very moment that formerly unfree citizens try to cross the moat, seeking inclusion in the public and private life of the new country. Mr Kriel's skewed definition of free association has no place in today's employment equity legislation. Debate over that legislation must be informed by historical realities and by a frontal facing of the past, not by a free-floating language of alibis.

One of the most hard-fought issues in the negotiation of the final South African Constitution was that of constitutional guarantees for Afrikaans-medium schools, supposedly designed to preserve Afrikaans culture. Those who most firmly opposed the inclusion of socio-economic rights (such as the right to education) in the constitution, ostensibly on some principled basis, had no trouble deadlocking the constitutional process with demands for a specific subset of such rights – a guarantee of racially exclusive Afrikaans schools. In the familiar racist alibi, the soothing terminology of preserving Afrikaans "culture" stood in for the more blunt defence of racial privilege.

In the February 1996 Potgietersrus school controversy mentioned above, this alibi – the alleged defence of Afrikaner culture – was very much in evidence. It was exposed as a pretence as it became clear that the school had a longstanding practice of admitting white English-speaking children and excluding black Afrikaans-speaking ones. It became starkly apparent that the issue was race, not language or culture. The Potgietersrus events pushed the issue of racially separate education to the forefront of the constitutional negotiations which culminated in mid-1996.

That race was in fact an issue in these constitutional negotiations was suggested by the way in which Freedom Front MP Constand Viljoen rejected proposals for own-language classes within multi-cultural schools. He flatly stated that "a class of 35 Afrikaans children in a school of 700 Black children will not be able to maintain its culture."[8]

This anxious version of culture defines itself by the ugly criteria of exclusion and by the explicit rejection of nonracialism. In addition, it conveniently pronounces well-funded Afrikaans-medium schools off limits to blacks, entrenching the inherited inequities of apartheid. It directly contradicts the spirit and promise of the ANC's 1955 Freedom Charter, which underpins President Mandela's ideals of reconciliation: 'The doors of learning and culture shall be opened." It is a standpoint that was rejected in the constitutional negotiations.

Similar issues have arisen, in suitably rarefied form, in the context of tertiary education. Professor Charles van Onselen, a well-known social historian at Johannesburg's historically white University of the Witwatersrand, has argued that such privileged universities were "organically" and "legitimately" linked to the mainstream (i.e. white apartheid) economy as opposed to the black universities which, he says, were "peripheral."

This deceptively bland and seemingly factual statement actually has extraordinary political implications, serving as a quiet justification for preserving apartheid's inherited educational imbalances in the new country.

Van Onselen objects that if the black universities manage to secure greater material support in redress of inherited inequalities, this would "further diminish the amount available to those with commitments to running expensive high-tech facilities at the core." Van Onselen takes the end product of apartheid, that is the creation of underfunded "bantustan" education for blacks and lavish institutions for whites, and effectively uses this shameful history as a legitimate basis on which to argue against corrective action in the funding of institutions of higher learning.

It is an approach that leads to the reproduction of inequalities and precludes the question of redress, and therefore of genuine reconciliation, from being addressed.[9] Van Onselen is refreshingly frank in acknowledging that his approach supplies new justifications for the patterns of the past:

> In the new South Africa, as in the old – but for different reasons no longer predicated on race alone – there will be a continuing need for a wide range of institutions of tertiary education operating at different levels which will seek to address the needs of a complex and diversified economy, a society informed by several cultures and traditions, and a political system that is sensitive to imperatives encountered over a vast terrain.[10]

This is little more than a tortured justification for the discredited rhetoric of "separate development." Nowhere does the question of equity – which schools should have which functions and why? – even arise. Van Onselen simply assumes that apartheid's patterns of specialisation must be perpetuated on the basis that whereas different institutions previously catered for different races, they now have different "functions."

This approach is unintentionally Verwoerdian in its unstated idea that bush universities must remain just that; and if they think they can rise above a certain level of institutional development they are mistaken – just as, for Verwoerd, the

"Bantu" was mistaken in aspiring to social roles above a certain level of personal development, hence Bantu Education.

On Van Onselen's theory, the ANC ought to reclaim its historical archives from Fort Hare University and give them instead to one of the historically white universities which, to Van Onselen's way of thinking, have resource advantages which they automatically deserve to keep. Corrective action and political morality disappear along with institutional history. This illustrates the pressing need for a careful reckoning of the past as a compass in navigating today's policy debates.

The very idea of functional differentiation, of different tasks for different categories of institutions, itself can have varying moral and political implications, dependent upon the tasks and categories that underpin the differentiation, and the precise manner of its proposed implementation. Thus, in debates over the 1996 proposals of the National Commission for Higher Education, some policy-makers attempted to use the concept of functional differentiation, underpinned by state funding, in a manner very different from the Van Onselen model. Under certain of the Commission's proposals, functional differentiation would mean placing the state's resources for career-oriented and product-related research in the preserve of the technikons (similar to UK polytechnics or US community colleges), while confining the traditional universities to more rarefied research and professional education functions. Predictably, the historically privileged universities favour a more flexible differentiation, which would not so definitively shut them out of lucrative vocational activities. They would like to be able to "cherry pick" across functional divides, performing vocational functions where prestige or large budgets are forthcoming, while abandoning the less glamorous or less lucrative of such activities. Only through detailed attention to the particular histories of institutions, and categories of institutions, can these seemingly abstract educational debates make any sense.

Another attempt at a laundering of history – an attempt to confer a present dignity on a past practice of collective looting – arose when, in their transitional local government proposals, the National Party sought to preserve the autonomy of previously all-white communities by defending their right to maintain their alleged "norms and standards."

As the Nationalists' 1991 White Paper on Land Reform put the point, "those who have already reached a high standard, are entitled to a higher order of services and to the maintenance of values appropriate to their lifestyle." Here again, forgetting (or ignoring) historical reality allows atrocity to be dressed up as the achievement of a high standard. Apartheid's ill-gotten gains become an actual entitlement that must be maintained in the new country. The Truth and Reconciliation Commission must assist the country to identify and reject such speciousness.

Similar audacious assumptions were present in the "Residential Environment Bill" tabled in Parliament along with the 1991 White Paper. Such statements, policies and legislative proposals almost make racial privilege and residential segregation seem like a product of hard work and moral rectitude.

But in fact, the skewed "norms and standards" of apartheid and its misallocation of "freedoms and rights" must be acknowledged on all sides to be indefensible. So to change this illegitimate spread of rights and freedoms, to alter these standards and norms, obviously affects things positively, for the better, even if those who were previously privileged experience this adjustment as a loss of "freedoms or rights." The alternative, as President Mandela said in 1991, is to "prevent majority rule having any meaning" and to ensure that the "accumulated privileges of white minority rule remain inviolate."[11]

In his opening address to the Federal Congress of the National Party in 1991, Mr de Klerk audaciously claimed that while he himself was "concerned about values and stability," his opponents in the anti-apartheid resistance were "obviously still concerned with a difference between Black and White, about things that happened in the past and about a bygone era," a contrast he has repeatedly returned to since then.

The problem with this wishful and forgetful approach is that past inequities will not disappear of their own accord; they must actively be dismantled. To avert our eyes from the past is to tolerate it as a continuing and phantom chauffeur in a seemingly new journey. The forgetting of history and truth in debates over current policy adds yet another to the accumulated blind spots that divide those who presided over the old system from those who seek, through corrective action, to speed nonracial democracy into all aspects of the new country's life.

The National Party's emphasis on "white" or "family" values and on norms and standards as veils to conceal illegitimate historical privilege is essentially identical to the language used in early 1988 by a white town clerk in the western Transvaal when he explained to the *Wall Street Journal* his council's decision to remove 600 black families from Koster township to a point 500 metres away from the town itself: "We need a buffer area for the same reason every other town has one. The Black's standard of living isn't the same as ours. Their culture isn't the same." A white farmer added, "They're different. They aren't on the same level as us; they aren't as developed. In the United States, you don't understand. Your blacks are more cultured and educated, just like the whites. Our blacks aren't."[12]

Thus, past deprivation surges back to underwrite new waves of itself.

The underlying problem is that the pilots of the old system still hope, as in previous periods of apartheid "reform", for a semblance of democracy without its substance. This is clear from the dismissive assumption, voiced by the National Party's Gerrit Viljoen during the transition, that a mere "arithmetic majority" could not be given "all political power for a period." This dismissiveness of the majority (for, of course, all majorities are "arithmetic" ones) was little more than a desire to confine the country's previously voteless population to an updated apartheid role of participation without power.

Only an absence of collective memory permits such disingenuous constitutional formulations to seem other than absurd. What is most interesting about the National Party's "reformist" constitutional agenda – in the early transitional 1990s as well as more subtly today – is its lack of novelty. In 1977 Nationalist minister Dr Piet Koornhof spoke of a "sophisticated parliamentary system" based on the Swiss model and protecting "cultural pluralism." Earlier, in 1970, as a Minister who had perfected racist Group Areas arrangements, P W Botha mooted a "canton system."

These earlier versions of the Nationalists' more recent proposals and continuing policies are united in one goal: to avoid black participation or else to render it toothless, in deference to the ultimate principle of white rule. Dealing with the South African past means retaining a memory of such continuities of policy at the forefront of national debates.

Past failures of collective memory left the country, particularly its privileged citizens, vulnerable to manipulative rhetoric. For instance, in a 1974 speech to the United Nations, apartheid Minister of Foreign Affairs Pik Botha made comments that were widely interpreted as a promise to dismantle race and colour barriers in South Africa. Yet in 1977, without having renounced the UN speech, Pik Botha could comment on German television that his government would "never in 100 years agree to share power with blacks, Coloureds and Asians."[13] The same man who was a decade later disciplined by apartheid President P W Botha for acknowledging that there could after all be a black South African president, told an American television audience in August 1976 that South Africa was working towards an "African dream of a White South Africa."[14]

The hope was and is that, in the absence of collective memory, the more that South Africa might seem to change, the more it might stay the same. Failures of collective memory place obstacles of blindness in the path of corrective action.

Moreover, mildly updated segregationist fantasies survived well into the negotiation period and, arguably, into the new South Africa – and not only among right wing Volkstaat separatists. Similar claims underlay, for instance, the calls in mid-1995 for privileged and exclusive local government electoral districts to be established in the Western Cape and in Gauteng province.

Another example of an attempt to protect past segregationist gains from present-day correction was the vigorous debate over the scope of the new constitution, specifically as to whether it should govern relations only between the state and citizens or should, additionally, prevent powerful private entities and individuals from abusing their illegitimate historical advantage. In the end the new constitution unambiguously adopted the latter approach, but the extent of the opposition to this result suggests that many South African constituencies have yet to catch up with the real significance of their own pasts.

Ultimately, technical constitutional mechanisms and seemingly arcane policy debates cannot be viewed in moral and historical vacuums. A shared process of corrective action must be rooted in a shared basic vision of the old order and the new country alike. The latter – a vision of the new country – must be continually debated and ceaselessly revised. But the renunciation both of apartheid and of its tenacious legacies must be unequivocal. That is why we cannot ignore the past and its implications for present debates in the new country.

The ANC's Special Commission on constitutional negotiations, presenting its 1992 report to the ANC National Policy Conference that year, chose the credo "From corruption, murder and mismanagement to democracy, justice and good government." This transition from the one to the other cannot be effected if we continually lose sight of what the one was and thus of what the other can be. A thorough reckoning of the South African past is crucial in ensuring that corrective action processes do not lose their historical moorings and condemn us to moral and political drift.

9

Confronting the Roots of Violence

"The National Party can't say they didn't know what was going on. They didn't stay in power because the majority of people supported them. They were in power because of people like me."

– Eugene de Kock, accused apartheid death squad commander (March 1996).

"Depending on the circumstances, I don't have a problem with killing children."

– J P Opperman, former apartheid intelligence officer and hit squad commander (March 1996).

Early in 1996, workers renovating an auditorium in the Cape Town parliamentary complex discovered a bomb-proof bunker hidden under a bust of apartheid's architect, H F Verwoerd.

They found a bomb shelter under what ought to have been the country's cradle of democracy and uncovered a vital truth about the place of law in apartheid. The bomb shelter, and a concealed lift linking the auditorium to an underground tunnel, were apparently built in the early seventies under the premiership of John Vorster and at a time when apartheid's "outward policy" was to present a benign reformist face to Africa and the world.[1]

A bomb-shelter at the heart of governance; this could scarcely be bettered as a metaphor for a terrorist regime for whom parliament was a cockpit of war rather than the forum of a society in conversation. "We have reached the stage in our national life where we realise more and more that there are times in a nation's history when not only reason must speak but blood as well – and that time is now," said Vorster in 1963, when he was Minister of Justice. In that same year, having congratulated the police and defence force for their allegedly sterling contribution to social stability, Prime Minister H F Verwoerd bluntly put parliament in its place: "I will not hesitate to place the security of the State and its citizens above technicalities . . . in the ordinary administration of justice." Governance cowered in the shadow of violence.

The sixties in South Africa saw the intensification of a long process of restructuring the so-called forces of law and order, the police and the army, into instruments of vicious oppression. In June 1968, the then Defence Minister P W Botha announced at a Republic Day festival that the commando units, a conscripted Citizen Force, would have to be restructured and trained for "conventional as well as unconventional methods of warfare."[2]

Murderous state-sponsored hit squads have been in existence at least since the formation of the "Z-squad" in the late 1960s, and are widely acknowledged to have stirred up much of the so-called black-on-black violence in the period leading up to the 1994 democratic elections. The police were trained to extract confessions from political prisoners by torture, and the army to hunt down and exterminate so-called terrorists and subversive elements. By January 1994, the Goldstone Commission confirmed the involvement of senior South African police officers in "a horrible network of criminal activity" intended to spread disruption and violence.

This terrifying war machine stood between a largely irrelevant parliament and the majority of the people of South Africa. Parliament regularly voted in favour of the defence budget, without questioning its details. Of an overall defence budget of close to ten billion rand in the 1980s, well in excess of five billion was voted blindly every year. In such a system, ideals of legality were necessarily a tatty afterthought. Alongside home-grown military technology of the very highest efficiency stood constitutional theory and practice that were derelict to the point of incompetence.

These were not new ideas. After a surprisingly strong electoral showing in September 1930 as he worked his way towards power, Adolf Hitler addressed a rally in Munich to clarify for his followers that parliament was merely, as he put it, one "weapon" among many. "For us Parliament is not an end in itself, but merely a means to an end . . . We are not on principle a parliamentary Party, [only] by compulsion, under constraint."[3] In South Africa, leading architects of apartheid had already demonstrated, in their violent extra-parliamentary resistance to the war against Hitler after parliament voted in favour of that war, that for them, too, parliament was merely one option in an arsenal of force.

Apartheid's falsehoods and systems of state-sponsored lawlessness bred contempt for language, including legal language. Under apartheid, law, which should have been a pillar of justice and social stability and a wall against violence and chaos, became instead an agent of injustice and social instability and a catalyst for violence and chaos. Law was systematically reduced, as one observer has commented, to a continuation of violence by other means.

There were several strands to the violence of law under apartheid. South African law always lacked, even before apartheid, vital ingredients of democratic legitimacy, a defect which apartheid exacerbated. Second, it lacked, particularly as apartheid legislation accumulated, a basic attribute of all laws, and that is the simple ability to provide rational guidance for lawful conduct. Much apartheid legislation was so capricious, in its drafting as well as its application, as to defy all efforts at good-faith obedience. Third, a whole battery of laws made political dissent a crime. The normal functions of a responsible citizenry became the business of the country's jailers. Fourth, the apartheid state increasingly conferred forms of lawless discretion on its functionaries in the civil service, the police and the military; it humbled and co-opted what should have been an independent judiciary. Fifth, the government sought vainly to control the very fabric of reality through its censorship laws. And finally, the cumulative logic of this wholesale and varied contempt for law triggered the ultimate expression of bomb-shelter governance – the deployment of the state's resources to inflict random terror and assassination on the state's own citizens. Each part of this declension is examined in more detail below.

1. Law and Democracy

What separates the rule of law from the rule of force is, among other things, the felt legitimacy and voluntary allegiance that the lawmaker enjoys among the governed. In a very real sense, therefore, laws cannot exist where the majority of those subject to their dictates have no voice in the formulation of them. This was the case in South Africa in every election prior to that of April 1994. As President Mandela commented in 1991, the 1983 Constitution "derived from the support of just over 1 million voters," and the then government itself was elected by slightly more than one million people of a total population approaching forty million, so "we speak of a government without a shred of legitimacy."[4]

The 1983 Constitution consolidated a long history of illegitimate South African governance, wholly inconsistent with the rule of law in its fertile and legitimate sense. The 1909 Union Constitution incorporated the pre-existing (and varying) franchise laws of the several colonies. A right as fundamental as the right to vote was determined, in the unitary South Africa of 1909, by the accidents of the prior histories of the disparate colonies. These limited black voting rights, found only in the Cape and Natal, were circumscribed by property qualifications or granted as a privilege on a case-by-case basis, for example, to handpicked Africans "exempt from the Native law" in Natal.

Even these faint glimmerings of the principle of a nonracial franchise were aggressively attacked by apartheid legislators during the 1950s. The Nationalists' failure to muster the required two-thirds majority laid down in the 1909 constitution as a precondition to altering the franchise rules led them into extended clashes with the courts, including attempts to divest the courts of relevant judicial functions in favour of a so-called "High Court of Parliament," which was to be the final arbiter of the validity of Acts of Parliament.

These manoeuvres – more than a little bizarre from a standpoint of judicial independence, let alone nonracialism – were nevertheless ultimately successful through reliance on the device of an artificially enlarged Senate stacked with Nationalist appointees. An all-white electorate was thus established, free of even the inadequate marginal representation of blacks that had previously existed. By 1977 the last Coloured common roll municipal franchise disappeared in the Cape, Prime Minister Vorster having ten years earlier declared his party's determination that "Whites and Whites only will be represented in Parliament in Cape Town."[5]

In 1965, when it appeared likely that the Progressive Party opposition would capture the four Coloured seats in Parliament, the Nationalists did not hesitate to misuse the law. The Prohibition of Improper Political Interference Act was unveiled, making interracial political mobilisation unlawful. It forced parties to organise on strictly racial lines.

Earlier, the 1959 Promotion of Bantu Self-Government Act had removed the meagre surviving pockets of enfranchisement among Africans. And before that, in the immediate aftermath of their slender electoral victory in 1948, the Nationalists moved to expand the white supremacist vote by granting the 24,000 whites in occupied South West Africa (Namibia) representation in the South African parliament on a numerical basis more favourable than even South African whites were granted. (South Africa's all-white constituencies each averaged roughly 9,000 to 12,000 voters in the 1950s; Namibia was given six seats, resulting in 4,000 voters per constituency.) The Nationalists accurately calculated that Namibia's Afrikaner and German whites, some of whom had been deported by Smuts for wartime Nazi sympathies, would be solidly Nationalist in their loyalties.

Hence South West African whites enjoyed representation without taxation in the South African parliament, while South African blacks faced taxation and extraordinary regulation without representation. Moreover, one of the four white South West African senators (these were in addition to the six elected representatives) was by statute required to be appointed by the apartheid government itself on the basis of the appointee's perceived knowledge of the "reasonable wants and wishes" of the "Coloured races" of the Namibian territory.

The naked manipulation of parliament's lawmaking ability in order to reshape parliament's own accountability to its electorate, from which that lawmaking power theoretically derived, was too much even for some Nationalists to stomach. Japie du P Basson, who was expelled from the National Party for his opposition to the 1959 Act, commented that:

> Parliamentary democracy is never exposed to greater and more actual danger than when a political party which is in power at a specific moment and which has been given a limited mandate for a period of five years, uses the parliamentary machinery to change the constitution of parliament in a way which, deliberately or otherwise, strengthens its own political position.[6]

It was, in short, a deliberate form of parliamentary banditry. Quite apart from the abhorrent nature of apartheid's substantive agenda, that agenda was pursued in a manner that demonstrated complete contempt for parliamentary democracy, disdain for voters, including white voters, and an unambiguous pattern of manipulating law rather than upholding it. All this reduced the unjust legislative system that apartheid inherited to something even more vulgarised: a profoundly lawless bureaucracy wielding brute force with only the skimpiest pretensions to democratic norms of legality.

2. Law As a Guide to Conduct

Moreover, in implementing thuggery, apartheid legislators neglected the basic requirements that any lawmaker, legitimate or otherwise, needs to observe if her laws are to find compliance: there must be clear guidance, settled and pre-dictable patterns of enforcement, and an absence of caprice.

Where such preconditions are not fulfilled, the law's attempts to direct conduct fail because its directives are vague, incomprehensible or shifting. Like a blunt knife that cannot cut anything, imprecise law fails to get its own job done because it fails really to tell people what to do. By this test, South Africa's apartheid laws must rank as a model of failure in the post-war era. Apartheid laws comprised large areas of ungoverned discretionary power.

But this legal failure is not only (or always) a practical failure from the point of view of the legislator's intention. It is also a moral and political abuse of the governed. For the failure to supply clear guidance for lawful conduct was not accidental. It disabled those subject to apartheid laws from remaining law-abiding – because they had no way of knowing what compliance required of them. They could do nothing to avoid infringement and so simply had to hope that they were never held to have infringed, rather than deliberately acting so as to ensure non-infringement.

Such circumstances reduce law's subjects to a position of legal insecurity and place the commission or non-commission of an infringement more in the hands of the responsible administrators than in the hands of the legal subject as a responsible citizen. In this precise sense, by ignoring the basic human agency of the governed, apartheid dehumanised those who were subject to its dictates.

And therein lay the paradoxical usefulness of fuzzy law for apartheid law-makers. Arbitrary power (especially over blacks), and the insecurity that went with it, were both part of their design. These factors assaulted the morale of those subject to law and assisted the attempt to manufacture a passive black citizenry, an attempt that, while never wholly successful, was always at the heart of apartheid. What failed as law could succeed as a more brutal form of social control, passing under the legitimising label of law. There was a special jurisdiction of "Native" courts to facilitate these goals of lawless social control.

Moreover, it was not only blacks who were subjected to such forms of arbitrary social control under colour of law. The regulation of apartheid's predominantly white media institutions was subject to such caprice that Kelsey Stuart's authoritative *Newspaperman's Guide to the Law,* intended as a straightforward guide for practising journalists, could do no better than the following in relation to offences under the 1982 Internal Security Act (which itself was supposed to have consolidated and clarified prior law): "Editors and journalists should be wary of *unwittingly*" infringing the security laws and thus facing jail terms as high as ten years (emphasis added). The end result of this was to chill anti-apartheid reporting, undermine independent reporters and effectively co-opt the press as part of the security apparatus.

In respect of reporting on organised campaigns of resistance – simple civil disobedience – Stuart's *Guide* warned: "The safest course is to examine all campaigns against laws very carefully before in any manner becoming associated with them. In reporting any such campaigns, the 'dead pan' approach is the wisest unless it is absolutely certain that illegal acts form no part of them."[7] This state of affairs was an insidious assault on the morale of potentially decent journalists who, unless they had unequivocal anti-apartheid commitments extending to a willingness to incur punishment, were forced to think twice before telling things as they were. The coverage of the Soweto Uprising in 1976 is a clear illustration. Journalists often did not believe the stories filed by the newly appointed black journalists and preferred to give the regime's version of events.

While whites were thus not wholly exempt, the caprice directed at blacks was all-pervasive. For instance, the entire apartheid system was underpinned by the legal mechanisms of racial classification, set out in the 1950 Population Registration Act.

But in practice, given the innate incoherence of racial categories, it proved difficult to define a white person. So over the years the definition changed from time to time, hovering between "appearance" and "acceptance," with even the most zealous officials experiencing acute frustration in their attempts at rational enforcement. The law absurdly specified that a white person is one "who in appearance obviously is, or who is generally accepted as, a White person, but does not include a person who, although in appearance obviously a White person, is generally accepted as a Coloured person."

Absurdity multiplied when the definition was altered in order to accommodate the Japanese (who were concluding important trade arrangements with South Africa) through according them "honorary white status," so that the privileged category then included any person "who is generally accepted as a White person even though obviously not in appearance a White person." Maverick black West Indian cricketers, forming part of sanctions-busting "rebel" tours of the old South Africa, were also accorded this status of "honorary whites," a fact which exposed them to intense ridicule and contempt in their home countries and, moreover, did not insulate them from the vagaries of racist abuse in South Africa.

Such capricious definitions were supplemented by tests of the most grotesque imprecision, such as the infamous test of running a pencil through the hair on the theory that even invisible black curliness would detain it, while truly white hair would release it. These tests were applied by administrative courts appointed by the Minister without any appeal to the ordinary courts. Rights of voting, residence, property, schooling, movement, marriage and conjugal relations, among other cradle to grave matters, could all be affected by the largely unfettered decisions of administrative bodies implementing these vaguely worded and inherently unscientific racial classifications.

The initial divisions into White, Coloured and Native groups were extended by a regulation in 1959 when the Coloured category was subdivided into Cape Coloured, Cape Malay, Griqua, Chinese, Indian, Other Asiatic and Other Coloured. Whatever this law achieved, it did not set up clear guidelines for separating one supposed racial group from another, as the stubborn phenomenon of "borderline cases" attested.

In 1967, the Population Registration Amendment Act, making descent the main factor in determining racial classification, attempted to close the gates on borderline cases and racial hybridity and to give some semblance of rationality to the basic concepts that underpinned the entire superstructure of apartheid. But this attempt, in the responsible Minister's words, to end the "gradual" and "dangerous" process of racial integration, was no more effective than its 1950 and 1959 predecessors.

It had retrospective effect, breaking up existing communities; it arbitrarily gave precedence to the classification of the male parent over the female in the case of a child born into a subgroup of the Coloured group, leading to such absurdities as the segregation of cousin from cousin. The legislation remained an incoherent morass incapable of providing clear guidance of any sort; it was the opposite of law.

The difficulties of racial classification were compounded by novel challenges of criminal detection when these racial categories served as the basis for the prohibition of interracial marriage and sexual relations, just as the Nazi Nuremberg Decrees forbade marriage and extramarital relations between Jews and Aryans.[8]

In South Africa, detection of such so-called crimes of miscegenation involved the careful examination of bedsheets, the creative use of mirrors, binoculars, tape recorders, cameras and two-way radios to facilitate observation, the arrest of offenders in the veld and in gravel pits, the concealment of investigating officers in cupboards, under beds, in long grass, in trees or in car boots. This all provides entertaining anecdotes about the enforcement of the racial classification system, but also underlines the necessarily random and often tragic nature of that enforcement.

The laws restricting the right of Africans to free movement in their own country caused terrible suffering to many more than did the laws prohibiting interracial marriage and sex. The pass laws, restricting the physical movement of Africans to those areas endorsed in the pass books that they were required to carry, resulted in over 381, 000 Africans being arrested in the year 1975–76, at the height of their use; and in over 12 million arrests over the period from 1948 to 1985.

Every year tens of thousands of Africans were "endorsed out" or summarily evicted from urban areas at the behest of labour bureaux officials who were barely accountable to anyone but themselves. The 1963 Aliens Control Act provided that foreign Africans not in possession of appropriate documentation could be detained, deported without trial and made to perform prison labour pending deportation; after 1974 this applied to African South Africans who were suddenly dubbed foreign too, arbitrarily stripped of citizenship and reassigned membership of homelands.

Through this deliberately capricious superintendence of their personal movements, people were reduced to units of labour, imported and exported in accordance with the perceived labour needs of white business. Most importantly, the imagined smooth and efficient process of importing and exporting people remained a fiction. In reality the system was inept, cruel, wasteful and, most importantly, lawless. It elevated tinpot bureaucrats, for all practical purposes, into *de facto* lawmakers.

The entire system of criminalising job-seeking in the cities also flew in the face of economic rationality. In the eighties, a person from Ciskei could earn three times as much by working three months in Cape Town and spending nine months in jail as would be earned by working for the whole year in the Ciskei – where, anyway, jobs were invisible.

Apartheid's internal security statutes, such as the Terrorism Act of 1967, were examples of statutes that imposed harsh sanctions, including death, while giving little meaningful guidance about how to avoid contravention of the law. These are more fully discussed in the following two sections.

Apartheid's legislators were in large part concerned to paralyse individuals and whole communities, rather than to galvanise a united country in the pursuit of shared societal goals. This meant that their laws did not uniformly seek to deliver crisp guidance to an eager and highly motivated citizenry, as would be the case in a well-functioning rule of law system. Apartheid legislation that sought to demoralise rather than to build may have tried to pass under the banner of law, but it always lacked true law's essential ingredients of allegiance and civic-mindedness.

One unwitting apologist for apartheid has argued, in *The Liberal Slideaway*, a book that upon its publication in 1995 received much attention in South Africa, that apartheid was not merely equivalent to its opposite (the resistance), but that apartheid was actually, in some ways, more defensible than the forms of resistance that grew up against it. In a romanticised view of the apartheid legal regime, this author argued that its "structural violence at least has the quality of being structural, with its own bureaucracy, rules, reports, files, trials, and inquests, and can be challenged within its own terms ... The other violence [*sic*] has no boundaries, only a vastly sinister impetus of its own and weird shifting rules which no one who wants to be safe can work out how to obey."9

This is the certifiable voice of apartheid's safe suburbanites for whom that lawless system could somehow seem sane and reassuring, compared to the distant vagaries of the resistance to apartheid. The myth that apartheid was a system of rule-bound and orderly violence is not only inaccurate but chilling. Nazism too had some of this false fragrance of orderliness, which, however, did not increase its legitimacy; it merely created a new homicidal class – the desk murderers.

The apartheid system was predominantly a runaway bureaucracy, not an orderly and rule-bound system; and to the minor extent that it was rule-bound, that banalisation of evil made apartheid more shocking, not less.

3. Criminalisation of Dissent

In a properly functioning society, genuinely underlain by the rule of law, the legislative process forever wants to throw its arms wider and wider, so that law can be a final product of exhaustive societal dialogue. Such has, for instance, been the process of writing the final constitution in the new South Africa, where hundreds of thousands of submissions were received from across the country. By contrast, under the old system, legislating was almost surreptitious.

But more than that: the legislature itself set about actively dictating and curtailing the scope of political debate. Apartheid's parliament tried, in vain, to kill ideas. Such attempts to remedy intellectual weakness with brute force are as familiar as the bully on the playground. This fundamentally childish authoritarian endeavour, really a shying away from the rigours of adult intellectual process, accounts for much of the brutality of apartheid. The civic, moral and intellectual challenges of the resistance movement's Gandhian tactics in the 1950s were met by legislative responses – such as the 1950 Suppression of Communism Act – designed to crush dissenters rather than engage rationally on the issues underlying their dissent.

What is interesting about this sort of apartheid legislation, in common with all measures intended, flailingly, to score violent body-blows against intangible ideas, is its incompetence. Statutes, while they may authorise the use of force, are also inevitably part of the world of the written word and therefore of ideas. It is partly the coherence of the statutory text that separates brute state violence from civic-minded and legitimate legislation. In the end, a statute is seldom any more (or less) brutal, nor more (or less) ignorant, than its authors.

In this vein, nothing better illustrates the moral and intellectual dereliction of apartheid than the Suppression of Communism Act itself. The head of the apartheid Security Branch, General van den Bergh, who was appointed in 1968 as security officer to Prime Minister Vorster, reported directly to Vorster himself and was given effective command over the intelligence services of the police, army, navy and air force. He was obviously a leading figure in the fight against the alleged communist menace.

His understanding of this supposed menace, it is clear, had an enormous influence over the apartheid regime's efforts to contain it. However, that understanding was seriously flawed, as appears from his comments at an international symposium on communism held in Pretoria in September 1966. General van den Bergh, who as an extra-parliamentary opponent of the war against Hitler had been interned along with Vorster during that war, confided to the symposium that he had often been asked why Jews joined communist organisations and were involved in communist-inspired sabotage. He uncritically accepted the suggestion that Jews were disproportionately communist and added that "they became Communist because Communism was the highest form of capitalism."[10]

Such absurdities were shared by Adolf Hitler himself, who declared with murderous incoherence in January 1939 that "if the international Jewish financiers in and outside Europe should succeed in plunging the nations once more into a world war, then the result would not be the Bolshevising of the earth, and thus a victory for Jewry, but the annihilation of the Jewish race in Europe."[11] Thus, for apartheid's functionaries as for the Nazis, international capital and its most bitter opponents were one and the same.

Such incoherence would be merely amusing were its historical consequences not so hideous, in both Germany and South Africa. In the latter place, "communism" became a catch-all phrase directed at all forms of opposition to apartheid. The idea that communism and universal suffrage were identical was a widely held view within the security forces and in the Nationalist press. *Die Burger* commented, for instance, on the "simple truth" that a policy of "one man, one vote . . . differs so little from Communism as to make precious little difference to the minority groups in South Africa."[12]

As South Africa's transitional negotiations got under way in earnest in August 1990, there were sensational revelations of an alleged "communist plot," masterminded by Joe Slovo, to subvert the negotiations and seize power by force. But investigation revealed that this was an ANC contingency plan for the resumption of hostilities should negotiations have failed. Slovo, who was indeed a communist, was not involved.

Apartheid's vacuous definitions of communism found their way into the Suppression of Communism Act, which was initially used to ban the Communist Party. But its definitions were so vague that it could be, and was, subsequently used to outlaw almost the whole spectrum of anti-apartheid dissent. Adolf Hitler, who said he entered politics to become, more than a mere Minister, a "destroyer of Marxism," added on another occasion that "if necessary, by one enemy many can be meant."[13] It was a lesson that the apartheid regime adapted masterfully for local conditions as they waged a lawless war against blacks under cover of a war against communism.

Among other things, the South African Suppression of Communism Act forbade agitation in favour of "any doctrine or scheme" aiming at "any political, industrial, social, or economic change within the Union" or aiming at "the encouragement of feelings of hostility between the European and non-European races of the union."

This amounted to a legal command that people should like the way things were under apartheid rather than seeking change of any sort and should, failing that, simply grin and bear it rather than indulging in illegal "feelings of hostility." Failure to heed these commands amounted to the commission of the criminal offence of furthering the objects of "communism." This crime was not confined to the commission of acts intended to further the objects of "communism," but merely required that the acts could be said, "objectively" (effectively, in the judge's largely unfettered subjective opinion) to have furthered such ends.

In practice, few activities of a public or political nature can have fallen outside of this definition of "communism." Unsurprisingly, not all qualifying activities did in fact receive unwelcome attention in terms of the legislation. Rather, the legislation conferred open-ended discretion upon enforcement officials, permitting them selectively to harass disfavoured groups at will and to criminalise them.

Among other things, the Act made it a criminal offence to record, reproduce, print, publish, or disseminate (except in legal proceedings) any speech, writing, utterance or statement made, or purporting to have been made, by a listed person. This consigned those listed to what critics called "civil death."

Thus it was that when ANC leader Govan Mbeki was released from jail in 1987 after decades of imprisonment, a planned rally for him in Port Elizabeth was banned. Mbeki may have been nominally freed, but he certainly was not free to exercise rights of simple speech in ordinary politics. This weighty determination was made by a mere mid-level securocrat, General Hennie de Witt, Commissioner of Police.

But even these ample provisions of almost infinite scope are not the whole story. The 1960 Unlawful Organisations Act was aimed specifically at the ANC and the PAC, which were banned pursuant to that Act in April of the year of its passage. The Unlawful Organisations Act focused on organisations that threatened so-called public safety and order; it omitted any reference to the promotion of communism, a concept itself already so broadly defined as to include the whole universe of activism.

An organisation could be banned as unlawful under the 1960 Act if, in the unfettered and subjective opinion of the State President, it constituted a serious threat to the safety of the public or the maintenance of public order. A declaration of unlawfulness meant that many provisions of the Suppression of Communism Act became applicable to the targeted organisation.

While the scope of the Suppression of Communism Act was absurdly broad, actually capturing more than a few anti-communist objectors to apartheid, the Act expressly exempted from criminal or civil liability any person who referred to listed persons (and designated others) as communists. A stigma of communism was manufactured based on involvement in any activity challenging the government's apartheid policies; then free rein was given to the regime's media allies to discredit all opposition to apartheid as "communist."

Failure, for instance, to comply with a notice restricting the accused to a certain place, which was a lapse that could be committed even by a virulent anti-communist, would entitle all comers to characterise the offender as a communist. This label carried, in certain circles, severely distorted and negative connotations at the time that the Act was passed; indeed some of these connotations survived until very recently and perhaps survive even today. Internal security legislation was reshaped to serve pro-apartheid propaganda.

The criminalisation of ordinary politics continued in the Prohibition of Improper Political Interference Act of 1968, which created a novel crime: participation in racially mixed politics at the levels of membership, voluntarism (e.g. unpaid canvassing), candidacy or even electioneering (e.g. making platform speeches). Offenders faced a fine or imprisonment for not less than six months or up to a year or both.

This phenomenon of using law to criminalise ordinary politics was also present in the 1962 Sabotage Act, which labelled as sabotage such lesser acts as politically motivated trespass and embarrassment of the administration of the state. The penalties for this so-called sabotage were to be the same as those for treason, which meant anything from a minimum of five years' imprisonment to the death sentence, penalties to which minors were liable. It was a piece of savagery that horrified the world.

The 1967 Terrorism Act, made retroactive in its application to 27 June 1962 despite the fact that it carried the death penalty, also covered a whole range of activities classed as "participation in terroristic [sic] activities." These activities included possession of explosives, ammunition or weapons; undergoing training which could be of use to a person intending to endanger the maintenance of law and order, or merely attempting or consenting to undergo such training, or inciting another to undergo it.

The acts that served as the factual basis for a terrorism charge need not in themselves have been unlawful. And once any of these acts was committed, the crime of terrorism was proven, unless the accused could show that these acts were not committed in order to secure any of a long list of results, including embarrassing the administration of the affairs of the state, hampering or deterring any person from assisting in the maintenance of law and order, or securing a political aim in concert with a foreign or international institution. The onus was on the accused to prove innocence, often a virtually impossible task as it was a question of proving an intention, not an actual deed.

The 1974 Affected Organisations Act gave the State President the power, by declaring an organisation "affected," to criminalise any effort by the organisation to seek foreign funding. It also criminalised anyone who handled foreign money destined for the organisation.

As late as 1989, the apartheid state was still actively hounding people for the capital crime of treason, for instance in the celebrated Alexandra treason trial and others. Half of the twenty-two accused in the 1988 Delmas treason trial were convicted, and afterwards issued a message from prison stating that the 1988 trial was an "interim affair" and that "somewhere in the future lies a date when white and black South Africans will take a second look at these moments of our history. They will evaluate afresh the events now in contention and our role in them [and] they will vindicate us."[14] That moment is now.

While the Delmas accused were convicted, the judge in the Alexandra trial commented openly on the dubious and jerry-built nature of this crime of treason, given the peculiarity of South African conditions. The judge commented that treason "is a crime of a very special category," especially in a "strange and complex" society like South Africa where political differences were severe so that "a charge of treason should be very carefully considered and reconsidered before it is brought before the court."[15]

This realisation, dawning only in the last year of the eighties even for this judge himself, was wholly absent from apartheid's decades-long violent war on ideas. Apartheid governments brutally sentenced moral and intellectual resisters to prison and even to death.

In its deliberately all-embracing definition of political crimes, its abolition – and even reversal – of basic requirements of criminal procedure, its slapdash invocation of the sanction of death, and its eccentric enforcement habits, apartheid's mis-named internal security legislation was a system of naked authoritarianism. And that system was at the disposal not merely of the executive, but of particular individuals within it (usually the State President and the Minister of Justice). It was also a system of propaganda: it attempted to harness the opprobrium that usually attaches to criminal convictions in order to direct that social disapproval at its moral and political opponents who were engaged in ordinary, profoundly moral, political activities.

As argued above, these criminalisations must be nullified through formal – if necessary statutory – means as part of the new country's dealing with the past.

4. The Rise of Permanent Emergency

Every legal system makes provision for those moments, rare in the history of a country, when severe and illegitimate disorder threatens a body politic to which most citizens are loyal. In such circumstances the state, on behalf of its citizens, may allow itself emergency powers for the brief period necessary to restore normality.

In South Africa, paradoxically, the state did not enjoy the allegiance of the majority so that disorder, the attempt to "make South Africa ungovernable," was as legitimate as it was resilient.

Even the quisling "Coloured" and "Indian" houses (collectively, "Bantustan Chambers") of the illegitimate tricameral parliament established in 1983 – even such dubious representative bodies – refused to pass apartheid's draconian emergency legislation, the 1986 Public Safety Amendment Act. This demonstrates that apartheid's emergency laws went far beyond the legitimate self-preservation of a society in the interest of its inhabitants. The Bill had to be forced into law by resort to the President's Council, a white-dominated executive body with power to override the Bantustan Chambers.

The apartheid state's inability to command the allegiance of its citizens, the persistent resistance of those citizens, and the regime's refusal to acknowledge the legitimacy of that resistance, all led to a decades-long anomaly: temporary laws, such as those covering detention without trial, were left in place indefinitely, and a state of emergency, usually a transient thing, became normal. As one critic noted, apartheid inaugurated a peculiar state of emergency affairs, which was the permanence of the temporary.

In a similar (un)constitutional fashion Adolf Hitler, throughout the Third Reich, ruled by administrative *fiat*, based on an emergency decree of 28 February 1933 which the aged President Hindenburg, who shortly afterwards died, signed under the sway of Hitler's assurances that there was a grave danger of communist takeover.[16]

However, apart from those periods in South Africa, notably 1960 and the 1980s, when emergencies were formally declared pursuant to the 1953 Public Safety Act, there were ordinary statutes which effectively undermined the rule of law and created an ongoing, undeclared state of emergency.

The 1953 Act permitted the State President to proclaim that an emergency existed if, in his personal opinion, there was a serious threat to the safety of the public or the maintenance of public order, and the ordinary law of the land could not meet the challenges posed to stability. Proclamations remained in force for twelve months and were immediately renewable without any limit on the number of consecutive emergencies that could be declared.

Regulations promulgated by the State President under his emergency powers could be retroactive in effect and could authorise confiscation of goods and property associated with an offence. Subject to the limited constraints stated in the Act (e.g. barring the President from imposing fines above R1 000 or prison terms exceeding five years), the State President's power to legislate in an emergency was equal to that of Parliament.

The emergency regulations promulgated in 1960 allowed for the prohibition of gatherings and meetings and for their dispersal by force, including deadly force. They created new crimes, including an offence of circulating "subversive statements." The 1960 regulations empowered the Minister of Justice to investigate any organisation that he suspected to be "in any way connected with any matter relating to the state of emergency"; he could order it to discontinue its activities and failure to comply constituted an offence. In the 156 days of the 1960 emergency, 11,503 persons were detained without trial and only a small fraction were subsequently convicted of any offence.

The Commissioner of Police was given power to issue orders for the control of traffic, the closure of industries, the control of essential services, the occupation of streets and other public places and all other matters deemed by him to be desirable for ending the emergency. The law enforcers were themselves inventing the laws that properly ought to have bound them. The guards were avowedly guarding themselves and even defining the very content of guardianship itself. The State Security Council, composed of the most senior Cabinet Ministers and the top military brass of the security forces, became in the 1980s the country's real government.

Meanwhile, the role of the courts was curtailed: the security forces were granted in advance indemnity from criminal and civil actions arising from good-faith implementation of the regulations. According to the 1960 regulations, no court of law was competent to entertain any application or action arising out of anything done under the regulations.[17] Additionally, parliament was given no legal role in emergency procedures. The executive was literally a law unto itself and it in turn was driven by the police and military bureaucrats.

Some hint of the more subtle attempts to enlist the courts in systematic lawlessness can be gleaned from an incident where Durban magistrates and prosecutors were notified to attend a courthouse briefing conducted by the police on 15 November 1985. There they were lectured by police on the unrest situation and on the regime's favourite notions such as the "communist onslaught," and the "terrorist" nature of the resistance. Through a combination of such initiatives and others, as well as the domination of the bench and the magistracy by privileged adherents of the old system, it is unsurprising that judicial officers often entered fully into the spirit of government thinking.

In a 1986 case one judge, Steyn J, accepted as fact without any need for evidence (what lawyers call taking "judicial notice") the unrest situation in the country, which relieved government of any need to prove that an emergency existed, thus insulating the assumed facts from forensic challenge. In what amounted to a textbook statement of the government's onslaught ideology, he pontificated at length about "mob action," "acts of gruesome cruelty," and necklacing which were "usually instigated by agitators" and extended to "acts of organised terror" as well as a "political, psychological, socio-economic and terror onslaught upon the Republic of South Africa from beyond its borders."[18] Thus was the voice of the common-law guardians of liberty as they confronted the apartheid state.

The powers contained in the 1953 Public Safety Act overlapped with others declared in the 1956 Riotous Assemblies Act, 1957 Defence Act, 1958 Police Act and the 1966 Civil Defence Act, creating an abundance of arbitrary power and conflicting jurisdiction which add up to a bureaucrat's (or securocrat's) paradise, accountable to no-one.

In 1982 the government consolidated these assorted security laws into one Act, the Internal Security Act. In line with the familiar *modus operandi* of the apartheid regime, a judicial commission (in this case, the Rabie Commission) was appointed to make repressive recommendations, smoothing the way for repressive legislation and directly involving the judiciary in parliamentary lawlessness.

The draconian 1982 enactment gave the Minister of Law and Order continued power to declare organisations illegal, to compile lists of people who could not be quoted, to ban individuals or place them under house arrest, to ban meetings and gatherings, to ban newspapers and other publications, and to hold people in indefinite detention. The pre-existing definition of communism was only superficially altered and still included any doctrine aiming at "any political, economic, industrial or social change."

The same Act confirmed and elaborated on existing powers of detention without trial. People could be detained to prevent them from committing an offence; they could be interrogated because they were suspected of committing an offence or having information about an offence; or held because they were potential witnesses in a forthcoming trial.

And yet the 1986 Public Safety Amendment Act went further, removing any need for the State President to proclaim a state of emergency and instead authorising the Minister of Law and Order to declare any area (or the whole country)

an "unrest area" and to apply regulations deemed necessary. The June 1987 regulations authorised the Commissioner of Police to issue orders, and this power
could be exercised by divisional police commissioners who thus achieved *de
facto* legislative power over internal security matters. The law enforcers were
given enhanced powers to make the laws that bound them.

The above litany of acts passed by the apartheid parliament recalls the
German Reichstag's formal abdication of its legislative functions to the Nazi government in the March 1933 "Enabling Act."[19] Under apartheid, to an extreme
extent present only in a few cases elsewhere, law descended to violent self-
mockery.

5. Manufactured Truth

In a well-functioning society, talking to itself through healthy and unharassed
media institutions, a shared debate over right and wrong gradually emerges. The
public consciousness of the country acquires a perpetually self-critical sense of
itself and evolves a benign cluster of shared imagery and precepts that the country comes to call its own plural brands of patriotism. Shared lines are drawn
between sanity and excess; old lines are ceaselessly redrawn. Jingoism and triumphalism are beleaguered. Wit thrives. Satire – what Gore Vidal terms "simply
truth grinning in a solemn canting world" – abounds. And all this makes it relatively easy to tell secular heaven from secular hell.

These ideal circumstances are rare at the best of times and have been absent,
except in pockets, in the recent history of the world's most prominent western
democracies. But in apartheid South Africa, these ideals were not merely absent;
they were reviled and actively rejected in favour of an uncritical mediocrity of
public debate. The result was to put political culture and debate among the
South African privileged into a dizzying spin in which heaven and hell could
each seem like the other.

In November 1985 during the extraordinary press restrictions of the state of
emergency, a South African newspaper published a full length interview with
ANC President Oliver Tambo (the Devil Himself, according to apartheid's lexi-
con). Nelson Mandela, hospitalised when the interview appeared and waking up
to find it at his bedside, jokingly said he thought that he had died and gone to
heaven.

Nelson Mandela's grace and wit, durable through humiliation, decades of
imprisonment, and temporary illness, contrast strikingly with the witless insecurity and inwardly consuming rage of P W Botha, at the time State President
and to all superficial appearances a man at the height of his powers and of his
career. Apartheid could never lose this corrosive inner sense of its own fraudu-
lence and mediocrity. As Brian Bunting has said in his *The Rise of the South
African Reich*:

> Ask for guns, armoured cars, baton charges, detention without trial, hang-
> ings, lashes, and all the other trappings of physical intimidation, and the
> Nationalists can prove their advantages. But ask them for an idea which can

stand the moral scrutiny of the world, and their deficiencies are immediately exposed.

When Botha, previously architect of apartheid's cross-border aggression, rose to the leadership of the country in 1978, a front-page cartoon in one newspaper depicted one nervous Egyptian saying to another, "Man the ramparts, *effendi*, P W is their new PM." Apartheid lacked any intellectual basis, or even merely the coherence, with which to fight these battles of the thinking and the satirical sorts.

Instead, its response was the kind of solemn canting petulance that Foreign Minister Pik Botha, for instance, dished out to the Foreign Correspondents' Association in 1988. He accused the assembled journalists of ignoring the country's "beauty, promise and goodwill" in favour of a relentless focus on the "dirty work." Invoking Paul Kruger, Pik Botha addressed the assembled international press corps as "friends, citizens, thieves and enemies." He was forced to retreat from the hall under a hail of hisses, boos and shouts of "Go home."[20]

From the very beginnings of its rule, the National Party made determined efforts to control the media. Television, which had been displayed as early as 1936 at a Johannesburg trade fair, was prohibited until 1976 because the regime feared that it would have an undesirable "liberalistic" influence on the electorate. H F Verwoerd himself suggested that television posed risks of a magnitude similar to those posed by poison gas and the atom bomb. The Minister of Posts and Telegraphs, Dr Albert Hertzog, warned in 1967 that: "Friends of mine recently returned from Britain tell me one cannot see a programme which does not show Black and White living together; where they are not continually propagating a mixture of the two races."

When the regime finally succumbed to pressure to allow television – and also saw TV's propaganda potential – the technology was permitted, but only along segregated lines. Programmes were aimed at either blacks or whites, never both, and programmes for Africans were required to be in one of the five principal African languages.

The radio also was firmly under Government control and, through a combination of subtle and ham-fisted manoeuvres, constant attempts were made to manipulate the press. The Afrikaans language press, though generally well behaved, occasionally fell foul of the Nationalists. The editor of the Afrikaans Sunday newspaper *Rapport* left his job, squeezed out after P W Botha's interference; and there are other examples of media industry job losses following upon clashes with the government and with P W Botha in particular.

In the view of Verwoerd's friend and ally, pro-Nazi Piet Meyer, who was appointed chair of the South African Broadcasting Corporation in 1959, Afrikanerdom's sacred mission was beleaguered by "Russian and Chinese communism, Indian imperialism, Eastern, Middle Eastern and North African Mohammedanism, West European liberalism, American capitalistic sentimentalism, and fervent anti-white Bantu animism in Africa."[21] Powerful media bosses thus carried the laager mentality far beyond unintended self-satire; yet most of apartheid's privileged citizenry rallied earnestly around such cultural claustrophobia.

The gravelly voice of an anonymous Nationalist Lord Haw-Haw distorted the truth for a whole generation through the SABC's Current Affairs talks, billed as the equivalent of a leading article. In 1963, the SABC produced and broadcast radio propaganda under the paranoiac title of "Know Your Enemy." According to one observer, this programme "was a McCarthy-style anti-Communist series of total one-sidedness. These and similar broadcasts accused the World Council of Churches of being Communistic; denounced America's Attorney-General as being a tool of the Communists; called the integrity of the United States Supreme Court into question because one of its members was allegedly not a Christian."[22]

Aside from monopolising the broadcast media (and later, in the eighties, granting concessions to friends), the regime built a large apparatus of straightforward censorship. The extent to which such apartheid censorship drew sustenance from, and also intensified, the experience of repressive regimes elsewhere, is directly evident in the SABC's treatment of censorship in neighbouring Zimbabwe (then still officially Rhodesia).

Upon the 1965 Unilateral Declaration of Independence by the white supremacist Rhodesian regime, an official South African radio broadcast openly defended Ian Smith's embrace of censorship on the simple basis that "the Rhodesian press not only clearly opposed Mr Smith's government in the face of the clearly expressed wishes of the [all-white] electorate, but even adopted an attitude at times which can only be described as hostile."

Thus, said the SABC broadcast, Smith was justified in gagging any newspaper that criticised him since, had he failed to do so, he would have exposed himself to considerable criticism. 'The Rhodesian press," continued the SABC, "and those in South Africa who are now bewailing the hardships of censorship, should not forget the extent to which censorship was brought upon themselves by the Rhodesian newspapers."[23] Through this breathtaking spiral of illogic, media disagreement with the Rhodesian government became, in and of itself, an ironclad justification for censorship. And the victims of censorship somehow became, through an alchemy of unreason, its cause.

In a comment that surely belongs in the *Guinness Book of Records* under the heading "Mindless Tautology," the SABC further defended the Rhodesian censors as follows:

> Reference has also been made to blank spaces in current Rhodesian newspapers. These blank spaces are supposed to indicate the high-handedness of the censors – but the censored articles, written in newspaper offices, can only be removed for one reason: because they are dangerous to Rhodesia. If the articles are genuine, it shows their hostility. If they are deliberately written in such a way as to be censored, it means that the censors are being provoked, in an attempt to create an impression of ruthlessness in the public mind. So in either case the blank spaces prove, for all to see, the extent to

which censorship was necessary.

Soon enough the SABC's defence of racist censorship next door would circle back to justify, with exponential illogic, censorship at home in defence of apartheid. While the apartheid state fought secret wars and committed hidden atrocities within its own borders, it wanted public debate to be a blunt humourless weapon in its arsenal of force, rather than remaining an intellectual counterweight to society's coercive resources.

In Pik Botha's view, the suspended anti-apartheid *Weekly Mail* – today the left–liberal *Mail and Guardian* – was one of the most "vicious" newspapers he had ever seen and was responsible for "more violence in this country."[24]

When in the mid-eighties Capital Radio in the Transkei (a so-called independent state) declined to heed Mr Botha's editorial directives, he reported to the State Security Council that "it is being considered to buy out the radio station in order to bring that situation under control."[25]

In all this, however, nothing better sums up the apartheid ruling caste's abdication of intellect in favour of coercion than the report of the 1982 Steyn Commission headed by Justice Tienie Steyn. This body was a further step in the apartheid tradition, traceable to Prime Minister Malan's press commission headed by Judge van Zyl, of appointing judges to horse-whip the press.

Ostensibly a critical investigation of the mass media, the report of almost 1,400 pages was largely an ill-executed attempt to legitimise the then government's "total onslaught" propaganda. Over 900 pages of the report offered an approving exegesis of the idea that South Africa faced a dangerous communist onslaught.

This "onslaught" concept is an article of faith for those who claim that the supporters and opponents of apartheid clashed with equal idealism. They suggest that if the resistance was idealistically seeking to overthrow an unjust system, the apartheid regime itself was, equally, seeking to avert the arrival of a barbarous one: communism. The apartheid regime presented itself as "The West in Africa," a vital bulwark against encroaching communism.

But in fact, it has been clear for decades – not least to the West itself – that, in the words of former British Conservative Party Prime Minister Edward Heath, "the South African government believe . . . that they can always use the Communist threat as the argument with which to handle Washington and Whitehall." He went on to note the irony that it was apartheid, more than anything else, that created the real risk of driving black South Africa towards the Soviet bloc.[26]

Arguments about the alleged communist threat in southern Africa fit neatly into a discussion of apartheid's propaganda machine. Indeed, the alleged Soviet threat was little more than a creature of that machine. And to the extent that there were undeniable – but fairly low priority – geopolitical issues at stake in southern Africa, it had been clear for decades that the easiest way to avert Soviet geopolitical gains was to end apartheid.

Indeed, in erecting a justification for apartheid's violence in the 1980s, the

Steyn Report could not entirely ignore such realities. It actually defined the alleged onslaught as a threat from both the western and the eastern blocs, said to be equally bent on interfering in southern Africa.

To rebuff the hostile foreign onslaught, the report urged, the country had to "gird its loins and marshal all the forces at its disposal, as such an onslaught demands total manning of the ramparts and mustering of the sallyports." This militarised vocabulary seems so outlandish as almost to be self-satirising. Yet it holds an important truth: violence was ingrained in the language of the apartheid ruling caste itself; critical faculties retreated as the Casspirs advanced. Apartheid lacked an intelligentsia; its thinkers were merely soldiers with inkpots.

Unsurprisingly, the Steyn Report, lengthy yet insubstantial, was not a coherent text. It for instance pronounced democratic theory "intellectually . . . [and] politically bankrupt" while at the same time insisting, even as the segregationist 1983 constitution was on the drawing board, that South Africa was a "developing and expanding democracy." Compounding its confusions with racist dogma, the Commission concluded that since "power remains the ultimate frame of reference in African politics" and since democracy is "properly workable only in a state with an ethnically and culturally homogenous population," democracy was impractical in South Africa.[27]

In a country like the Steyn Commission's South Africa, where cultural heterogeneity meant democracy was inherently unworkable, what could the role of the press possibly be? The press is generally one forum through which a healthy democracy enters frankly into conversation with itself. If democracy was rejected, as in the Steyn Report, the press would need to find something else to do. But what?

The Commission's terms of reference were significant in this respect: "to enquire into and report on the question whether the conduct of, and handling of matters by, the mass media meet the needs and interests of the South African Community and the demands of the time and, if not, how they can be improved." Clearly, any parts of the press that were mistakenly pursuing the bankrupt democratic model of the press as a vigilant counterweight against government and private sector abuses would have to be "improved." The Commission, in language that was overtly paranoic, pointedly rejected this democratic idea of media vigilance:

> We are told that the press is a "watchdog." But just what does that mean? To whom does the watchdog belong? Whom is it watching and for what reasons? If the press is a watchdog, presumably it is protecting something. Just what is that? Is it the people's watchdog, watching the government, and keeping the government from doing harm to the people? . . . Who gave the watchdog this task? Did the "people" buy this dog for this purpose?[28]

Here a supposedly neutral press commission went beyond an approving summary of the onslaught mindset and became visibly the embodiment of an hysterical and authoritarian state. The authoritarian idea – that the press should join hands with the governing ideology – was expressly stated by P W Botha as he tabled the Report in parliament:

> ... we have a right to be proud of the large measure of freedom which the press continues to enjoy here ... But I wish to repeat my appeal ... Let those who, in common with myself and the government, value sound working relationships between the public, the press and the authorities in South Africa, now offer their co-operation to help put an end to certain abuses which have become unbearable and a threat to the nation.[29]

This was a blatant call for the press to join in apartheid's social engineering, abandoning criticism. In the florid language of the report, it was time "not only to gird our loins for the struggle now upon us but also to clear our own domestic decks of any damaging perception breeding impedimenta and to tend the dykes of goodwill and stability." In the Commission's view, the security and preservation of the apartheid state constituted a "Highest Law" justifying the "curtailment" of the rights of the press or of others.[30]

In all of this there was a quite deliberate manipulation of the rhetoric of patriotism. The narrow interests of the apartheid privileged were identified with the patriotic best interests of the country as a whole, so that dissenters (like the End Conscription Campaign, the sanctions campaign, and the so-called treason trialists) could be painted as traitors. A false patriotism became not merely the last refuge, but actually the most favoured rhetoric, of a scoundrel government that pretended to speak for a whole nation, while violently rejecting the largest part of it.

Apartheid's agenda for the press was echoed in its ideas for the educational system. A school cadet system inculcated militarism and narrow forms of Afrikaner nationalism; veld schools peddled the myth of a "communist onslaught" and taught survival training and a range of military skills. They made patriotism seem synonymous with violence, ethno-chauvinism and xenophobia.

Education and "national security" became so directly linked in the apartheid 1980s that the Minister of National Education, F W de Klerk, actually had a seat on the State Security Council (the shadowy militaristic inner circle of the apartheid government) in these years. Moreover, secret documents and SSC minutes that have emerged as evidence in the trial of former Defence Minister Magnus Malan show Education Minister de Klerk apprising the SSC of "efforts by undermining elements to create dissatisfaction with the authorities" over "compulsory school uniforms." According to these records, National Education Minister de Klerk actually recommended that the National Intelligence Service (the South African spy agency) investigate these activities and that the work of the End Conscription Campaign, which was opposed to the apartheid draft in white schools, should be "resisted."[31]

Unsurprisingly, apartheid's twisted veld school ideologies occasionally claimed as victims their own schoolchild adherents. In May 1996, the mother of an assassinated right-wing student told the Johannesburg hearings of the Truth and Reconciliation Commission that her son had acquired his ideological proclivities on a "school leadership course" in 1991, organised by the South African government's Department of Education.

When her son sought to withdraw from the unsavoury activities of the right-wing "World Apartheid Movement" which he had subsequently joined, he was found dead in suspicious circumstances, victim of an alleged "suicide" shortly after having been apprehended by the police in the northern Cape. "He knew too much about the organisation and had to be silenced," she told the Truth and Reconciliation Commission.[32]

This false patriotism was to the fore in the Steyn Report, which in 1982 promoted the idea that South African patriotism was inconsistent with criticism of apartheid: "No journalist can report or comment with real insight, impartiality, and truth on people or institutions he dislikes. *Journalists reporting in such a state of mind perform a disservice to the country*"[33] (emphasis added). Likewise, internal opponents of apartheid's militarism, such as the End Conscription Campaign (ECC), faced high-level and systematic attacks on their commitment to a democratic and demilitarised South Africa.

In August 1988, the ECC became the first white organisation to be banned since the Congress of Democrats in the 1960s. Defence Minister Magnus Malan said ECC supporters were "lacking in the moral fibre to defend the country."[34] Shortly before the banning, the *Citizen* newspaper urged that "the government will have to act firmly to prevent the rot spreading and it will have the support of most South Africans."[35]

The fact is that such manipulative and seemingly high-minded appeals to false patriotism were not wholly without effect at the time; and are not without residual effect today. There were clear benefits to those journalists, parliamentarians, and other individuals who accepted the alluring invitation to enter an inner circle where they had privileged access to information and to the untiring blandishments of office-holders. P W Botha only narrowly failed, for instance, to tempt the Newspaper Press Union with an exemption from the restrictions of the 1986 state of emergency – while non-members would have suffered its full force.

That particular initiative may have failed to co-opt the press, but others succeeded. Thus an express agreement was struck in 1981 between the Newspaper Press Union and the Commissioner of the South African Police. As amended in 1983, it provided for *de facto* police certification of journalists through a system of carefully issued press cards. The agreement was further modified orally from time to time.

The Newspaper Press Union had already struck an agreement with the Minister of Defence decades earlier, in 1967. As amended in September 1980, the agreement set up a joint "Liaison Committee" to meet at least once a month "to consider matters of policy and principle including the amendment" of the agreement itself.

The agreement provided that the press "must abide by" any request by the Defence Minister that "no reference be made to the fact that he had been approached and refused to comment as even a 'no comment' reply could embarrass him." Additionally, the Minister of Defence was given a right of pre-publication comment and the guidelines further provided that reporters "should understand that there are to be no arguments with the Minister or the [relevant] officers on matters that have leaked out somewhere in their publication. A request that a report or comment should not appear is to be accepted as such." In 1980, participation in this agreement was extended to the state-owned arms company, Armscor, which was given a seat on the Liaison Committee. These agreements were voluntarily entered upon by the Newspaper Press Union.

Given such unabashed and formalised collaboration, it is no surprise that the apartheid regime's 1977 White Paper on Defence could comment confidently that "as far as reporting and commentary are concerned, the SA Defence Force enjoys the cooperation of all the local news media based on an agreement reached with the South Africa Newspaper Press Union . . . The news media remain an essential link in the total national strategy, because of the great influencing role they can play through proper cooperation."[36]

The apartheid government's conduct discloses a pattern of threat, negotiation and eventual voluntary restraint on the part of the press. This pattern can be traced back at least to 1960 when, almost twenty years before his rise to Prime Minister, P W Botha, then Deputy Minister of the Interior, introduced the Undesirable Publications Bill, making provision for pre-publication censorship. The Bill was watered down and the major print media were largely exempted after the South African Newspaper Press Union agreed to draw up its own Guidelines, which were published in 1962.

Despite such formal and informal accommodations between the press and the apartheid rulers, there was also a formidable and wide-ranging statutory apparatus for the straightforward suppression and banning of ideas, including statutory requirements that all newspapers should be registered, as well as a fully-fledged system of censorship including a "Directorate" of publications which in turn appointed committees of individuals to judge the "undesirability" or otherwise of publications. Appeals against the determinations of any committee were heard by the Publications Appeal Board (PAB) which overwhelmingly had the final say, subject only to an appellant's limited right of review in the Supreme Court. On the PAB sat the truth Czars.

The Act compounded the PAB's lawless power by its vague definitions: "undesirable" publications included those that in whole or part were "prejudicial to the safety of the state, the general welfare or the peace and good order." In construing this language, the PAB explicitly set out to serve the moral and political status quo under apartheid. It stated: "Generally, the present state of affairs must always be taken into consideration. If a revolutionary or quasi-revolutionary state of affairs exists, a finding of undesirability would of necessity follow more readily."[37]

As the international sanctions campaign mounted, reporting on straightforward commercial matters such as trade in petroleum products became a matter of national security, and restrictions were imposed by the 1977 Petroleum

Products Act. Also that year the Central Energy Fund Act 38 provided for a fine, imprisonment, or both, if any information in respect of any levy paid by government to the Fund was disclosed, including by its publication. It was an offence to tell taxpayers about the use of their own money in subsidising a state-sponsored commercial exercise.

Apartheid's authoritarian press management, handmaiden of its violent strategies, was not only directed at internal political opponents but also at external sovereign states that opposed it. The invasion of Angola in 1975 to 1976 was not only violent and brutal but also secret.

This was part of a broader pattern of clandestine activity. In the Muldergate or "Information Scandal," secret government defence funds were poured into various pro-apartheid ventures, including the creation of a government-supporting newspaper given a patriotic-sounding title, the *Citizen*. The responsible Minister Connie Mulder, then a fully risen star – and even heir apparent – of the National Party, lied outright to parliament in denying that the government had funded the newspaper.

Outside the country's borders, funds from the same military secret slush fund were deployed in elaborate attempts to buy influence, including attempts to purchase the right-wing *Washington Times* and other US newspapers, the funding of pro-apartheid "research" and lobbying efforts, and a range of assorted dirty tricks against prominent overseas foes of apartheid, including Senator Dick Clark, who lost his seat apparently in part because of the "Info" project's success in discrediting him.

At its height, apartheid's pattern of secret governance, its intellectual mediocrity, and its compensatory violent assaults on wit and ideas, led wholly away from genuine parliamentarianism, the heart of which is skilled and robust debate based on open information. In the end, apartheid's patterns of secret funding (as in the Infoscandal), hidden militarism (as in Angola 1975) and contempt for the citizenry (pervasive) converged in a grotesque but predictable onslaught: a secretly funded terrorist war against the country's own people; a murderous assault on anti-apartheid campaigners – both within and outside of South Africa.

6. State Terrorism

As apartheid shrugged off debate in favour of violence, it triggered new resistance rather than quelling it and the apartheid regime came to realise the futility of systematic violence under colour of law. It increasingly resorted to random terror directed against both its own (disowned) citizens and neighbouring states. As one church leader told a visiting delegation of lawyers in 1987, "the uncontrollability is part of the design because it is only by sheer terror that you can continue to hold people down."[38]

Terrorism, properly defined, involves the indiscriminate use of force or violence in order to intimidate or coerce alleged enemies. At no time was it ever the policy or the practice of the ANC and its military wing to target systematically the civilian population, or randomly to target its opponents for the purpose of intimidation.

This was not the case for the apartheid regime, either within or beyond its borders. Outside the country, the regime sought to justify its own terrorist initiatives by alleging that these efforts were actually attempts to control the alleged terrorism of the resistance. But this transparent propaganda was swiftly dismissed by the international community.

For instance, following the regime's 1982 attack on Lesotho, and notwithstanding the shift of certain of its veto-holding members towards "constructive engagement" with apartheid, the Security Council unanimously recognised (Resolution 527) that the apartheid bureaucracy was not entitled unilaterally to characterise persons seeking refuge in the front line states as "terrorists." Then five years later, following the apartheid bureaucracy's attacks on a number of houses in the capital of Botswana, the Security Council's Resolution 568 condemned the apartheid bureaucracy's systematic military "practice" which was intended, it said, to "*terrorise* and destabilise Botswana and other countries in the Southern African region" (emphasis added).

Additionally, South Africa funded and assisted the Renamo terrorists in Mozambique, who were, according to the US government, guilty of "systematic atrocities" including the slaughter of more than 100,000 civilians. The terrorist activities of the Koevoet counter-insurgency unit in Namibia are also well known. Even Koevoet's defenders admit its use of "ruthless" and "unorthodox" measures but allege, in the usual fashion, that such were the necessities of combating the alleged terrorism of those who resisted apartheid.

Within the country, the regime's terrorist initiatives were equally undeniable. According to a management directive issued to General Joubert, commander of the South African Defence Force's covert Special Forces in 1986, the responsibility of this secret branch of the SADF was "to disrupt maximally the enemies of the state in support of other parts of the force."[39] Within the country, according to the testimony of those who were directly involved in these activities, "maximal disruption could conceivably consist in anything from breaking a window to killing a person."[40] A monkey foetus was hung from a tree in the garden of Archbishop Desmond Tutu.

Nor was the practice of state terrorism confined to the national government. The facts disclosed by the 1990 Hiemstra Commission's investigation into a spy network lavishly funded by the Johannesburg City Council "fully warrant," according to the international group Human Rights Watch, "findings that death squads have been supported by both the SAP and the SADF . . . and have targeted anti-apartheid leaders in a calculated plan to terrorise opposition figures."[41]

Among other things, terror served to discipline, and to ensure the loyalty of, apartheid's own loyalists and functionaries. Even after the negotiations towards democracy were well under way, the most robust and courageous of the government's own officials still felt the strain of the regime's habits of intimidation.

In November 1992, Justice Richard Goldstone, an internationally respected jurist, commented that he was "just terrified" of making public statements about his findings as investigator of ongoing violence because of the feared reaction of elements within government.

With common criminals and some captured members of the resistance, the apartheid government's systematic deployment of terror was even more effective. It was a well-known practice for such people to be subjected to torture and detention until they "turned," becoming "askaris" and agreeing to perform services ranging from spying to assassination. Joe Mamasela, an askari who participated directly or indirectly in at least 53 killings of anti-apartheid activists, told the Pretoria Supreme Court in 1996, during the trial of death squad commander Eugene de Kock, that:

> Myself, I am a victim. I was acting against my own will and made a killer machine against my own people. I was captured by the police. I was assaulted severely. I was brutalised. I am telling you. And then the police used me against my own people . . . [if] I did not commit one of them I will have been dead, I will have been Brian Ngqulunga [an underperforming, and therefore executed, askari] today. If I did not become productive by killing these people, I will have been killed. I have no doubt in my mind about that.[42]

When in the 1980s the press was prohibited from publishing the names of detainees, there were immediate and justified fears in some quarters that the laws "could be used as a weapon of state terror" and a "fearsome psychological weapon," with citizens "disappearing into the clutches of the state," without any possibility of sensible or informed intervention by concerned individuals.[43] In a calculated process of manipulating terror to beget exponentially more terror, systematic torture and detention were used as recruiting devices to fatten the ranks of apartheid's death squads.

Over the years, detention became longer, torture more savage, and methods of extorting information more sophisticated.

In 1960, 11,000 people were detained under the Public Safety Act. In 1961, between 8,000 and 10,000 people were arrested for periods of up to 12 days. From 1963–64, under a new law which allowed people to be detained for up to 90 days, over 1,000 people were detained. In the final desperate years of apartheid between 1986 and June 1990, detention for indefinite periods without trial accelerated. There was random terroristic incarceration on an unparalleled scale.

Between 1963 and 1990, at least 68 people died while being held under security legislation. According to official explanations, they died from such unlikely mishaps as slipping on soap, and falling out of a window, through suicide, or what human rights lawyers began to call the "induced suicide" of people who killed themselves rather than give information. Torture of detainees took many forms, from sheer physical brutality, beatings and whippings, to the use of electric shock treatment and sophisticated methods of sensory deprivation. Many detainees were kept in solitary confinement for months, with no access to family, friends or a lawyer. They emerged disorientated and traumatised. Some had mental breakdowns; all were mentally and emotionally scarred.

A widely cited study of South African detainees conducted between 1974 and 1984 disclosed that 38.5 per cent had no access to external light and 38.4 per cent no opportunity to exercise; 83 per cent of the sample said they had been physically tortured, while all of them reported mental torture varying from verbal abuse and threats to sleep deprivation and sham execution.44

In one common ritual, two warders dangled the torture victim by the legs outside a window far above the ground and each would successively let go of one leg, the other attempting to catch the remaining leg in time to avert an "accident." In several cases where the victim did end up crashing to the ground below, the deaths were recorded as suicides.

Detainees were systematically made to sing freedom songs while being subjected to torture, a form of mockery designed to demoralise them while apparently entertaining their interlocutors. "I used to scream and shout and they used to laugh like mad hyenas," said one victim recently, describing the conduct of warders as they banged his head against walls and battered his penis.45

Ms Nohle Mohapi answered a door-knock one night to be informed by a police officer that her anti-apartheid activist husband had allegedly hanged himself with his own jeans. "They call themselves leaders and they kill themselves!" she was taunted by a black policeman at the mortuary, as she confirmed the identity of the body.46 On the bodies of some supposed suicide victims, fingernails were torn out and electrical shocks had clearly been administered. Shock machines were familiar tools of interrogation in police stations; in one police station, officers even gave their machine a nickname, Sophie.

Sometimes these things were done to children, some as young as 11 years old. An article in the British medical journal, *The Lancet*, published on 19 March 1988, summed up the experience of a few of them, based on their accounts given to the 1987 Harare Conference on Children. The author wrote:

> The children described their experiences of physical abuse. Moreover, they talked about the widespread use of psychological torture, including solitary confinement, sleep deprivation, and humiliations such as being stripped naked. The conference was told of children who had been made to lie down naked in mortuaries with bloodstained walls. Threats of many kinds were made, and in one instance police put a rubber tyre round a schoolchild's neck, doused it with petrol, and threatened to set it alight. One youngster recounted his arrest in the middle of the night without explanation to his parents. He was kept in solitary confinement for several days; attempts by his parents to find him were prevented; and police ate the food brought for him. He described electric shock torture to which he had been subjected for half an hour, then how he had been put in a refrigerator for half an hour before undergoing electric shock torture again. He was kept in a cell and frequently heard the screams of other children. To this day the boy's sleep is disturbed; the screams of others seem to haunt him more than his own dread-

ful treatment. An eleven-year old boy had been assaulted during his two-month detention, with the loss of four teeth. He began to give evidence about his incarceration, but became frightened, saying "Vlok [the Minister of Law and Order] will get me."

Such policies of wanton state-sponsored violence actually intensified within South Africa itself during the negotiation period. In September 1990 a veteran political commentator on the *Cape Times* remarked of the sudden spate of seemingly random violence that "not since this series of weekly surveys of the political scene began in 1966 has a single dominant theme persisted for so long, week after week. Every time the killing and burning seems to be easing, it suddenly starts up again," suggesting that there was a strategy to "alarm white opinion to the point where negotiations collapse."[47] According to the Human Rights Commission, as many political assassinations took place in 1992 (ninety-seven) as occurred in the entire decade of the eighties (roughly ten per year).

In November 1992 the Goldstone Commission uncovered a covert military project, *Project Echoes*, to discredit the ANC by infiltrating criminals into its ranks. This was a terrorist government deploying its own terrorists in sheep's clothing to discredit its humanist opponents. And all this happened at the height of the intense and hard-fought negotiations towards democracy. It represented continuity with the pre-negotiation period, during which the security forces committed atrocities and attributed them to the resistance.

In the case of the December 1989 Motherwell bomb, four security officers were killed. In June 1996 three other security police officers, one a former hit-squad operative, were found guilty of the Motherwell murders by a Port Elizabeth court. These attacks, previously attributed to the ANC, had served a double purpose of propaganda as well as silencing apartheid's own operatives who were threatening to disclose security police misdeeds.[48]

When, in October 1988, a Supreme Court judge found that the SADF had involved itself in "dirty tricks against a political opponent" (the End Conscription Campaign), the SADF argued in its defence that the courts had no jurisdiction to evaluate its conduct since a state of war existed. The court gave this claim short shrift, but the fact that it was even offered by the SADF remains unequivocal evidence that an arrogant lawlessness had gripped the security forces and that these forces operated, in practice, overwhelmingly beyond the reach of judicial supervision.

Confirming such suspicions, an April 1992 Goldstone Commission Report on the conduct of 32 Battalion at Phola Park concluded that the Battalion "acted in a manner completely inconsistent with the function of a peace keeping force and in fact became perpetrators of violence," including alleged rapes of innocent residents. The captain in command of the Battalion sought to explain his troops' conduct by alleging that they "were involved in what amounted to war," an explanation that only heightened the Goldstone Commission's concerns.[49]

Central to the strategy of wanton violence within South African borders was the concept of "deniability," the insistence that the state should not seem responsible for violent unrest which was, in the official government explanation, blamed on township radicals and non-state right-wing extremists. Even the severely flawed 1990 Harms Commission, in many ways a simple exercise in exculpation of the apartheid state, confirmed the existence of a government policy to the effect that apartheid's covert forces "had to operate in such a way that its operations could not be traced back to the SA Defence Force or the state."[50]

According to a supplementary indictment in the ongoing trial of former Defence Force General Magnus Malan and others, Malan, at a death squad meeting with the Inkatha leadership on 21 March 1988, cautioned that "Inkatha should not be linked to the South African government and [the Inkatha leader] should not identify himself with the South African government during overseas visits."[51]

A central document in the case adds that "open SADF support" for the Inkatha leadership and other collaborators "will clearly have a negative impact on their power base and must not be overlooked. Any support must be clandestine or covert. Not one of the leaders must, as a result of SADF support, be branded as marionettes of the South African government by the enemy." Finally, the minutes of the State Security Council clearly demonstrate that F W de Klerk (then Education Minister) and Pik Botha (then Foreign Minister) were both present at a 3 February 1986 meeting where this terrorist scheme was discussed.[52]

Much of the unrest resulting from these apartheid government initiatives was called "black-on-black" violence, suggesting to the world that barbaric natives were predictably going for each other's throats as the necessary constraints of beneficent white overlordship were relaxed. The truth, parts of which are now well known but much of which remains to be revealed, was somewhat different.

The security forces contributed to the violence by establishing and funding hit squads which harassed, intimidated and murdered apartheid's opponents. In addition, the state manufactured violence both passively (by omission) and actively (by sponsorship, training and protection of violent marauders). We shall outline each of these specific terrorist initiatives in turn.

(a) Hit Squads

The existence of callous assassins, funded by the apartheid state and given the job of killing South African people, has been beyond doubt for some time. "It is hard to avoid the conclusion that a clandestine force is carrying out a systematic campaign of assassination of local leaders of the African National Congress," wrote the liberal *Cape Times* in July 1991.

From the 5-man "Z-squad" of the 1960s, to subsequent divide-and-rule killer divisions, such as the hundreds of recruits secretly trained for an "offensive unit" established under Operation Marion in the late 1980s, which is at the heart of the trial of former Defence Minister Magnus Malan, the full story of apartheid's killing machine remains to be told. We must look to the Truth and Reconciliation Commission for further light on these systematic terrorist cells.

In late 1989, Brigadier Floris Mostert, commander of the Brixton Murder and

Robbery Squad, in the course of his investigation of the assassination of anti-apartheid activist David Webster, established that a secret organisation "was responsible for different incidents of murder, arson, bomb explosions at buildings, assaults and intimidation . . . I established that the mentioned secret organisation was actually a unit of the South African Defence Force that was known as the Civil Cooperation Bureau."

In making these statements under oath as part of Supreme Court proceedings, Mostert added that the "general purpose" of this state-sponsored secret organisation was "to sow fear among leftist radicals by violence and intimidation."53 This is a classic statement of the terrorist creed.

The most vivid early confirmation of these state-sponsored terrorist activities was the 17 November 1989 *Vrye Weekblad* interview of former death squad commander Dirk Coetzee who subsequently fled the country: "I was the commander of the South African Police's death squad. I was in the heart of the whore. My men and I had to murder political and security opponents of the police and the government. I know the deepest secrets of this unit, which is above the law. I myself am guilty of, or at least an accomplice to, several murders."

When the apartheid laws proved insufficient to ensnare activists, the security services simply turned to extra-judicial execution. "Make a plan with Griffiths Mxenge. He is a former Robben Island convict and an attorney who gives us a lot of trouble. Mxenge defends accused in terrorist trials. We tried to build up a case against him, but failed. We just do not have enough evidence to charge him."54 This was the voice of Brigadier Jan van der Hoven, chief of the Security Branch in Natal, shortly before the assassination of human rights lawyer Mxenge in 1981. Law was merely one means of apartheid violence; when law proved inadequate, more direct means were available.

A document authored in 1985 by C P van der Westhuizen came to light in mid-1992, by which time he had risen to chief of staff of Military Intelligence. The document ordered the "permanent removal from society" of anti-apartheid activist Matthew Goniwe and two companions who, shortly afterwards, were found murdered. Implementing P W Botha's determination in 1988 to impose what he called law and order, the Secretary of the State Security Council declared that the primary goal was to "command, coerce, *and eliminate* the revolutionaries" in the townships (emphasis added).55

In February 1991, after a Walkman personal stereo had arrived for him in the post, anti-apartheid lawyer Bheki Mlangeni donned its headphones in order to listen to the accompanying audio cassette – labelled "Hit squads, new evidence." Seconds later his head was in pieces, his brains splattered on the curtains; it was his mother who found him like this.

In July 1992, two SADF intelligence officers were arrested in Britain trying to recruit Ulster Loyalist killers to assassinate Dirk Coetzee, who had deserted his former masters for the ANC. Pretoria's assassination of ANC Paris representative Dulcie September was more conclusive, as was their bombing of the ANC's

London headquarters in the 1980s. Joe Gqabi, the ANC representative in Harare was assassinated outside his home there. ANC human rights lawyer Albie Sachs lost an arm to a Maputo car bomb that was intended to kill him. There were similar bombings and attempted killings in Harare, Bulawayo, Brussels and elsewhere.

In September 1992 it emerged that a murderous bomb blast a few years earlier in the Harare suburb of Avondale had been carried out by an operational commander of the CCB, Christopher "Kit" Bawden, who had afterwards escaped safely to South Africa. Pleading for intervention in favour of five associates who remained in custody in Zimbabwe, Bawden wrote that "all of these men were loyal members of the South African Defence Force Special Forces and were serving their country with pride and distinction during covert operations officially sanctioned by the SADF ."[56]

In November 1991, after he had left the job of Minister of Defence, Magnus Malan commented in public that the CCB, of which he had previously denied any knowledge beyond the press reports, had achieved "phenomenal results." Prior to his removal from the Defence portfolio, in an attempt to justify the CCB activities, Malan commented in parliament in 1990 that "Southern Africa is a marshland of international agents of the Western and communist secret services. It is a grey world of which John Public often only hears. It is a world with its own rules and morality. South Africa is, because of its safety needs, also necessarily involved in this grey matter . . . we can't talk about these matters in public."[57]

This suggestion, with its contemptuous dismissal of "John Public," reflected the onslaught mentality run amok. Such thinking was a widespread and accepted feature of apartheid governance, even during the political transition. Upon the 1990 appointment of the Harms Commission to investigate hit squad allegations, a National Party MP commented that "if I should discover that my government, in the circumstances in which South Africa finds itself has not got a special unit such as the CCB, I would have blamed the government bitterly."[58]

The apartheid parliament effectively endorsed this onslaught-mania by voting blindly to approve enormous and secret military budgets throughout the 1980s. Ultimately the security forces [sic] could only act with murderous abandon because they were granted the impunity of limitless funds, no questions asked, by the government. Apartheid security official General van den Bergh, testifying before a commission inquiring into the secret slush fund Infoscandal in the late 1970s, proclaimed unrepentantly, "I am able with my department to do the impossible . . . I have enough men to commit murder if I tell them: Kill! . . . I don't care who the prey is."[59]

Parliament's failure to police its own armed forces was part of a more pervasive decay and non-existence of the rule of law. Governance, with the active consent of the governors, gave way to a meticulously implemented and randomly murderous killing machine.

(b) Omission

The consent of the governors in the criminal horrors of apartheid involved, beyond the active atrocities of assassination and harassment, the nudge-and-wink tactics of complicity. As was widely noted in commentary at the time, the apartheid government may have been armed to the teeth and fearfully effective in tracking down its opponents, but it proved oddly inefficient in bringing to justice those who killed, attacked and harassed opponents of apartheid.

It was a revealing coincidence that the police completely failed to find the perpetrators of the Khotso House bombing, the bombing of Cosatu House, and the bombing of the Catholic Bishops Conference headquarters at Khanya House, among other incidents. All these targets were prominent anti-apartheid organisations. Rather than launching an effective investigation, the Minister of Police, Adriaan Vlok, engaged in a transparent attempt at misinformation, for instance detaining ANC activist Shirley Gunn as an alleged suspect.

These machinations left commentators with "an uneasy feeling that rightwing terrorism is not taken seriously – or is even condoned"[60] by the then government. Despite mounting evidence of SADF and police force abuses under General Magnus Malan and Minister Adriaan Vlok respectively, the then State President de Klerk resisted widespread pressure for their dismissal, until the ANC made their removal from security-related posts a prerequisite for continuing negotiations.

In April 1996 a former security policeman, Inspector Douw Willemse, testifying in a death squad trial, confessed involvement in the Khotso and Cosatu House bombings in Johannesburg as well as the bombing of Khanya House in Pretoria; he further admitted involvement in cross-border violence in Swaziland and elsewhere. Willemse also confirmed that Minister of Law and Order Adriaan Vlok had visited the death squad headquarters "from time to time" to congratulate the terrorists on their bombings of anti-apartheid activist targets; and that other high-ranking security officials were directly involved: Brigadier Willem Schoon, a police commander, attended a party with the death squad terrorists after one of the Johannesburg blasts.[61]

Meanwhile, right-wing extremists were given astonishingly free rein to pursue their tactics of havoc. Thus on 22 July 1987, a delegation of prominent Afrikaners, returning from talks with the ANC in Dakar, was forced to cancel a scheduled press conference and use side exits in order to avoid a band of thugs, led by Eugene TerreBlanche, that had assembled at the airport to molest them. The press, not the thugs, were bundled into vans and driven away from the scene.

Apart from the obvious convenience to the regime (which had opposed the talks) of the cancelled Dakar press conference, this intimidatory conduct had the almost explicit sanction of the Botha government. On 1 August Magnus Malan questioned the patriotism of the Dakar delegation and suggested that they condoned a bomb blast that had occurred in Johannesburg during their visit. (Evidence has since emerged that the blast was organised by the South

African Police in an attempt to discredit the ANC.)[62] In leading a parliamentary delegation into the so-called "operational area" – the apartheid military's occupied territories in southern Africa – the following month, Malan pointedly excluded two MPs who at the time advocated discussions, leading to negotiations, with the ANC.

After long delays in the face of intense pressure following the CCB disclosures, President F W de Klerk in 1990 eventually appointed a Commission of Enquiry into "Certain Alleged Murders" and other unlawful acts. This was subsequently known as the Harms Commission. This Commission's terms of reference were limited to offences within the borders of South Africa, despite substantial evidence that CCB activities had cross-border scope.

While paragraph 3 of the terms of reference empowered the one-man commission to "inquire into and to report on any other matter which, in your opinion, is relevant," Justice Harms chose to construe his already restricted mandate in the narrowest possible fashion, alleging for instance that the commission was "not mandated" to "investigate the security arm of the state, the so-called Civil Cooperation Bureau."[63]

Yet Harms made an *ad hoc* exception to the cross-border prohibition in the case of Anton Lubowski and investigated cross-border money transfers and other activities calculated to substantiate Defence Minister Magnus Malan's allegations, stated in parliament, that Lubowski was a paid agent of South African Military Intelligence. And while going out of his way to reach a conclusion on Lubowski's alleged functions as an informant, Harms was conspicuously sceptical of allegations against the police, apparently even commenting to one witness who made such allegations, "How must I believe this crap you're talking."[64]

Apart from the scepticism displayed by the Commissioner himself, the Harms Commission's investigations were hampered by the deliberate destruction of documents and assorted non-cooperation from the South African Defence Force, which the then State President, F W de Klerk, the Defence Minister and parliament made no effective interventions to correct.

The Harms Commission's Report, while unsatisfactory in most aspects, did confirm the existence of a secret arm of state, the Civil Cooperation Bureau. Yet State President F W de Klerk exonerated Malan from political responsibility for the CCB scandal and turned a blind eye to the fact that, on his own version of events, Malan had no explanation for the large expenditures (R 29 million annually) that funded the CCB out of Malan's own Special Defence Fund.

Between 1990, when the CCB scandal first broke, and 1992, Finance Minister Barend du Plessis and Defence Minister Magnus Malan officially allocated another R28 million (and unknown unofficial amounts) to the CCB. And this was the tip of the iceberg. In the 1989/90 budget, fully R5 816 billion was voted into the secret Defence Special Fund; an undisclosed proportion of this was earmarked for covert activities of unspecified scope and objectives.

In September 1990, after the Goldstone Commission had found certain shooting incidents at the Vaal township of Sebokeng wholly unjustifiable, there were new shootings in the same township. This recurrence ought to have created substantial alarm. Yet General Magnus Malan arrogantly rejected Nelson Mandela's claim that the South African Defence Force was at fault for the renewed killing of eleven people (and the injuring of many more) at Sebokeng. Despite reports that balaclava-clad whites were involved in the unrest, Malan, rather than launching an independent investigation, brazenly challenged Mr Mandela to substantiate his claims to a military or police inquiry – a procedure which could have carried little credibility at any time.

Thus there was a corrosive and systematic practice of apartheid governance until its very last days in 1994. It looked the other way, or pretended to be looking the other way, in order to allow the commission of terrorist acts against the resistance. In February 1991, Defence Minister Magnus Malan made the astonishing suggestion that it was not his fault if members of the SADF broke the law. Apart from suggesting a failed grasp of the responsibilities of his job as Minister of Defence, this can only have signalled a contempt for legality and fanned the flames of defence force impunity in continuing their patterns of human rights abuse.

(c) Vigilantism

Apartheid's leading military strategists, such as Army Chief General C Alan Fraser (not to mention P W Botha himself), realised early on in the 1960s that conventional military strength might be, in Fraser's phrase, "quite useless," in isolation, against revolutionary insurgents. Rather, it was essential to obtain the support of a "neutral or uncommitted majority," said Fraser. Apartheid's militarists never doubted, as Defence Minister Magnus Malan commented decades later during the 1986 state of emergency, that

> There are at the moment only a small portion that are really interested in political participation. I think that for the masses in South Africa democracy is not a relevant factor. For them, it concerns the satisfaction of their own requirements. These requirements change from time to time, and are presently being exploited by the revolutionaries.[65]

This was a constant theme of apartheid's violent assault on the South African majority – the idea that only a small minority of "agitators" was stirring up trouble and that most blacks were, or potentially were, loyal adherents of the apartheid system. In the early days it was even said that the small band of agitators were all white communists, since blacks could not, it was said, contrive and execute sophisticated strategies of subversion.

Such thinking, a form really of the traditional imperial mindset of arrogance and racism ("We know our natives better than anyone else – themselves included"), had in the end murderous implications. Apartheid's militarists set about implementing a strategy of divide-and-rule, turning community against community in an attempt to create a popular counterweight to the anti-apartheid resistance.

An official document circulated to government functionaries through the

National Security Management System (NSMS) in the 1980s advocated the promotion of a "counter revolutionary guerrilla force which ... must be supported by the security forces ... and which is employed according to guerrilla tactics to annihilate the revolutionary guerrillas and take over the population."[66] In this variant of apartheid's terrorist tactics, selected sub-groups of apartheid's victims were to be mobilised as human cannon fodder against those resisting apartheid.

A December 1985 military intelligence report at the centre of the ongoing trial of former Defence Minister Magnus Malan and others confirmed this strategy. Entitled "South African Defence Force Support to Chief Minister Buthelezi and Bishop Lekganyane" it spoke of a "golden opportunity to pull a meaningful and influential section of the black population into a counter-insurgency and mobilisation programme."[67]

This reinforced the police role as a partisan player in a violent divide-and-rule strategy of alleged counter-insurgency. In January 1988, Minister of Law and Order Adriaan Vlok stated brazenly in a speech in Pietermaritzburg that: "the police intend to face the future with the moderates and fight against the radical groups ... Radicals who are trying to destroy South Africa [sic] will not be tolerated. We will fight them. We have put our foot in that direction, and we will eventually win the Pietermaritzburg area."[68]

Natal warlord David Ntombela, found by an inquest to have been responsible for killing a woman and a child in October 1987, was treated indulgently by the Pietermaritzburg security chief, Brigadier Jacques Buchner, who commented that "Ntombela is a legally appointed representative of the KwaZulu government; he has to rule with an iron hand or he loses respect and authority."[69] Regional fascism was openly condoned – indeed relied upon and cultivated – by the beleaguered apartheid regime.

The Goldstone Commission in June 1993 concluded that there was "every justification for the perception by many people that the SAP were working" with Inkatha-aligned violent gangs.[70] Such comments are a telling counterweight to claims by State President F W de Klerk that, while individual policemen may have acted improperly, the force as a whole was impartial.[71]

As violence continued and intensified, and despite loud protestations of concern, President F W de Klerk, for reasons that remain ill-explained to this day, repeatedly refused to ban the carrying of spears and battle axes (so-called "traditional" or "cultural" weapons) which had become a prime tool in vigilantism.

Apart from deliberately inadequate and partisan policing, there were also active partisan initiatives by the apartheid government to create, arm and train enemies of its political opponents. According to the relevant Goldstone Commission Report, issued in June 1993, the SADF in the mid-to-late eighties trained Inkatha-aligned recruits in the use of weapons, "including the AK47, the Uzi, the G3, and the Tokarev. They were taught how to fire, dismantle and reassemble these weapons. They were taught how to use and fire RPG7 rocket launchers. They were given instruction in urban and guerrilla warfare; and how to attack buildings using hand grenades and smoke grenades. Structures made of corrugated iron and piled sandbags were repeatedly repaired and rebuilt after being destroyed during practice exercises. They were taught . . . how to interrogate captured persons using both violent or aggressive styles as well as gentle or protective styles. They were taught how to abduct people as well as surveillance."[72]

Those thus trained were being prepared only for bodyguard duties, claimed State President de Klerk in 1990. Consistent with the "deniability" approach, counsel for the SADF argued that if the SADF trains people it cannot be held responsible if such persons "thereafter go out and employ their skills for illegal purposes."[73] The Goldstone Commission rejected this claim but nevertheless rather inexplicably declined to find that the SADF rendered this training with the specific intent to establish "hit squads." Subsequent disclosures have put the existence of hit squads beyond doubt, a fact that the Truth and Reconciliation Commission must unambiguously acknowledge.

In July 1991 it emerged that the National Party, despite their ostensible abandonment of apartheid's policies of divide-and-rule, had secretly funded the Inkatha Freedom Party as a counterweight to the ANC. One support payment was made in March 1990 – on the wrong side of the February 1990 speech of the then State President F W de Klerk, often taken as the moment when his party finally broke with apartheid. Pik Botha, in an explanation widely dismissed as unpersuasive, defended these payments as part of the government's desire to oppose the international sanctions campaign.

President Mandela commented accurately at the time that "the transformation of Natal and many parts of the Reef into killing fields must be laid squarely at the door of the government."[74] In the 1988 Trust Feeds case, the trial judge found that the massacre of eleven people (including a four-year-old child) by the local police chief Brian Mitchell and four black underlings, was part of a "planned operation to disrupt a community, oust the residents' association, and give Inkatha control of the area."

Such disclosures conform to a longstanding pattern of cultivating black groupings as a manipulated vanguard in apartheid's desperate attempts to impose military control over the South African population while minimising white casualties. The introduction of the "kitskonstabels" – essentially untrained blacks sent to police the black townships – was a related strategy of using black bodies to defend white supremacy. The training, funding, arming and even overt armed support for government-aligned marauders was a potent extension of the kitskonstabel concept.

This deployment of state-backed vigilante groups proved an effective strategy of pro-apartheid repression. For instance, as early as the last months of 1976, allegedly Zulu hostel dwellers, going into battle against the anti-apartheid resistance, ended the Soweto uprising that had begun on 16 June. In the Cape, between Christmas and New Year 1977, bands of "witdoek" migrant labourers mounted attacks on the anti-apartheid resistance in the townships, with the tacit support of the security services. The unrest in the Peninsula quickly subsided.

The destruction of the Crossroads/KTC squatter camp in 1986 was a brazen and overt instance of police-backed vigilantism, with uniformed police and Casspirs openly protecting the marauders as they made their way towards their targets.

On a grander scale, the ideologically driven process of incorporating black communities into homelands often had the useful side-effect of fanning rivalries and battles for scarce resources among black groups, thus diverting energy from the collective resistance to apartheid. A striking example was the incorporation of the Moutse district into KwaNdebele as part of the so-called KwaNdebele "independence," where partition placed diverse cultural groupings under the iron grip of the bantustan leadership. This apartheid policy deliberately fostered conflict between the Sotho-speaking Moutse people and the KwaNdebele government. It was described by the *Washington Post* as "one of those fateful moves that causes a . . . full scale war."[75]

Summing Up

"The law should not take its course."
– Mangosuthu Buthelezi, objecting to the Malan trial (1996).

The rule of law suffered inner decay under apartheid. The ideal of equal law for all was – early on and not merely in the 1980s – shouldered aside by the twin imperatives of white supremacy and of the militaristic garrison state. Law made no effort to guide conduct towards rational goals of nation-building. It instead became a word-shield for a state bent on assassination and wars of aggression.

The disturbing thing about such historical facts is that their effects remain with us today. One newspaper reported on 18 February 1996 that "members of the now-defunct Kwazulu Police are obstructing efforts by Third Force investigators to arrest suspected Natal hit squad operatives, using methods ranging from 'hiding' suspects to the issuing of death threats."[76]

In an echo of the difficulties experienced by the 1990 Harms Commission, investigators in Ulundi today face obstacles such as the sudden disappearance of witnesses, the withholding of information such as home addresses, personal files that go mysteriously missing, locked offices, and refusal by police to execute warrants of arrest on behalf of the Third Force investigating team. Sometimes all exit routes have been blocked in areas where a suspect has been arrested. Witnesses and police officers have been intimidated. Investigators' vehicles have been sabotaged. One investigator was told straightforwardly that if he sought to arrest a certain suspect he would be killed.

So some parts of the past are still with us. This must not continue for long. We must face the past in order to overtake it. And we are succeeding.

Acknowledging the Humanity of the Resistance

"We must at all times act justly in our own ranks, train our people in the procedure of justice and establish the embryo of the new justice system we envisage for a liberated South Africa."
  – African National Congress, Code of Conduct, 1985.

"The United Party comes and whines, 'the constitution'. Anyone would think that the constitution was of greater importance to them than the maintenance of White civilisation in our country."
  – S M Loubser, National Party MP, 1952.

In choosing between the starkly different apple trees of apartheid and of the resistance to it, it is helpful to examine the moral, political and constitutional roots of the latter.

Born in 1912, the African National Congress spent nearly fifty years seeking acknowledgment of the rights of the South African people by peaceful means: through petitions, demonstrations, strikes and all the campaigning methods that would be normal in a democracy. No liberation movement in the world can surpass this history of methodical non-violence in circumstances of relentless state violence. The young Gandhi himself pioneered his technique of passive resistance in 1915 as part of the struggle against apartheid.

Indeed, amid the multiple injustices visited upon blacks at this time, the main thrust of the ANC in its formation was resistance to the gross new unfairness of the Land Act, not the accumulated injustices of the *status quo*. Moreover, at the time of the ANC's founding, European nationalism was full of the ideas of blood and sacrifice as the legitimate price of nationhood. It was a path that the ANC rejected.

In the interwar years the ANC maintained a practice of dignified dissent from the prevailing racism. Throughout the 1950s, the ANC's tactics were those of the passive-resistance Defiance Campaign in 1952 and the anti-pass campaign.

Only when it was banned, its leaders hunted, and its membership restive for a new phase of struggle did the armed campaign (in support of ongoing attempts at a civic campaign) see the light of day. And the decision to enter the new phase of armed and civic struggle was thoroughly discussed within the organisation, in so far as the need to preserve secrecy allowed. The decision, for instance, to establish MK as a separate armed wing was a product of these deliberations and flowed from a desire to protect the legal status of the ANC's organisational allies.

The ANC, despite the exigencies of the time, managed to sustain at least some of these internal democratic practices. It hardly learned these from the National Party, which had been thoroughly authoritarian from its inception. The historical pattern is obvious: apartheid was, in its every aspect, a rejection of the twin ideals of nonracialism and constitutionalism; whereas the African National Congress has always embraced both these ideals.

On 24 May 1923, the South African Native National Congress, held in Bloemfontein, adopted South Africa's first nonracial Bill of Rights, which was predictably ignored by the white supremacist parliamentarians. Alarmed by the systematic erosion of the rights of the African people and "their Coloured brethren," the delegates called for "the constitutional right of an equal share in the management and direction of the affairs of this land."

This was a natural evolution from the founding of the ANC eleven years earlier. It was a logical response to the white supremacist 1909 Union constitution, which shut blacks out of governance. It represented resistance to the policies underlying the 1913 Land Act, which dispossessed Africans, disrupted their economic and agrarian security, and rendered them dependent on white employers.

In order to define a different vision of South Africa, the five clauses of the 1923 Bill of Rights demanded the right to live in South Africa, to own land, to be equal in the eyes of the law, to be treated equally irrespective of race, class, creed or origin and to have direct representation in government. It was these systematic constitutional claims that fuelled the ANC's protests against specific government legislation throughout the 1920s and 1930s.

In December 1943, this constitutional kernel of five clauses was expanded into a comprehensive Bill of Rights for South Africa, which anticipated by five years the provisions of the Universal Declaration of Human Rights. A core demand was that there should be a place for all in the parliamentary machinery of the country and the extension of voting rights to all adults irrespective of race.

The Preamble of the 1943 Bill of Rights called unequivocally for full citizenship rights "such as are enjoyed by all Europeans in South Africa." In addition, the Bill of Rights raised the following issues: access to land across the country, including fair distribution of land; rights of urban residence, including the inviolability of the home against police arrest; equal justice in the courts, including nomination to juries and appointment as judges, magistrates and other court officers; competitive examinations for the civil service; careers open to talent; free and compulsory education; freedom of movement; and equal access to social services.

Prime Minister Smuts, presiding over the white supremacist parliament, rejected these carefully considered and evolutionary demands, rooted in three decades of methodical protest, as "wildly impracticable" and "propagandist." In particular, he suggested that "tremendous snags" precluded the granting of parliamentary representation to Africans. On Bills of Rights, as on so many other policy matters, Smuts's rule was the precursor of outright apartheid.

In 1955, seven years after the white supremacist Parliament was captured by the National Party, a 3,000-delegate multiracial ANC conference in Kliptown adopted the world-renowned Freedom Charter, which remains a global model of inclusive politics. Its preamble declared that "South Africa belongs to all who live in it, black and white, and no Government can justly claim authority unless it is based on the will of the people." After rejecting the apartheid government as "founded on injustice and inequality," the preamble emphasised the fact that the struggle bound "the people of South Africa, black and white, together."

The body of the Charter itself proclaimed that "all national groups shall be protected by law against insults to their race and national pride" and "shall have equal right to use their own languages, and to develop their own folk culture and customs." There were to be full voting rights for all as well as rights of participation in government and in institutions of property and industry. All were to have "equal rights to trade where they choose, to manufacture and enter into all trades, crafts and professions." Racially discriminatory land ownership and dispossession were to be ended. Equality before the law was guaranteed. Civil liberties and socio-economic rights alike were to be safeguarded. And there was a commitment to the ending of all international disputes "by negotiation – not war."

The Freedom Charter, which became a beacon for liberation across the globe, both anticipated and contributed to the global human rights consensus that has been so important in ensuring the victory of democracy in South Africa.

In its traditional 8 January statement in 1987, the ANC reaffirmed its commitment to a justiciable bill of rights – one enforceable by the courts. Following the ANC's 1987 Lusaka conference, the movement's "Constitutional Guidelines For a Democratic South Africa" were published in 1988, significantly before the fall of the overcentralised European states began in late 1989. The Guidelines reiterated the ANC's longstanding commitment to humane and democratic governance.

This commitment was ignored by the apartheid regime for as long as its anti-communist propaganda remained credible. After the events of 1989, the myth of a communist onslaught, which had always been absurd, became manifestly untenable and the regime lost an important justification for ignoring the real nature of the decades-long resistance to it.

The 1988 Guidelines put to shame the travesty of rights contained in the regime's proposed 1990 Bill of Rights. In that document, the National Party sought to hamstring democracy with rules that in effect provided for a white veto. The liberation movement successfully argued that an effective Bill of Rights could not become a bill for whites. Instead, in 1990 it proposed a model *Bill of Rights for a New South Africa*, as "the fundamental anti-apartheid document," ensuring a basic level of physical and material security to all.

Additionally, Article 16 of this 1990 document stated that "provision shall be made for the establishment of a constitutional court" and that "any law or executive or administrative act which violates the terms of the Bill of Rights shall be invalid . . ." This proposal was the first that unequivocally subjected South African governance to fundamental principles of legality. Proposals for proportional representation and the entrenchment of a constitutional court as the guardian of the Constitution were also of ANC provenance.

It is instructive to compare these 1990 proposals, as well as the others outlined above, with the final outcome of the transitional negotiations – the 1993 interim constitution as well as the 1996 final constitution. Such a comparison makes overwhelmingly clear the extent to which the anti-apartheid resistance, and the ANC specifically, are the primary authors of the new South African democracy.

As Nelson Mandela said in his statement from the dock in the Rivonia show trial, "The African National Congress has spent half a century fighting against racialism. When it triumphs it will not change that policy." The oral history and personal narratives of figures within the ANC resistance are replete with concrete examples of the ways in which, despite the unpredictable problems of resistance, the ANC managed, in practice, to teach the principle of nonracialism to its followers and activists. This was the unbreakable golden thread of the movement.[1]

In the light of the ANC's demonstrable and heavily documented history of nonracialism and constitutionalism, one can only describe as ignorant the view, held by at least one reputable South African commentator, that to project the democracy and human rights of the interim constitution of 1994 as the kind of democracy the ANC has always fought for is to produce a gigantic optical illusion; and that to have supported the ANC in the 1980s out of allegiance to human rights would have been a long shot. Such views can only seem true to someone more absorbed in battles with Afro-pessimism, and the neuroses of complicity in the past, than by an honest appraisal of the ANC's history of constitutionalism and nonracialism.

In stark contrast to the ANC's long history of constitutionalism and human rights, the National Party State President's statement of 2 February 1990, announcing a move away from apartheid, was also the first occasion on which that party accepted the idea of the constitutional protection of the rights of the individual. It is no accident that only with the move away from apartheid could the National Party accept basic tenets of constitutionalism. While decades of white supremacist violence assaulted the very ideas of the rule of law and constitutionalism, the anti-apartheid resistance was the dutiful safe-house of these ideals.

South African history pitted the world's most law-abiding liberation movement against the world's most lawless bureaucracy; nonracialism confronted its racist opposite. It pitted an internationally recognised and respected resistance movement against an internationally reviled pseudo-state whose credentials were rejected by the United Nations in 1974. It was such realities that repeatedly pushed frustrated apartheid governments into recurring denunciations of the

United Nations and the whole world.

It is uncontroversial to observe that the African National Congress is the only liberation movement to have initiated a formal investigation of its own human rights infringements. It established not one or two but four separate investigations (in 1984, 1989, 1992 and 1993) to find the truth about events in its camps in southern Africa. The first of these was set up in 1976, born of the necessity to deal with apartheid's deliberate strategies of infiltration.

The 1993 Motsuenyane Commission Report, an unsparing account of significant human rights infringements in these camps, proclaimed:

> It would be wrong to ignore the historic significance of the investigation the ANC, through this Commission, has undertaken – *a first in the annals of human rights enforcement.* By its commitment to this inquiry, the ANC seeks to breathe life into the lofty principles proclaimed in the Freedom Charter – to render fundamental rights the Golden Rule, to be applied in good times and bad, peace and war. (Emphasis added.)

In striking contrast to the liberation movement's commitment to human rights "in good times and bad," the South African Police have expressly disclosed that because of an alleged "revolutionary onslaught" the government ordered its security forces to take all measures deemed necessary to sustain apartheid:

> This included actions not covered in normal legislation and created moral grounds of justification for the contravention of existing laws. Structures like the State Security Council under the chairmanship of the State President, the Co-ordinating Intelligence Committee and other multi-disciplinary bodies gave direct, but in most cases indirect, orders to the security forces, culminating in the commission of various crimes.[2]

The difference between apartheid and the resistance to it, in their respective disregard for and allegiance to human rights, could not be sharper. The ANC's 1993 Motsuenyane Commission Report into human rights abuses in the ANC's southern African camps acknowledges that "it is difficult to apply the formal structures of documents such as international treaties to the complex situation of a national liberation movement in exile, struggling against a racist regime that imposes its power by all possible means, including its police force." Yet, despite its complex position and severe shortages of resources, the resistance embraced the large tasks of human rights discipline.

Remarkably, in November 1980 the African National Congress made a solemn Declaration to the International Committee of the Red Cross in Geneva that it would abide by the Geneva Conventions, and Protocol I of 1977, on the treatment of combatants and civilians in liberation wars. Members of MK, the armed wing of the ANC, were trained in the requirements of the Conventions.

Many ANC members who were put on trial by the apartheid regime for their military activities mentioned this training, and were clearly aware of their duties in this regard. One such was Andrew Sibusiso Zondo, who was hanged by the apartheid bureaucracy for causing an explosion which killed five people in Amanzimtoti in December 1985.

Zondo's story illuminates the contrasting moralities of the anti-apartheid resistance and the apartheid police. He joined the ANC after police attacked a peaceful prayer service in which he was at worship. He then left the country but soon returned and was promptly arrested. According to his father, the young man had become "mentally deranged" and was under great stress as a result of the abuse to which he was subjected. He fled to Maputo, only to encounter the grisly SADF raid on Matola. Finally he went for military training and returned to South Africa in 1985, shortly before the SADF raid on Maseru.

It was clear from his trial testimony that he was a sensitive young man who had been driven beyond endurance by the violence of the regime. It was also plain that he had not intended to kill people, and was profoundly sorry for the deaths he had caused. He was, he said, "happy to be arrested so as to face it because the outcome of what I did . . . five people dead . . . . If ever I have part of flesh to give to those who remain I can do it with pleasure." He continued that "as an ANC member, I was supposed to prove the difference between the South African Defence Force and Umkhonto we Sizwe, and ensure that civilians did not get hurt." His MK colleague Robert McBride, whose attempts to target off-duty security force officers resulted in collateral civilian deaths, has expressed similar remorse.

In contrast, the well-resourced apartheid state simply shrugged off not only human rights restraints, but even its own self-indulgent legislation, which proved too onerous a fetter on the atrocities in which the regime wished to indulge. As the ANC National Executive Committee's statement in response to the Motsuenyane Report emphasised, they were its own laws that the regime broke.

As for the 1977 Protocols to the Geneva Conventions, the regime refused even to consider signing them; and while it had ratified the 1949 Geneva Conventions, it failed to incorporate them into municipal law as then required. It continued to hang captured prisoners of war in defiance of binding international law and humanitarian standards.

The ANC as an organisation, and President Mandela personally, frankly accepted moral and collective responsibility for ANC contraventions, a step which the National Party's present-day representatives have yet to undertake in respect of their own systematic and inordinately more culpable system as a whole. As with every aspect of the anti-apartheid resistance, the ultimate, causal, responsibility rests with the apartheid regime, since the necessity for and the very existence of these camps would have disappeared in the absence of apartheid. As the ANC's National Executive Committee wrote at the time, the lapses recorded in the Motsuenyane Report "occurred as a result of the resistance and opposition to apartheid."

Moreover, there was no finding of any pattern of systematic abuses. These infringements represented lapses in the liberation movement's structures of authority and accountability. They were the opposite of what the movement's authority structures intended. The problems of maintaining command and control while vulnerable to cross-border attacks and infiltration by the apartheid state were formidable. The imposition of adequate checks and balances on a security apparatus is a difficult task in the most settled of circumstances; the difficulties multiply dramatically when the organisation seeking to exert control is outlawed in its own country, is essentially living on the run, and faces material constraints such as the simple shortage of money.

On the other hand, apartheid's systematic and well-funded violence was deliberate and crucial to the regime's survival. As the old South African Police force has conceded, the governmental structures that directly and indirectly ordered violations of apartheid's own laws were not only "formed by the nationalist government, but [also] the actions of the security forces were fully sanctioned by it and senior members of Cabinet were briefed on a continuous basis."3

Ultimately, apartheid and its administrators avowedly rejected human rights as a form of what apartheid Prime Minister Vorster called "misguided" humanism. They had as much contempt for black people as for civilised international norms.

According to the South African Police, the apartheid government's "Simonstown Deliberations," held in 1979 with the security forces, gave specific orders to them in respect of information gathering and cross-border operations. These orders, according to the South African Police, placed an "emphasis" on confessedly "abnormal intelligence gathering methodology and not according to international norms and practices." Subsequent to the Simonstown Deliberations, decisions were taken by formal structures created by government and the security forces "over a number of years" to implement these "abnormal" measures. Moreover, according to the South African Police themselves, "these structures were fully sanctioned by the Nationalist Government and senior members of cabinet were briefed on a continuous and structured basis."4

It has emerged from a supplementary indictment filed in the trial of former Defence Minister Magnus Malan and 19 others that 1988 duty sheets issued to SADF officers directed that "offensive actions" (for which read hit squad activities) had to be authorised in advance by Military Intelligence and targets had to be approved by military officers and the police's security branch.5

On 12 March 1990, one month after the release of Nelson Mandela and the regime's supposedly definitive parting of ways with apartheid, a document issued by apartheid General Jannie Geldenhuys, Minister of Defence Magnus Malan and Minister of Finance Barend du Plessis confirmed that "the present state president was briefed on a broad spectrum of sensitive projects and reacted as follows: a) Approval in principle is granted for the running of Stratcom [i.e. irregular covert] projects; b) There should be a revaluation of areas and the allocation of responsibilities. In the meantime the Defence Force should continue running [them]; c) A central controlling body will be looked at." The document contained a list of at least 45 covert projects, including the one at the centre of the Malan hit squads trial. Each project was, based on a brief description of it, specifically approved for covert funding by the Finance Minister.

In the same document, the hands-on control that Cabinet Ministers including former State President F W de Klerk himself exerted over violent projects through the State Security Council (SSC) is confirmed: "Covert Stratcom Projects are controlled and directed by the secretary of the SSC. This includes the separation and allocation of areas to departments. The SSC secretary receives decisions and orders in this regard from the state president and passes them to the departments involved."[6]

This principle of high-level accountability applied as much to cross-border aggression as to internal repression. The then Foreign Minister Pik Botha commented at the time on SABC TV that he had known beforehand that the December 1986 attack on Swaziland would take place; that he accepted full responsibility for the killing of a teenage child; and that he regretted nothing.[7]

On 9 May 1984, Foreign Minister Pik Botha told parliament that during the period of massive cross-border destabilisation leading up to the Nkomati Accord which brought Mozambique to its knees, "I was in absolute agreement with all decisions taken" and that the successes such as the Accord owed as much to "military action" (including support for the murderous Renamo forces) as to "diplomatic action."[8]

While direct documentary evidence, the proverbial smoking gun, is difficult to find because of lost and destroyed archives, it does sometimes emerge: Ministers Pik Botha and De Klerk, according to the minutes of the State Security Council, were explicitly party to a decision in the mid-1980s to use "violence over the border" in order to prevent Lesotho from aiding the ANC.[9]

Such patterns of internal and external homicide and violent abuse against its opponents were a longstanding feature of apartheid. When in 1963 Minister of Justice John Vorster introduced in parliament the notorious Sabotage Act which facilitated violent police interrogations, he left no doubt that deliberate and legalised torture was on his mind. "It is not a very nice thing to see a human being broken," he said. "I have seen it . . . The man taking these powers must take the responsibility for them."[10] Decades later in 1986, following the disclosure of widespread torture of Port Elizabeth detainees, MP David Dalling read victims' affidavits into the record so that "when the Nuremberg trials are held in this country – and it will happen – I do not want any members of this House to say: 'I did not know.' "[11]

The ANC's armed wing, MK, eked out a precarious existence in the southern African countries surrounding South Africa. It knew and feared the attempts of the regime to infiltrate its ranks, and its members were forced to be on constant alert for raids from the air or attacks by land. Some succumbed to this climate of terror unleashed by the apartheid regime and used the enemy's instruments of torture against suspected spies. But we must emphasise that these infringements of human rights were comparatively few, and were never condoned – were actually forbidden – by the ANC leadership. Under apartheid, torture was a deliberate systematic practice, expressly on the mind of the Justice Minister as he introduced detention legislation in parliament. By contrast, abuses in ANC camps and conduct such as "necklacing" – setting alight rubber tyres after placing them around people – were the result of failures in the command and control structures of the resistance. The ANC expressly condemned necklacing.

The anti-apartheid resistance, under-resourced and reduced to the status of exiles and refugees by a few men who hijacked a whole country, committed scattered human rights infringements amounting to departures from its primary humanist goals. The inadequacy of available means of resistance resulted in unintended civilian casualties, some of whom were supporters of the resistance movement. Such was the case, for instance, where a grenade targeted at the Bophuthatswana Consulate in Kimberley accidentally killed one anti-apartheid protester and injured thirty-nine others. Resistance could have unpredictable and sometimes tragic results.

In contrast, apartheid's administrators, deliberately rejecting humanism and civilised international norms, formally implemented avowedly "abnormal" measures in the conscious and deliberate defence of a crime against humanity. These things inhabit different, fundamentally incompatible, moral universes.

The Morality of Armed Resistance

Choosing an apple tree was not a simple act; it was choosing a whole ethical world, choosing moral headspace, choosing who, exactly, one wanted to be. It is simply not true, as some have suggested, that people on both sides were only puppets in an armed and violent struggle. Among those who upheld apartheid, this argument is often a plea for exculpation under a doctrine of "superior orders," though in fact such an argument was ruled out of court at Nuremberg. It has no validity in international law.

The interesting point, however, is that no one on the side of the resistance seeks (or has sought) to invoke this argument as a tactic to evade moral responsibility. Being part of the resistance was profoundly an act of ethical self-expression. Each participant had individually, as Albie Sachs puts it, "embarked upon a certain road out of proud and conscious choice."

In particular, those individuals who chose armed struggle have, with the exception of those few guilty of human rights infringements, nothing to apologise for. In no European country has the resistance movement been called upon to acknowledge the illegitimacy or condemn the conduct of those resisting occupation or Nazi rule. In fact, in liberal democracies such as Denmark and Norway, a curtain is drawn across this reactive violence of the resistance. Additionally, historians have, by acknowledging the inequality of resources in combat, fought shy of apportioning blame to the combatants on the side of the anti-Nazi resistance or the anti-colonial struggle.

This is an important point because certain voices have suggested that apartheid's liberal parliamentary opposition is the only group to have emerged from the South African past with clean hands; that they alone rejected violence.

This claim of liberal clean hands is certainly not true, given their acceptance of South African aggression against those countries in southern Africa which were in the front line against apartheid at the time; or given parliament's acceptance of whites-only military conscription, which meant mandatory white violence against a predominantly black population; or given parliament's acquiescence in murderous states of emergency; or its blind annual approval of billions of rands of secret defence spending, which included the funding of hit squads, without asking or knowing, though certainly suspecting, to what use the funds were being put.[1]

It is an oxymoron to speak, as do the parliamentary liberals of the old order, of having pursued a "non-violent parliamentary path in opposing apartheid."

There was no such luxury. The apartheid parliament was a primary, if unsuccessful, legitimiser of apartheid's horrendous violence.

Ambivalence towards apartheid's internal and cross-border violence is the cross that all apartheid parliamentarians must necessarily bear. To renounce that apartheid violence unambiguously is to renounce aspects of their own complicit past; it is something with which, clearly, they have yet to come to terms. Yet despite this selective blindness to the violence of its allies, South African liberalism's reputation for nonviolence survives, proving once more Milton's comment that hypocrisy "is the only evil that walks Invisible except to God alone."

It needs to be emphasised again that the oppressed majority had no access to normal democratic channels, no vote and no right to peaceful protest. In these conditions, armed struggle was not a choice but a necessity, a burden taken up with reluctance, but also with integrity and dignity.

The intention is not to belittle or downplay the real courage and genuine contribution of the small liberal parliamentary opposition to apartheid: the Liberal Party through people like Mrs Margaret Ballinger, and the Progressive Party which broke from the highly conservative United Party in 1959. But the fact is that the whole parliamentary institution was a sham. And as the late Harold Wolpe emphasised at the 1987 Dakar talks on ending apartheid, the dynamics of white electoral politics were flatly irreconcilable with the liberation movement's goals of self-determination: "What satisfies the white electorate does not at all satisfy and would be regarded as betrayal by the mass democratic movement."

No issue better demonstrates this truth than that of the armed struggle itself. The struggle was not a disposable adjunct of the mass democratic campaign. It was rather a vital inspiration for that campaign, particularly after the 1960 bannings of open political self-expression. As President Mandela mentions in his autobiography, in 1960 the ANC's constituency was far ahead of the ANC on the issue of armed struggle. The armed struggle was mandated and supervised by the movement, which maintained political oversight throughout. As Joe Slovo put it: "The struggle can no longer be centred on pleas for civil rights or for reforms within the framework of white dominance; it is a struggle for people's power, in which mass ferment and the growing importance of the armed factor go hand in hand."[2]

It is important also to recognise that opponents of apartheid who chose the path of armed struggle did not merely differ as to means with those who rejected armed struggle. Rather, they differed as to ends. In the 1960s, when the armed struggle of the anti-apartheid resistance began, self-determination and the universal franchise were not part of any significant parliamentary party's manifesto. By the late seventies when such ideas had begun, in diluted form, to appear on the agenda of the white parliamentary opposition, these dissenters were too few to have any substantial impact on the apartheid regime, which had become ever more openly authoritarian.

For the resistance movement, by contrast, self-determination – a vote for every adult in an unfragmented South Africa – was an intrinsic value sanctioned by international law. And it was a basic requirement of simple dignity. It was legitimately an end in itself. Even had the "hardships" of apartheid been ameliorated by a white liberal government, this basic issue would have remained as a crucial aspect of human dignity: it is the governed who must directly endorse government policy, not merely a beneficent élite chosen by a racially exclusive electorate, however well meaning. But many liberals remain unable to digest the full implications of such truths about the past.

Beginning in 1961 with a formal resolution of the Pietermaritzburg All-In Africa Conference, Nelson Mandela and the resistance repeatedly appealed for a National Convention to resolve the country's manifest problems. According to the Pietermaritzburg resolutions, the Convention, elected on a nonracial franchise, was to have "sovereign powers to determine, in any way the majority of the representatives decide, a new nonracial democratic Constitution for South Africa."[3]

These calls were ignored and no such convention transpired. Instead, there was increasing repression, including killings of innocent protesters at Sharpeville, Langa and elsewhere.

The apartheid government then exploited the ensuing mass unrest to impose a state of emergency and to ban the ANC and the Pan Africanist Congress. Thousands of people were arrested or detained, and any attempt to organise demonstrations or strikes was immediately repressed. The ANC felt it was no longer justified in putting unarmed demonstrators in harm's way. It hoped, by embarking on armed struggle, to compel the apartheid regime to change course and thus avoid further suffering.

As a result of this wilful indifference alongside escalating use of state violence, the Manifesto of uMkhonto weSizwe (MK), the ANC's armed wing, was released on 16 December 1961. The Manifesto expressed full support for the resistance movement. And MK members "jointly and individually" placed themselves "under the overall political guidance" of the resistance.

The Manifesto referred to the longstanding nonviolence of the resistance movement and the fact that "the people prefer peaceful methods of change," an attitude that had withstood years of "government-inspired attempts to provoke them to violence." Nevertheless, the government had interpreted adherence to ideals of nonviolence as weakness and had seen nonviolent strategies as "a green light for government violence." In these circumstances the only choices were to submit or fight: since submission was not a legitimate option for a movement to foist upon its people, "we have no choice but to hit back by all means within our power in defence of our people, our future and our freedom." The Manifesto emphasised that there was no alternative, as the Nationalist Government had rejected every peaceable demand by the people and answered every such demand with force and yet more force.

The Manifesto expressly hoped that the imminence of armed resistance would "awaken everyone" to the disastrous path being plotted by the National

Party. "Let the Government, its supporters who put it in power, and those whose passive toleration of reaction keep it in power, take note of where the Nationalist Government is leading the country."[4]

This was a textbook case of an oppressed people employing a measured threat of resort to force in order actually to avert violence. ANC President Oliver Tambo was called a "reluctant revolutionary." This is why MK's manifesto has been described as "one of the most eloquent assertions of revolutionary morality in the period after the Second World War."[5]

It may seem curious that one of the reasons for embarking on the armed struggle was actually to avoid greater and more intense violence, which would have destroyed South Africa. But this is not a novel idea and was in fact the case in South Africa. The desire to avoid violence was based on the fundamental realisation, widely shared within the anti-apartheid resistance, that change relying solely on violent seizure of the state was almost necessarily superficial and reversible.

In her magisterial 1970 study of *coups d'état* in Africa, *The Barrel of a Gun*, Ruth First saw that "violence has nearly always been present; fundamental change nearly always absent." The armed anti-apartheid resistance was never a quest for a mere *coup d'état*; rather, its goal was to initiate basic change in the structure of apartheid society. This wisdom permeated the anti-apartheid resistance, ensuring that armed force was always an adjunct to a massive democratic as well as international quest for fundamental change.

Initially MK confined itself to acts of sabotage against public property. Even in the late 1970s and 1980s, the armed struggle was restricted in scope. Nevertheless it clearly played a vital role in overthrowing apartheid, both by the threat it represented to the security forces of the regime and by the inspiration and hope it provided to the South African majority.

The importance of the role of the armed struggle was emphasised in the Harare Declaration of 1989, which was a document drawn up by the ANC, setting out its conditions for negotiation. Actual negotiation would only begin when political prisoners were released, organisations and individuals were unbanned, repressive legislation was lifted, and so on. Until these conditions were met, MK would continue to operate. This document was endorsed by the Organisation of African Unity, the Front Line States, the Non-Aligned Movement and, with minor amendments, the United Nations.

Even after the regime lifted the bans on organisations such as the ANC in February 1990, MK activities were not suspended for some months. As Joe Slovo said on 6 May 1990: "The much vaunted open door offered by the State President F W de Klerk, still had a master lock. If this master lock is not removed, we will have to break it down . . . then the only peace will be that of the graveyard."[6]

Joe Slovo's point, coming at the height of the regime's attempts to force acceptance of various white minority veto proposals, the "master locks", illustrates the decades-long commitment of the liberation movement to real freedom, not sham democracy. It was a principle for which Nelson Mandela, as he said quietly at the Rivonia trial, was prepared to die. Peace, the end of the armed struggle, was not to be sought at the price of genuine self-determination.

MK's activities were suspended in August 1990, but the organisation was not disbanded. The existence of MK remained a vital ingredient in the negotiations over the future of the country. Terminating armed resistance (as opposed merely to the 1990 suspension after the unbannings) meant placing a degree of trust in, and conferring a certain legitimacy upon, the existing apparatus of state violence. It was to say that the apartheid state had become irrevocably committed to genuine debate over the longstanding goals of the resistance to it. Such a decision could not be lightly made.

Apart from the political arguments for and against ending the armed struggle, there were the practical perils of negotiating within an illegitimate state that retained crucial security responsibilities. This pragmatic argument is also important. The suspicion will, for instance, never die that events like the Boipatong massacre (which occurred during an impasse in the negotiations), the attacks on train commuters and the violence from the hostels, were orchestrated in a criminal attempt to weaken the resolve, and the negotiating position, of the anti-apartheid resistance movement. "Third force" disclosures have confirmed the existence and actual implementation of such violent and terrorist strategies.

The nature of the anti-apartheid resistance as a battle of truth against violence is clearest if one examines the relative place of militarism on each side. On the side of apartheid, the battle was never genuinely one for the hearts and minds of the majority (not even in the early eighties and early nineties, when attempts were desperately made to hide the iron fist inside a velvet glove).

If the apartheid machine used overwhelming military might in a failed quest to bury truth, for the resistance the situation was exactly the reverse. Its strength lay in its adherence to the truth of its human rights claims and the integrity of its ideals of non-racialism. Its campaign of "armed propaganda" was a vital prop of all this, designed to reassure a mass base of the movement's determination to transport theories into real political practice.

Fundamental to this strategy was the realisation that unless the armed struggle was supported by a popular base, served it and was guided by it, it would have had "as dismal a future as an isolated group of bandits would have."[7]

Victor Molefe is the only surviving direct participant in uMkhonto weSizwe's strike, in August 1981, at the heart of the apartheid military establishment: the Voortrekkerhoogte military base outside Pretoria. In an interview in 1996 he commented that by the time the first of five shells had been successfully launched, a crowd of the disenfranchised had gathered to watch, some of them leaning on his getaway car. It was "like being at FNB stadium."[8]

The deeply rooted mass democratic base underneath the armed resistance to apartheid vitally distinguishes it from the lonely violence of the apartheid state. It is, frankly, hallucinatory to suggest that "the anti-apartheid movement, intolerant of dissent, totalitarian in outlook, and violent in method, became the mirror image of the apartheid state . . . the instruments of terrorism were used to control populations, for and against."9

The surest sign of the humanism of the anti-apartheid resistance has been its performance in government. Confounding the pro-apartheid propagandists, nobody is hanging from the lamp-posts; indeed the death penalty stands abolished by virtue of the new constitution.

One judge, called upon in the old South Africa to implement certain apartheid legislation, dismissed defence counsel's legal arguments for an ameliorated reading of the statute. The judge rejected this suggestion, saying bluntly that it was nonsensical to attempt to grow flowers on the guillotine.

The new country has thrown the guillotine away.

12

Establishing Equality Before the Law

Apartheid South Africa, it was said, had as much need for a Minister of Justice as landlocked Zambia has for a Minister of Maritime Affairs.

As Ms Navi Pillay, a new South African judge, wrote in 1988: "In the perception of the black majority," the courts of the old South Africa formed "an integral part of the oppressive political system."[1] Through extra-judicial commissions which tapped the rapidly waning prestige of the judiciary in the pursuit of apartheid's political goals; through their straightforward role in implementing apartheid legislation, and especially because of their enthusiasm in so doing, the courts, with a few honourable exceptions, became active partisan upholders of apartheid.

The principle of equality before the law was an early casualty. In the 1962 case of *State* v. *Nelson Mandela*, a Transvaal magistrate's court rejected Mr Mandela's application that the magistrate recuse himself because of the potential for injustice were he (Mandela) tried by a white supremacist court. The magistrate rejected this application on the telling ground that "after all is said and done, there is only one Court today and that is the White Man's Court. There is no other Court."[2]

This system of white man's justice (powerful gender-critiques of the courts abound) was firmly rooted in the colonial era, gained new intensity after the 1948 victory of apartheid, survived until the last days of that system, and still exists residually today.

In November 1988, as was widely reported at the time, a white farmer was fined R3 000 by a northern Transvaal court for tying one of his labourers to a tree and beating him to death. The deceased, a black father of five children, was whipped and beaten with sticks; he was punched with fists and kicked. The farmer invited acquaintances to join in the assault. They did. Then the labourer was left tied to the tree overnight and the violence resumed the next morning.

He died very slowly and was killed in this way because he had angered the farmer by accidentally killing a puppy with a tractor in the course of his duties. "It seems we live in a place where a man's life is less important than a dog's," said a friend of the deceased. But the farmer disagreed: "We treat people differently here. People do not seem to realise what life is like out here in the countryside. I don't think there is anything wrong with South African justice. Things are done in the right way. The fair way."[3]

The farmer's view reflected a deep-rooted history of anti-black violence carried out under cover of law, most obviously in the legal institution of slavery in South Africa and internationally. The northern Transvaal case was not an isolated one in the South Africa of the late 1980s. Almost contemporaneously, a white farming duo in Klerksdorp escaped with a R600 fine and suspended sentence after abducting and beating a black man suspected of cattle theft; the victim died of a brain haemorrhage. In November 1984, a Van Rhynsdorp farmer and two prison warders each suffered merely a R1 000 fine and a suspended sentence for killing a prison labourer.

In April 1990, in the early months of the transition, it was clear to informed observers that white vigilantism rather than black revolution was the main threat to the safety of persons in areas like the Free State goldfields. Even in January 1992, the Free State platteland district of Verkeerdevlei was the site of something resembling United States lynch law, when an alleged criminal wrongdoer (who was black) was summarily beaten to death by white farmer vigilantes who rushed to the rescue of an elderly farming couple who had supposedly been attacked by the deceased. In Welkom, in mid-1990, young whites beat a black man senseless while most whites walked past looking the other way and only a few stopped – to cheer the thugs on. Such examples could easily be multiplied, although recorded examples become less frequent the further back one goes in time, since dead black farmworkers were not newsworthy in the good old days of South Africa.

The systematic denial to South African blacks of equality before the law has a history much longer than apartheid. Within the police force, theoretically the upholders of equality before the law, traditional *baas en kneg* (master and servant) attitudes still survive and sometimes dominate at the expense of the community policing models that are being introduced in the new South Africa. The 1992 Waddington Report, conducted by an internationally eminent British criminologist, concluded that the South African Police's handling of events surrounding the Boipatong massacre reflected "serious incompetence," an approach that was "tactically reckless," and an appearance of bias in favour of hostel dwellers who were complicit with apartheid, at the expense of anti-apartheid township residents.

Beyond the abuse of the criminal justice system, blacks were objects in the eyes of the political system and the law alike, rather than being viewed as citizens with rational and legitimate aspirations of their own, worthy of equal respect.

The white segregationist policies of separate development were never fully applied in practice, because the apartheid regime relied on black labour in the towns and throughout the white areas. However, for the African, presence in a white area was a privilege, not a right. Blacks were hedged about with rules and restrictions, denied free mobility, and not allowed to own property – or even to buy ordinary liquor, until the white businesspersons comprising the wine and beer lobbies pressed for and obtained a change, for purely commercial reasons, by the 1961 Liquor Amendment Act.

One third of African workers in the towns were migrant labourers who were employed on annual contracts; but the security of the rest was not much better. Such arrangements had a long history. The Masters and Servants Acts, passed in the pre-Union territories between 1856 and 1904, made a breach of an employment contract a criminal offence. In practice the courts applied these laws mainly to unskilled work, which was mainly performed by blacks.

Black convicts, but not white ones, were liable to be rented out to farms as prison labour – one of the post-war world's singular barbarities. It was this practice which in 1959, when it was exposed with all its attendant brutality, led to the international boycott of South African potatoes, and thus ultimately to a similar boycott of apartheid South Africa's agricultural produce. But this international uproar did not at the time produce any improvements on the ground in South Africa. It merely resulted in the passing of the 1959 Prisons Act, which effectively prevented the press from publishing any similar information in the future, except when cases managed to get to court.

In 1971, after a fresh scandal arose from a prisoner being beaten to death on one farm, the system was changed. Instead of prisoners being contracted out to farmers, approved farmers were encouraged to raise the capital to build a prison. It was a perversely motivated and early form of privatisation and it came extremely close to straightforward chattel slavery (especially given that blacks were imprisoned as "criminals" for infractions such as not having the required apartheid "pass book" to hand). Based on the value of his capital contribution, each farmer was allocated a specified number of prisoners per day, and was responsible for transporting them to work and paying a guard to supervise them. The cost to the farmer was estimated to be 40 cents per day. In 1976 farmers paid between 24 cents and R1,90 per prisoner per day (to the state, not the prisoners, who received nothing).

By 1972, there were already 22 farm jails in the country. Barberton farm jail gained particular notoriety in 1983, when conditions were so atrocious that a total of 11 prisoners died there, at least 4 of them after they had been driven by desperation to attack warders. One court heard that prisoners were compelled to load gravel into wheelbarrows on scorchingly hot days and were beaten with truncheons if they flagged. Such conditions of forced labour are forbidden under the International Labour Organisation (ILO) Convention and under various human rights conventions.

Even today, there are seasonal farm labourers in the South African winelands who earn as little as R1,90 a day, plus a bottle of wine, for a thirteen-hour day's work. This is a latter-day variant of the notorious tot system that historically prevailed in South African vineyards: workers received no cash and were instead paid in alcohol.

In March 1996, farm labourers produced current pay slips which showed deductions for punishment for backchatting the farmer, for failing to call him "baas" and for being absent due to illness. When 75 workers tried to depart from one farm, they were essentially kept captive by the farmer in six small dark rooms and were only released after the local ANC office intervened.4

These historical and contemporary events, extending even into the new South Africa, reflect a deep-rooted attitude, intensified by apartheid, to black South Africans. In 1975 a government spokesman stated with reference to blacks working in so-called white areas: "These people are here, as far as we are concerned, for all time on a casual basis; they are here because they have come here to work, but without land ownership and without political rights." A Deputy Minister described Africans in white areas as "surplus appendages."

This totalitarian system of population control was enforced through the notorious pass system, which was originally designed for slaves, but over the centuries was refined into an instrument for the oppression of all Africans. From 1952 onwards every African man over the age of 16 had to carry on him his "reference book," a document of some ninety pages containing his identity card, fingerprints, photo, employment record, tax receipts and permits to be where he was. African women were forced to do the same from 1953 onwards, despite mammoth protests.

Hundreds of thousands of people were arrested every year because their books were not in order, because they lacked an appropriate "endorsement," or often because they simply did not have the document in their pocket at the time. Overall, 12 million were arrested and convicted in summary trials between 1948 and 1985; 700,000 in the peak year of 1968; at least 250,000 annually from the 1950s through the 1970s, and an average of 200,000 annually in the 1980s.5

These laws exposed blacks to lives of humiliation and insecurity. Passes had to be produced upon the demand of any authorised official, a term that was defined to include any police officers and that, in practice, included any white who felt like harassing a black.

The mindset of racial caste deference that the system instilled in blacks is suggested by the following story: In the early eighties a young white conscript, dressed in his military uniform, set off on a driving lesson in downtown Johannesburg. Having stopped at a traffic light and intending to turn right, he nervously held his arm out of the window, indicating this intention. Within seconds, a respectably dressed middle-aged black man had scurried across the street and presented his pass book at the car window.6 Although there was good-natured laughter on all sides when the misunderstanding was clarified, the incident revealed volumes about the racial caste subservience that apartheid fostered.

Since Africans were already covered by the repressive 1913 Land Act and other legislation, it was members of the Indian and Coloured groups for whom the rigours of the Group Areas Act were a novel imposition. They had to hold a racial identity card for the first time. Coloured people were particularly affected by the Population Registration Act of 1950, which classified everyone into racial groups, since prior to that the fairer members of the group had been able – if so minded – to "pass" as white. The new rules brought tragedy to many families that were split up as a result. In 1984, a government commission studying the courts found that two pre-school children had been held in detention for three years while they awaited a government decision on their race.[7]

Communist MP Sam Kahn's suggestion in the 1950 Immorality Act debates that "the white man can never stay without the Coloured women," and his allegation that a Cabinet Minister had interracial "bastard" offspring, were expunged from the parliamentary record and – it was presumably hoped – from the realm of recorded truth. The goal in apartheid was to bolster white supremacy, not to shake its foundations, whether through over-meticulous attention to facts or overzealous enforcement of white supremacist laws against a proliferation of prodigal whites.

Paradoxically, the South African system of race classification never approached the purist zeal of, for instance, the "one drop" rule in the United States, according to which, regardless of physical appearances to the contrary, a person with the slightest documentable hint of black ancestry was deemed black for purposes of the Jim Crow laws.

The more indulgent South African approach to defining whiteness was directly linked to the sheer pressures of demographics: there were simply too few whites and too many blacks. Vigorous attempts to swell the ranks of the white racial caste were made through such straightforward means as encouraging white immigration from abroad and discouraging black reproduction. But the indulgent implementation of racial classification was also of assistance.

According to the famous research of the Afrikaner historian F A van Jaarsveld and others, several of the oldest and most established Afrikaner families, pillars of the apartheid establishment, possess a degree of racial hybridity. Betsie Verwoerd herself was widely rumoured, among her husband's rivals for the white supremacist leadership, to have had more than "a touch of the tar brush," as it was put.

Such was the well-known illogic at the heart of South African white supremacy, as of all doctrines of racial purity.

Whole structures and substructures of racial discrimination were built upon a barely suppressed knowledge of the absurdity – let alone immorality – of the distinctions central to the system. But an insistence on these distinctions nevertheless remained attractive to ambitious National Party politicians.

The 1985 repeal of the Immorality Act for instance, the belated legalisation of "miscegenation," was opposed by F W de Klerk,[8] a position that assisted his subsequent rise within the National Party to become apartheid's last state president.

The inequality of blacks under apartheid was fundamentally expressive not only of the legal system of the time, but of its moral, political and economic systems as well. If slavery was North America's peculiar institution of the nineteenth century, apartheid was South Africa's twentieth century attempt to normalise the peculiar. This effort to implement a rarefied twentieth century slavery of racial caste was a spectacular failure.

13

Placing Property on a Legitimate Footing

Another area where the past has vital implications for the present and for the future is in the area of property rights. Defenders of the old order frequently seek the protection of "established rights," or the indiscriminate protection of alleged property rights, as an essential part of the new democracy.

Such suggestions ignore the fact, one which ought really to be common cause, that decades of apartheid have resulted in an accumulation of established wrongs, not rights. At the extreme end of the spectrum, apartheid's hit squads often operated through privatised front companies, containing significant assets which, during the political transition, were essentially given away to the murderers who ran them. As a further example of illegitimate public activity translating itself into questionable private gain, millions of rands worth of assets were reportedly given away when two apartheid front companies engaged in chemical weapons research were wound up during the transitional 1990s.[1]

Beyond such extreme examples (which could be multiplied) of state asset giveaways to those who loyally advanced apartheid's violent and illegal agendas, lie whole illegitimate substructures of apartheid entitlements. Those who genuinely seek durable institutions of property and ownership cannot simply invoke the political transition, like a sorcerer's trick, to erase the illegitimate origins of what they now seek seamlessly to dignify as "property."

Instead, a more realistic understanding of the racially skewed history of South African property accumulation is necessary, a history that is substantially longer than the history of apartheid itself, but which apartheid vastly exacerbated. In addition, an awareness of the links between property rights, rights of free movement, and a society where careers are open to talent, is essential. Institutions of property cannot be viewed in narrow isolation from the moral and political legitimacy of the surrounding society.

Apart from the well-known prohibition on black land acquisition outside designated Native Reserves under the 1913 Natives Land Act, the 1937 Native Laws Amendment Act removed the surviving right of Africans to acquire land in urban areas from non-Africans. Thenceforth any such transactions would require the Governor-General's specific consent. Later, in the apartheid years, even the possession of freehold title did not prevent the forcible removal of thousands of African families who happened to occupy land coveted by whites.

Indian South Africans also suffered severe property losses, often with minimal compensation. As early as 1885, they were expressly prohibited by law from owning fixed property outside specifically demarcated areas. These restrictions were restated in the 1932 Asiatic Land Tenure Act, amended in 1936.

The 1943 Trading and Occupation of Land (Transvaal and Natal) Restriction Act, froze the *status quo* relating to trading rights and land ownership, pending the outcome and recommendations of a commission appointed by the white government. The commission's findings led to the introduction by the Smuts government of the 1946 Asiatic Land Tenure and Indian Representation Act, prohibiting Asians from acquiring fixed property from a white person in Transvaal or Natal, except under permit (or if the property fell within specified exempted areas).

The importance of such measures to the overall scheme of apartheid should not be understated. The dismantling of black property rights may have been an important aspect of the powerful and overriding pursuit of a society based on principles of white supremacy, but it is naive in the extreme to suggest, as some have argued, that, if only there had been a guarantee of property rights in previous South African constitutions, apartheid could never have happened. Such logic is as absurd as a suggestion that, since the Nazis deprived Jewish people of property, the presence of a sturdy property clause in the Weimar constitution would have averted the Holocaust.

Apartheid's objective was not to attack black property rights as an end in itself; it was to erect white supremacy, sweeping away all that stood in the path of its progress. And to create rootlessness and subjugation among blacks, all the better to entrench the intended racial caste system.

If one leaves aside the systematic and technologically adept extermination of Jewish people that intensified under the Nazis in 1941, and which really has no parallel, there is a striking overlap between early Nazi German solutions to the Jewish Problem and apartheid's ways of dealing with the Black Threat.

According to Harvard University's Daniel Goldhagen, the Nazi measures included: verbal assault; physical assault; legal and administrative measures to isolate Jews from non-Jews; driving Jews to emigrate; forced deportation and "resettlement" (the original Nazi word); physical separation in ghettos; killing through starvation, debilitation, and disease (prior to the formal genocidal programme); slave labour; genocide, primarily by means of mass shootings, calculated starvation, and gassing; and death marches.[2]

Here it all is: the racist abuse, the pass laws, the separate "citizenship" and forced emigration to supposedly independent "homelands," the forced removals of whole communities, the establishment of physically separate black township ghettos, the slow genocide of starvation in the homeland dumping grounds, the prison labour. Once the systematic extermination programme after 1941 is excluded, there are striking similarities in the range of these policies.

Indeed, while the systematic process of hi-tech Nazi exterminations had no equivalent in South Africa, apartheid nonetheless amounted, under international law, to a form of genocide (the point is argued on pages 198–202). Archbishop Tutu emphasised this point at a press conference in New York after receiving the

Nobel Prize in 1984.[3] What differed – and it is an important difference – was the means employed to achieve the goal of genocide. There were no gas chambers; but there can be genocide without gas chambers, which is what many apartheid dumping grounds achieved. It is as wrong to assert that every defining aspect of Nazidom was unique as it is wrong to assert that apartheid amounted to a duplication of Nazi policies. There was substantial overlap; but the one was not a carbon copy of the other.

What is clear is that the apartheid property rights of the privileged flowed from a deadly system of dispossession and death. In South Africa, the dismantling of black property rights was a necessary, but certainly not sufficient, condition for a more fundamental racist agenda: the deliberate fostering, over four decades, of a privileged propertied caste of whites. According to the United Nations Human Development Index, if the white 12% of South Africa were a separate country – as indeed it was conceptualised by Verwoerd – it would rank 24th in the world, just behind Spain; black South Africa would rank 123rd, just above Congo.[4] According to research published in 1984, the homelands produced about 1.9% of South Africa's gross domestic product, but 37% of the population was corralled into them.[5] Death there; wealth elsewhere. The pattern was not accidental; it requires deliberate undoing.

This necessary process of corrective action cannot be evaded by pretending that there are two South Africas, one belonging to the First World, and the other to the so-called Third World. There has always been one South Africa, the larger part of which was invisible to the country's policymaking organs. The line of the homelands, of Grand Apartheid, which separated the so-called Third World South Africa from its allegedly First World fellow traveller, was not a legitimate or geographical contour; it was apartheid's iron curtain of racism.

Existing property distributions in South Africa are saturated with the logic and history of white supremacy. This logic and history are not abstract entities floating somewhere in the ether; they are the concrete by-products of atrocities like violent forced removals.

There were six different categories of forced removals under apartheid, in which blacks were arbitrarily deprived of property, stability and any sense of worth and civic belonging; and through which apartheid's privileged caste benefited in manifold ways.

First, in rural areas, labour tenancies and so-called "squatters" on white farms were arbitrarily evicted as part of the policy against the existence of "black spots" in what were declared, under the 1913 and 1936 Land Acts, to be white areas. Second, black urban dwellers who lived and worked near a homeland were relocated into the homeland, even if this disrupted existing employment relationships and the worker's productivity. At the very least, the worker's family had to move to the homeland, while the worker could continue in the urban area as a single hostel dweller. Third, this process of individual removals was intensified and systematised in major metropolitan areas like Pretoria, Durban and East London, where whole communities were relocated across nearby homeland borders. Fourth, in the Western Cape, designated a "Coloured Preference Area," there was large-scale removal of Africans from urban and rural areas alike to resettlement camps and townships, located especially in the Eastern Cape and other remote rural areas. Fifth, the policy of consolidation, an ideological attempt to bring some semblance of coherence to the irrational patchwork of separate development, resulted almost exclusively in the removal of blacks from settled communities into unpromising Reserves which bred starvation and soaring infant mortality. Finally, under the pass laws, a constant stream of blacks was "endorsed out" of the white areas and forcibly deported to their homelands.

These measures were explicitly designed to create a demoralised and pliant labour force, to maximise white profit from lucrative land, and to serve the twisted ideological imperatives of white supremacy. They created huge social and economic problems and triggered massive homelessness and underdevelopment. The continuing results of these policies constitute some of the major challenges facing the new South Africa today.

These grave circumstances were exacerbated by the peculiarities of the apartheid labour law regime. The man who was to become the first Minister of Labour in the National Party government elected in 1948, B J Schoeman, wanted to keep the regulation of wages entirely in the hands of the state, and to fix racial quotas for all skilled, semi-skilled and unskilled jobs.[6] Such a totalitarian scenario was never fully implemented, but strict control over workers was achieved by a variety of means.

Apart from the deliberate racist constraints on education and geographical mobility, specific laws reserved certain categories of employment for whites, expressly in order to protect the higher-paid white workers from competition from blacks. Thus, in certain areas of the Western Cape, where 75% of building workers were Coloured, all future job opportunities in seven skilled crafts were declared in 1963 to be reserved for whites. In some places of employment, a fixed percentage of jobs was reserved for whites. In other jobs, different considerations seemed to apply: in 1968, for example, the National Liquor Board issued new regulations forbidding the employment of Indians in bars where women were served. These regulations survived well into the 1980s.

The apartheid regime audaciously argued that these laws would encourage blacks to succeed in their allocated employment spheres, but in fact if they became too successful even within these prescribed areas, they were seen as a threat to white workers or white owners of capital. The colour bar in jobs, for instance, induced many Indian South Africans to set up on their own in commerce, but the reaction of the then Minister of Planning, Mr Coetzee, was to complain at their success. "They must branch out into other occupations," he said. "I am sick and tired of seeing young Indians sitting on shop counters as if there were no other occupations open to them. Should they fail to do so willingly, I will be forced to take action."[7] On occasions like this, it became clear that sheer visceral resentment of black success in any manifestation was what fuelled much of apartheid policy.

The initiatives towards black economic empowerment in the new South Africa are often presented as a form of political patronage or an inessential aspect of the reconstruction of society. But in fact these measures are a vital corrective of decades during which black businesses were deliberately dismantled and black entrepreneurship destroyed and constrained.

Until 1963, African traders had to apply annually for trading licences. As attempts to enforce the homelands policy unfolded in February of that year, the Department of Bantu Administration instructed local authorities that the guiding principle of licensing was to confine African business to the "Bantu homelands."

Additionally, the Department instructed that trading rights in African townships should be granted only to those qualified for permanent residence in the area. The conduct of more than one business, whether of the same type or not, by the same African was forbidden, even in different African townships in the same urban area. No African business venturing beyond the provision of essential daily domestic necessities was thenceforth permitted, a significant reduction of the scope of previously permitted activities. It meant, for example, that licences for a dry-cleaning business or a garage were no longer available. The establishment of African companies or partnerships in urban townships was disallowed and African-controlled financial institutions, industries or wholesale concerns were forbidden.

In August 1968, further regulations prohibited an African who had business interests in the homelands from obtaining a site in an urban area for trading or business purposes. Even when some of these restrictions were relaxed by proclamation in 1976, an annexed schedule of permitted activities excluded important areas like small-scale manufacturing.

Such prohibitions established a clear field for white business, while the exclusionary tendering practices of state and parastatal institutions complemented apartheid's active dismantling of black business with equally proactive support for privileged citizens seeking to occupy a playing field from which blacks were forcibly excluded.

Throughout all of this there were no protests from white business groupings or individuals; rather, they treated these restrictions on others as opportunities to expand the scope of their own activities and profits. When in 1995 the new South Africa's Minister of Trade and Industry presented a policy document on small-business development designed to correct this history, the National Party pressed for the deletion from the document of all references to their history of demolishing black business. It was a vivid example of the attempt to impose historical amnesia specifically in order to avoid present-day momentum for corrective change – and to conceal the illegitimacy of the historical gains of many privileged businesses.

Aside from the ownership and operation of businesses, an integral part of a smoothly functioning economy is the right of workers to secure for their efforts their best estimate of what those efforts are worth, tested in a process of negotiation with employers. That is the logic of collective bargaining.

Yet the apartheid bosses did their utmost to prevent mixed unions, and those catering for African workers, from functioning effectively. From 1953 until 1979, the apartheid regime tried to prevent Africans from joining trade unions. The term "employee" was so defined in Labour Relations legislation as to exclude Africans, which meant that they could not continue as members of racially mixed unions, and that African unions could not be registered, and thus had no status in the official bargaining system.

In this way blacks were excluded from the usual processes for the negotiated accrual of incomes – and thus of property. Union leaders were constantly harassed. Between February 1963 and the end of March 1964, no fewer than forty-five union officials were banned. In the same period, over thirty officials were detained, of whom two, Looksmart Ngudle and C Mayekiso, died while in jail.

These apartheid policies drew condemnations from the International Labour Organisation (ILO). Apartheid South Africa remained for some time an ILO member, although refusing in 1948 to vote for the ILO draft convention because it guaranteed freedom of association and labour organisation for everyone, regardless of race. Eventually, in 1964, the Minister of Labour announced that South Africa was leaving the ILO because of "an accumulation of hostile acts."

The General Law Amendment Act of 1962, the so-called Sabotage Act, criminalised the ordinary tactics of labour relations and brought them within the scope of internal security regulations. Sabotage included any act which was committed with intent to "cripple or seriously prejudice any industry or undertaking," or bring about "any social or economic change in the Republic."

In December 1962 the Government listed thirty-six organisations, including the South African Congress of Trade Unions, of which any listed or banned person could not be an officer or even a member. Nevertheless, union organisation was not effectively suppressed, despite intensified violent attempts to do so. In the early seventies there were mass strikes in Port Elizabeth, where police fired on a peaceful demonstration of 10,000 workers; in Durban, where massive strikes took place, more people were shot.

With the formation of the Congress of South African Trade Unions, COSATU, in 1985, a new and powerful instrument of resistance to apartheid had arrived. The regime attempted to reduce its power under its emergency regulations, and in 1988 prohibited it from engaging in any political activity. The prohibition was disregarded.

Interestingly, in 1996 when COSATU went on strike to resist constitutional provisions that would potentially have perpetuated several of the foregoing abuses, critics objected to the unions engaging in "political" strikes, a criticism that unconsciously or deliberately echoed the view of the apartheid regime in the repressive eighties.

Throughout the period under review by the Truth and Reconciliation Commission, the apartheid bureaucrats constantly attempted to hamper legitimate trade union organisation; they persecuted and harassed union officials, thereby directly interfering with the rights of workers to have and earn the wherewithal to purchase property. Most strikes by African workers were illegal under the restrictive laws. And even where they were legal, strikers could be and were dismissed by employers, and new contract workers were taken on to replace them.

Given this background of apartheid's pervasive interference with ordinary processes for the generation of property by individuals, it is clear that what is needed is an orderly transition in property rights that will move the country away from a regime of murderous and ill-gotten gains and towards one wherein property rights will cement the new order rather than corroding it. As Professor Renfrew Christie of the University of the Western Cape commented during the transition, "a settlement cannot be achieved without adjusting apartheid's property patterns. The economy will not grow properly if property is completely illegitimate. Capitalism will not survive well in South Africa unless ownership is made legitimate."[8]

The necessary transition is well under way in the land reform legislation passed by Parliament in its 1995 session and in other policy initiatives. It is vital, in the words of a 1996 Green Paper, to address "skewed patterns of land ownership, which are a cause of conflict and social instability."

The plain wrongfulness of existing patterns of possession and dispossession flows from the more general illegitimacy of the apartheid system in all its aspects. The apartheid system intensified a formalised disregard for property rights that can be traced back at least as far as the Land Act of 1913, which denied blacks the capacity to own land outside limited and generally inhospitable areas. The 1950 Group Areas Act, one of the earliest initiatives of the victorious Nationalist government, systematised the restriction of ownership and occupation of land in proclaimed areas to specified population groups.

The proclamation of Group Areas under the Act uniformly disfavoured blacks, uprooting communities, destroying businesses and leaving property rights to the whim of a single government minister, administrative functionaries and local municipalities. The provisions for forced sales permitted widespread abuse and collusion in which government officials facilitated sales of valuable properties to friendly purchasers for a fraction of their value. Group Areas legislation facilitated widespread, and sometimes imaginative, variants of greed, avarice and looting at the expense of blacks. For example, the occupants of thirty-eight African farms in six districts of KwaZulu-Natal were evicted in 1973. Twenty-two of these farms had substantial coal resources and, by 1982, sixteen of these properties had been transformed into mines, having been sold to whites.[9]

On another occasion, in 1990, the bantustan leader Lucas Mangope conferred mining rights over land worth billions of rand and owned by the Bafokeng tribe upon a large white business, Impala Platinum Company, in perpetuity. During litigation initiated by the Bafokeng to contest the validity of these leases, an

Impala executive suggested that the current royalties being paid to the Bafokeng are sufficient, which "is why they are the richest tribe in Africa."[10]

The implicit suggestion seems to be that there exists a separate, lower and specifically tribal measure of wealth which somehow becomes relevant where tribal property rights are an issue. It illustrates the resilient alchemy of race and property rights, even in the new South Africa. Without the unstated neo-apartheid assumption that blacks above a certain station must necessarily be content, a tribe's collective well-being could hardly seem relevant to its legal dispute with a mining giant.

In another example of the greed and cruelty of apartheid, the Batloung people of the North West Province were moved 100 km from Putfontein to Ramatlabama, from fertile ground to dry and infertile new land. Their cattle and sheep fell off the government trucks and died along the way, and they were given tents for shelter. But as one of their number, Lulu Shole, put it, this "was made to sound like a gift and yet we were being sentenced to death." On the land from which they were expelled, white beneficiaries today grow mealies, farm cattle and sheep, and prospect for diamonds and platinum.[11]

As late as July 1992, days before a government commission on land claims began its work and a mere two years before the Mandela presidency, apartheid state officials attempted to rush through the sale of 6,000 hectares of public lands to six favoured white farmers. This land had been expropriated by the state between 1969 and 1974 and its inhabitants were moved 50 km away in order to facilitate their incorporation into the homeland of Bophuthatswana. Justice van Reenen, chairperson of the Advisory Commission on Land Allocation said at the time that this was not an isolated incident: "we are having a lot of difficulties in this regard."[12] Yet vigorous and effective measures to arrest such land-grabbing were not evident.

Under the Group Areas Act, the owner of the property had no automatic right even to the reduced proceeds of such collusive sales. Except in a narrow range of specified cases, the Minister had a discretion whether the proceeds should be paid to the former owner or rather confiscated into the Consolidated Revenue Fund. In many cases where whole communities were relocated, victims received merely nominal, if any, compensation.

Existing South African patterns of ownership and dispossession are based on a system of law that not only facilitated the forced removal of some three and a half million people, but that also brutally curtailed the right of education and the right to work – crucial pillars of an individual's capacity to generate resources for participation in property rights. Confining the majority of people to "Bantu education" – and thereby to serfdom – placed a deliberate ceiling on their income levels and thus on their capacity to buy and own property, not to speak of the direct legal restrictions on ownership. For the lucky few who had less restricted access to education, there remained formal and informal obstacles such as the practices of job reservation and land reservation in favour of apartheid's privileged.

Questions of education, training and job reservation aside, the pass laws dramatically restricted the ability of sectors of the population freely to seek and accept employment. Moreover, the penalty for pass law violations was often forced labour for the benefit of privileged farmers – whose thriving farms were therefore built in part with stolen labour, or even the systematic use of unpaid or nominally paid prison labour.

Alarmingly, such facts today often seem to have disappeared down an historical void. Thus the supposedly reformist apartheid government in its 1991 White Paper on land reform blandly dismissed a programme of reparations, saying simply that it was "not feasible." Education and Training Minister Stoffel van der Merwe said at the time that giving land back to previous owners would result in a "quagmire" (sic). Yet this view, despite its manifest contempt for property rights, can manage to pass itself off in current policy debates under the soothing rhetoric of respect for "established rights." Ultimately, such views betray an unwillingness to acknowledge the uncomfortable facts about wealth generation in the old South Africa, a failure to face the profound illegitimacy of the past, and a desire to erase the past rather than to deal with it.

It has become something of a cliché to observe that opponents of the Truth and Reconciliation Commission would like to see the past consigned to a blind zone of historical amnesia. Yet this remains powerfully and literally true.

As the Johannesburg *Sunday Independent* reported in 1996,[13] there are people who grew up in the town of Triomf, Johannesburg, who were for most of their lives unaware of Sophiatown, the multi-racial community in whose blood and rubble Triomf stands. For one young couple with two infants, Triomf was simply a conveniently cheap place to live. "These brand new houses were around R5 000 each, so we jumped at it." It was, as the *Cape Times* commented in 1969 in relation to similar goings-on at District Six, "a staggering example of communal advantage" and a "sociological crime." In short, it was state-sponsored looting.

The problem with the pleasantly suburban approach to the looted fruits of apartheid is that it continues to colour present-day political debates. Like a South African variant of the idyllic American settler story, *Little House on the Prairie*, the blood of the natives mostly flows off-screen. One of Triomf's urban frontiersmen, for instance, commented that "our move here was not politically oriented, we were all just poor young folk who bought here because we could." Yet, faced with the facts about the past, and with the fact that the evicted residents continue to refer to the place as "Sophiatown," this allegedly non-political resident of Triomf objected, "We just won't let them rename it Sophiatown – that is discrimination."

Even without any talk of reparations, let alone the return of property, the mere suggestion that some kind of symbolic rectification might be in order arouses an immediate pained reaction. Cries of "discrimination" are uttered, echoing the equally incoherent use of the "reverse discrimination" concept across a whole range of contemporary moral and political debates in the new South Africa and elsewhere. It is hard to decide whether this demonstrates blindness to reality, hypocrisy, or something more sinister.

Certainly it bears no relation to historical truth as experienced by the oppressed. As one evicted resident of Sophiatown, Peks Pekane, commented, "We were such a happy people, like one big family – it was safe and fun living in Sophiatown. We were the rainbow nation long before Mandela was even arrested." By contrast, for the frontiersman who bought cheap land in Triomf, "Sophiatown was full of brothels, shebeens and gambling holes – it was a horrible and dangerous place *and should be deleted from our past*" (emphasis added).

This is the unrepentant rhetoric of good riddance; like the Biblical Sodom and Gomorrah, Sophiatown apparently deserved its fate of oblivion and now even its memory should be "deleted." Moreover, in this version of reality, the destructive hand of apartheid becomes the biblical agent of redemption – the holy fire of destruction that led good (Triomf) to victory over evil (Sophiatown). It seems that the apartheid government, like the Voortrekkers before them, brought the guiding light of civilisation to a heathen, sinful place.

That this ordinary citizen of apartheid could, even in 1996, so casually voice a view so impregnated with virulent racism, so blind to historical reality, and so spontaneously in accord with orthodox apartheid ideology, should give us pause. In his address to the 1991 National Party Congress in Bloemfontein, F W de Klerk congratulated the faithful: "that is what you support, when you support the National Party – balance, realism and a proven and civilised value system." It seems absurd that a party whose whole history of governance was the history of apartheid could yet claim to have a proven record of civilised values. Yet the alarming thing is that, as the Triomf man's comment illustrates, this delirium has deep roots among apartheid's beneficiaries.

Another privileged resident of Triomf lived in the adjoining suburb of Hursthill at the time of the forced removals. "We saw riots and people burning homes, and the army and police often had to close off the area and teach those guys a lesson." Courageous defence of one's house, home and community could seem like yobbery and vandalism to the privileged settlers who saw only cheap real estate where, in fact, there was the grief of millions.

These misconceptions remain at the heart of current policymaking and impact even on the meaning of democracy. In September 1991, National Party constitutional proposals suggested that votes of greater value should be given to ratepayers (i.e. property-owners) in local government elections. Taken in isolation from the past, this might not seem an inherently wicked idea. But when one recalls the systematic dismantling of black property rights under apartheid, it is extraordinary to suggest linking voting rights in the new South Africa to alleged property rights rooted in the old.

Moreover, the emphasis on current ratepayers overlooks decisive facts of history. For instance, in 1972 a repentant former mayor of Simon's Town, previously a site of forced removals, lamented that "half the town's population who had helped over two centuries to build it up, pay rates, and raise thousands of charity and war funds, were uprooted and moved out with all speed into the bundu." Quite apart from the present value of their property at the point of expropriation, the dispossessed lost accumulated labours spanning generations. And these labours were appropriated by those who moved in. Additionally, close-knit communities were forcibly unravelled and intangible bonds destroyed.

So in interpreting the property clause of our new constitution we must keep in mind that property, in the strict sense of a legitimate and settled entitlement, is very different from the pillaged belongings that many people took under apartheid. The right to property now has a place in the final constitution. But properly understood the ideas of rectification and redress, not stasis, are at the heart of this new, legitimate, concept of property. Reparations (private and public, taking various forms where the measures are systematic, orderly and fair) are the vital underpinnings of legitimate property rights in the new South Africa.

In a comprehensive sense, apartheid denied property rights not only to blacks but ultimately also to whites. For blacks, property was largely unattainable and, in important respects, black people were themselves reduced to a kind of property, to civil chattels whose whole lives were at the disposal of the arbitrary action of the state and private individuals such as farmers, factory owners and homeowners employing domestic help.

Meanwhile, for whites, apartheid abolished merit. It delinked pay and performance. It therefore removed the possibility of legitimate rewards for effort, an idea that is integral to the concept of property – the idea that separates property from theft. This is what Democratic Party leader Tony Leon overlooks in saying that his "policy and political approach commences with an understanding that the quality of a person's life will approximately reflect the quality of the effort you put into it."[14]

That can only be a statement about some utopia elsewhere; it certainly does not apply to South Africa's past nor (as yet) its present. Under apartheid blacks were dispossessed while whites had possessions, but not property. Only now, in the new South Africa, is a regime of property rights dawning for the first time. As it dawns, black dispossession and white possessions will require orderly and sensible realignment.

These goals are reflected in the property clause (section 25) of the new South African constitution, which provides that property rights may not be expropriated except by a law of general application, without arbitrariness. Additionally, the constitution provides that the amount, timing and manner of compensation for expropriated property (which includes but is not limited to land) "must be just and equitable, reflecting an equitable balance between the public interest and the interests of those affected, having regard to all relevant factors, including:

(a) the current use of the property;

(b) the history of the acquisition and use of the property;

(c) the market value of the property;

(d) the extent of direct state investment and subsidy in the acquisition and beneficial capital improvement of the property; and

(e) the purpose of the expropriation.

In addition, the "public interest" is expressly defined to include "the nation's commitment to land reform, and to reforms to bring about equitable access to all South Africa's natural resources." This acknowledges the special status of land as a form of property distinct from mere movable belongings. Because it is a form of property fundamental to social organisation – in a way that, say, a television set is not – the importance of land restitution deserves this special emphasis.

The property clause further provides that "a person or community dispossessed of property after 19 June 1913 as a result of past racially discriminatory laws or practices" is entitled to restitution or equitable redress in accordance with an Act of Parliament. South Africa's new property clause thus makes it impossible to consider institutions of property without the guiding light of history – and it does so in the orderly fashion that is at the heart of the new governance.

The practical implementation of this and other constitutional mandates will require an open-eyed coming to grips with the harsh realities of the past in order to redress them. In 1971 an opposition member of the apartheid parliament charged that the government had gone on a "concession spree," granting fishing rights in the waters of South West Africa to "political pals and business buddies." Faced with calls for an inquiry, the Deputy Minister for Economic Affairs claimed that it was not his duty to "go and ferret out what happened in the past." This old approach, this preference for sweeping the past under an historical carpet, can only bring alleged property rights into disrepute. Too often, in the old system, property seemed the terrain of the legalised crook or the charlatan. It cannot be that in the new South Africa the old processes of looting survive.

Contrary to the urgings of those privileged individuals who have developed a collective sweet tooth for the narrow feasts of apartheid, an accurate grasp of history, and of historical patterns of corruption and mal-possession, is central to legitimate property institutions. The Truth and Reconciliation Commission must map this aspect of the past. The deprivation of property rights is a form of serious human rights abuse and, as argued above, such abuses are certainly within the broadly defined mandate of the Commission.

Facing Up to Collective Responsibility

"We Brought You Democracy."
 – National Party advertisement (May 1996).

"The people of this country did not seem to feel that they were being cowed and held down by an unscrupulous and brutal dictatorship. On the contrary, they supported it with genuine enthusiasm."
 – William L Shirer, contemporary observer of Hitler's Germany (1934).

Within the narrow confines of its racially exclusive constituency, apartheid was one of the great electoral success stories of the twentieth century. It had a strong support base on the ground and it actually reflected the notions of democracy that prevailed for decades among the privileged, on both sides of the parliamentary aisle. This is an important reason why such an abhorrent system survived for so long.

While hardly anyone today lays claim to having supported apartheid, many of the previously privileged today openly resist measures intended to undo its legacy. They oppose land reform, employment equity, redistributive tax, deracialised schools, antitrust reform, universal health care, and constitutional rights guaranteeing access to basic socio-economic needs. Some people even think that the crime problem can be solved by the tried, tested and failed remedies of capital punishment or states of emergency. In order to make sense of these contemporary debates we need to understand the tacit and active support that apartheid's grassroots practitioners offered the system. Only then will we understand that these new objectors are actually clinging to their old enthusiasms.

It has proven difficult, in other countries, to develop a full grasp of the nature and extent of peoples' complicity in atrocious pasts. For instance, despite decades of debate over the Nazi past, the extent to which ordinary Germans (that is, non-Nazi party members, people outside of the SS, and so on) entered into active support for that system is only now becoming clear in popular debates.

Whole German battalions composed of volunteer soldiers conducted their genocidal tasks with fervour, frequently going beyond the call of duty and beyond the scope of their orders; forgoing opportunities to be recused from orgies of racist violence. Officers invited their wives along on genocidal "Jew hunts" meant to expose and kill refugees hiding in the countryside. Conscripted footsoldiers wrote home enclosing before-and-after photographs of Jewish captives (before) and mass graves (after).

This popular culture of violent anti-semitism was directly tapped as an organisational resource by Nazi policymakers. In a high-level meeting in November 1938, Nazi boss Reinhard Heydrich explained to Goering that the Nazis could rely, within Germany, on popular surveillance. "The control of the Jews through the watchful eye of the entire population" would remove, he said, any need for the establishment of ghettos within Germany. Concentration camps and work camps were widespread in Germany and genocidal executions were frequently a public spectacle that attracted citizen audiences, much like contemporaneous lynchings of blacks in the southern United States. Nicely carved timber signposts to many German concentration camps depicted SS men beating bearded Jews.

Only fifty years after the fact, with the 1996 appearance of Daniel Goldhagen's chilling work, *Hitler's Willing Executioners: Ordinary Germans and the Holocaust,* have such facts moved from the dusty corners of academic debate to the foreground of popular understanding of the nature of Hitler's country. Previously, the idea that Nazi atrocities relied on a small band of dedicated zealots, or else on various forms of coercion or mass ignorance, clouded accurate collective historical memory.

In South Africa, because of the urgency of current policy debates and the pressing relevance of the past in correcting the present conditions of the country's majority, we cannot wait so long. We need an accelerated understanding of the full extent of the complicity of the South African privileged in the atrocity of the past. This is a major goal of the discussion that follows.

1. Undoing the Apartheid Culture.

Most privileged South Africans wilfully insulated themselves from the founding realities of the apartheid country. There was a day-to-day *cordon sanitaire*, an existential buffer zone, that assisted large numbers of people to avoid immediate confrontation with uncomfortable realities and thus to suppress daily questioning of themselves and the government.

The black townships were hidden from view beyond a railway line or an open space; the encroaching squatter camps were bulldozed away time and again. When Afrikaner spiritual leader Dr Beyers Naudé returned from a meeting with the ANC in Dakar, he asked his flock how many of them had visited Europe; most had. But when he asked how many had visited the nearest African township, hardly anyone had.

Privileged South Africans under apartheid lived less under a regime of ignorance than of carefully calculated avoidance. It is ironic that, in an otherwise excellent editorial in 1996 urging privileged South Africans to avoid self-serving claims of innocence through ignorance, a major Johannesburg newspaper nevertheless ended by urging apartheid's privileged to say: "Forgive us, for we knew what *they* did"[1] (emphasis added). In this final slide from the acknowledgment (we) to the evasion (they), the editorialist highlights the manifold ways in which apartheid's beneficiaries still dissociate their current privilege from their atrocious past. Even more directly, one journalist recently claimed that a "wave of cynicism" was sweeping white South Africa about the work of the Truth and Reconciliation Commission. Truth commissioner Mapule Ramashala, a clinical psychologist by training, interpreted this alleged cynicism as a device for denial of the past.[2] The old mechanisms of avoidance are seemingly intact even today.

But this cultivated blindness can only have been partial at best. Like the trams through German Jewish ghettos in the film "Europa Europa", with their cracked windows painted white in a failed attempt to blot out views of dying Jews, apartheid's moral and political self-censorship was inevitably a perforated blindfold.

People like Cosmas Desmond, who in the sixties and seventies catalogued the facts about apartheid resettlement camps and successfully penetrated "the cloak of secrecy which had prevented the White public seeing the truth of what was being done under this policy in their interest and legalised by their votes," were dismissed by the responsible minister as "villains" (*booswigte*, in the Afrikaans).[3] In this way the cracks were fitfully papered over and the vitriol that ought rightly to have been directed at the system and its consequences was instead wilfully deployed to vilify the messengers of conscience.

These callous popular responses were explicitly fostered by apartheid's top architects. General Constand Viljoen, then Chief of the South African Defence Force, expressed this strategy in 1984 when he said that [white] "South Africans must be prepared to accept certain levels of discomfort, disruption and even violence in their everyday lives." In 1977, General Magnus Malan commented that the anti-apartheid resistance posed "a threat that makes essential the transition from a prosperous society to one that is geared for survival."[4] The propagandist undertones, suggesting a virtuous Spartan nation beleaguered by barbarians, could not always obscure the plain violence and injustice underneath the South African troubles.

The moral and political shock-absorbers which allowed the privileged imperfectly to rationalise the horrors of apartheid were not always discrete and easily identifiable mechanisms. They were a pervasive set of social constructs involving formal and informal conventions, patterns of behaviour and cultural self-regulation that eased the tasks of apartheid's legislators and its militarists. Prime among these was the simple assumption, often – but not always – taken as too obvious to require explicit statements, that whites were superior humans and blacks subhuman, if human at all.

In apartheid's heyday, alongside its main legal pillars, an extensive set of minor, seemingly secondary, struts sustained it further. These struts were not confined to "petty apartheid" – the rules about segregated toilets and beaches and benches and buses; they were the more diffuse patterns of conduct and of expectation, the innumerable forms of subtle and implicit homage, that apartheid's privileged paid to the system. While each secondary support might seem trivial if taken in isolation, the cumulative impact of these diverse and slender threads was to create a formidable web of steel, preventing any move away from the daily practices, habits and instincts of white supremacy.

Exactly because each of these threads, taken in isolation, could be dismissed as trivial, there is a taxing methodological problem for those seeking a full picture of this part of the past. Commentary on these informal webs of practices must necessarily be anecdotal and suggestive rather than exhaustive. Such commentary suffers from a paucity of sources. The South African press under apartheid, even at its most critical, lacked the resources, and sometimes the inclination, to document these micro-mechanisms of apartheid. Indeed, it might even be said that this task is more the job of the novelist than the newswriter. Yet poets and novelists were too often forced into exile and their works demonised or banned when they threatened apartheid's existential foundations with a too-honest self-knowledge.

So there is only sparse light to guide us in discerning the small truths about the loyal body politic of apartheid. Still, the task cannot be ignored. Some have already taken up the challenge. Professor Njabulo Ndebele's suggestively entitled collection of essays, *The Rediscovery of the Ordinary*, is a major step both in uncovering the ignored and manifold dignity of South African blacks and in the undoing of apartheid's instinctively white supremacist ways of seeing.

The task of undoing pro-apartheid populism is not only one of exposing apartheid's privileged devotees, but also one of directing critical and sympathetic attention towards the previously oppressed. Ndebele's work is exemplary of this latter part of the task; so is Charles van Onselen's *The Seed is Mine*, a painstaking reconstruction of the life of a sharecropper, who would otherwise have slipped silently into an historical void.

The unveiling of a culture of complicity in apartheid (the chief task of this chapter) is not a vindictive end in itself. Rather, it is part of the collective exercise of rejecting past wrongs and finding a new country – one that has a place, finally, for its previously ignored and collectively rejected people.

The fate of a black South African woman, Saartje Baartman, is a vivid metaphor of this process of restoration. Ms Baartman was transported in the early nineteenth century to England and France in order to be exhibited as a circus freak, and after she died her pickled brains and genitalia were passed to the Museum of Man in Paris, where they remain in a back room. Today negotiations are under way for her return to South Africa, for her restoration to the ordinary ranks of the human dead and her deliverance from a dehumanising posthumous circus.

And this year, in April 1996, at the Truth and Reconciliation Commission's first formal hearings, Ms Nombwyselo Mhlawuli, widow of one of the Cradock Four murdered in the mid-eighties, urged the Commission to assist in the return of the hand severed from her husband's body at the time of his death. It is apparently preserved, pickled, in a bottle in Port Elizabeth. She wants it back for a proper burial; it would mark her husband's joining the ranks of the ordinary dead.

Likewise widow Sindiswe Mkhonto, whose husband, another of the Cradock Four, was found dead with hair ripped out, his tongue stretched, fingers chopped off and parts of his body eaten by dogs; she too craves for him posthumous normality.

Present and future generations of South African citizens need no longer be imprisoned within an ugly political circus; but avoidance of this fate may be neither automatic nor comfortable. It is something that we must earn. Paradoxically, this task of restoring normality requires an unorthodox awareness: "the capacity to be surprised by the apparently extraneous and to detect, in the smallest shards of village life, the impress of history."[5] We need to breathe new life into the pickled and neglected remains of our real, humane, history.

A further vital part of this undoing of white supremacist eyesight is the recovery of South Africa's pre-colonial past, a project that was lost during the apartheid years in what Deputy President Thabo Mbeki has called an "audible silence"; and that has attracted much attention and heated debate in the new moral and political climate.[6]

Moreover, a current generation of cultural critics is renewing the ways in which post-apartheid South Africa both educates and learns from the world beyond.[7] New archival institutions, such as the Mayibuye Centre at the University of the Western Cape, are assembling the necessary building blocks for effective research to assist these developments. These institutions are attending to the neglected truths and seeking to repair the "historical vandalism" – the destroyed archives and devalued realities – of the past. And all this is changing the country's self-knowledge.

Yet a strange way of seeing survives among the privileged. It is exemplified by the correspondent to a Johannesburg Saturday newspaper who, in June 1996, described the democratic South African government as "incompetent" and continued: "In the US there is no apartheid, yet the jails are 95% filled with blacks. Why? Why are blacks always in trouble?" This kind of dubious contribution, emanating from our privileged suburbs, still litters the letter pages of the South African press.

This sort of attitude is not limited to individual suburban letter writers; political rallies, even today, can be mobilised around such themes. "De Klerk believes that God protects this land and therefore is much better than Mandela," said one National Party supporter who was part of a gathering that jeered the President and called him a "kaffir" during the 1996 Western Cape local election campaign. "He mustn't try and come to Hanover Park again, we'll chase him away like the dog that he is," said another.[8] This example, arising in a Coloured community, highlights the complexity of the complicity in apartheid: its painful hierarchy of relative oppressions has created divisions even among the oppressed, divisions that the National Party continues to exploit for electoral gain in today's South Africa.

Nor can one blame only the Afrikaans speakers and longstanding National

Party supporters. The revered figures of the anti-Nationalist parliamentary opposition were also implicated in the birth of apartheid. "There are certain things on which all South Africans are agreed. The first of these is that it is a fixed policy to maintain White supremacy in South Africa," said Jan Smuts, speaking as South African Prime Minister prior to the 1948 electoral victory of the National Party.9 Understanding the deeply rooted popular base of apartheid is a crucial part of retrieving the lost history that apartheid's champions still hope will stay hidden. Let us look at some of that lost past.

2. Apartheid's Eager Electorate.

Apartheid placed blacks under the dictatorship of an all-white electorate. Elections were frequent and that electorate always had the power to undo its own racial overlordship. Instead, privileged voters endorsed their own overlordship for decades with ever-increasing majorities.

More than that, the actual implementation of apartheid's dictatorship of racial caste relied upon the voluntary cooperation of the privileged electorate. Thus for instance, section 11(1) of the 1950 Population Registration Act, in implementing its goals of racial subordination, directly enlisted apartheid's loyal body politic. In analogy with Heydrich's Nazi reliance on the watchful eyes of supportive Germans to oppress Jews, section 11 enabled neighbours to object to the classification of any fellow-resident as a white person.

This opened the way for private vendettas to be played out within white communities in the spirit of a demented biological witch-hunt. More subtly, it invested the privileged with a sense of gratitude for their status. By fostering a mindset of "There but for the grace of God go I," apartheid's witchhunts against the racially impure created a rising currency in whiteness.

The Group Areas Act was not imposed, top-down, in the teeth of opposition from white local electorates. Rather, the mechanisms of the Act encouraged, required and relied upon local municipalities to concoct proposals and submit them to a centralised Group Areas Board. These locally generated proposals were often so zealous in the cause of racial segregation that they were regularly (but superficially) toned down by the Group Areas Board. The centralised Board had an abundant supply of willing foot-soldiers at local level.

In Cape Town especially, apartheid's privileged citizenry pursued these tasks of social engineering with great enthusiasm, and sometimes also with guilty knowledge of the wrongs that were under way. One privileged lawyer, who purchased very cheaply the house of his Coloured next-door neighbours following their forced removal, afterwards deliberately held on to both properties – just in case somehow, later, a return of the ill-gotten acquisition became necessary. Apartheid's privileged profiteers were very often not *bona fide* purchasers of apartheid bounty in the familiar legal sense. They were often simply looters and chancers.

In the 1980s, as the neo-Nationalist modernisers attempted to implement their strategy to ameliorate – rather than end – apartheid, they found that pro-apartheid populism had to be handled carefully. Thus after a Free Settlement Board was established in 1989 to facilitate exemptions to legally enforced segregation, the Board's chairperson commented that the Board was encountering "more resistance to the proclamation of free settlement areas than it expected."[10] This resistance comprised the immovable mass of apartheid's grassroots beneficiaries.

Decades ago, Nationalist leader H F Verwoerd dismissed the official parliamentary opposition by saying that its constituency voted for the United Party but went to bed at night thanking God for the National Party's vigour in safeguarding racial privilege. That Verwoerd, like Hitler, had a shrewd and accurate understanding of his constituency was seemingly confirmed in South Africa's first nonracial election in 1994. Faced for the first time with an enfranchised majority, erstwhile liberal constituencies bolted to the National Party in droves, apparently calculating that they needed a consolidated voice in defence of privilege. A repeat performance arose in the Western Cape local government elections of mid 1996, where traditionally liberal-voting white constituents defected to the National Party.

So it is wrong to attribute all of apartheid's ills solely to monstrous individuals like Verwoerd and P W Botha. If we rest after acknowledging their monstrosity, we will not have explored the equally important popular pillars of their electoral success. Verwoerd's ideological klansman Adolf Hitler, who faced no general election after 1933, nevertheless took it as a first principle that "no great idea [sic], no matter how sublime or exalted, can be realised without the effective power which resides in the popular masses."[11]

Apartheid was the organising principle of the old South Africa; it was a principle around which large numbers of people actively rallied, as they rallied around anti-semitism in Nazi Germany. As late as 1992, privileged rugby fans at Ellis Park ignored a call for a moment's silence in memory of the thousands of blacks who had died in political violence; they instead threatened mayhem in demanding that their familiar old anthem, *Die Stem*, should be sung.

The 1992 whites-only referendum (for or against political change) was fought on the basis of the National Party's longstanding power-sharing ideas, which used the language of democracy as a façade for continuing white primacy. The campaign itself was fought entirely on the terrain of narrow self-interest – the economy faced an abyss – and on an assumption that a "yes" vote meant a vote for "power sharing."

The National Party's 1989 Action Plan had emphasised power sharing as a guiding principle for constitutional negotiation: that "all groups should agree before an important decision can be taken." In addition, the Action Plan pledged to "place before the [white] electorate any new constitutional principles before such principles are finally implemented."

The 1992 Referendum campaign thus remained firmly within the old expectations of white leadership, as Mr de Klerk himself inadvertently confirmed. Responding in 1992 to criticism of the all-white nature of the referendum, De

Klerk replied that "it sounds in an element of justice that we, who started this long chapter in our history, were called upon to close the book on apartheid."[12]

This statement, with its ill-defined (even incomprehensible) claim of "justice" and its exaggerated claims for the authority of an all-white electorate, is really not at all far from P W Botha's directive, in designing the fraudulent 1983 Constitution, that unconsulted blacks should uncritically use the constitutional mechanism that he had personally put in place for them.

The "reformist" 1989 Action Plan carefully reassured the privileged electorate that their "residential areas will be protected" by "firm, yet sensitive" application of the Group Areas Act. The National Party additionally pledged that new "notification points will be created where transgressions" of the Group Areas Act could be reported. Thus this Plan ostensibly offered at most a kinder, gentler apartheid regime, while actually intensifying Group Areas supervision in order to placate privileged whites.

Similarly, in the run-up to the October 1988 municipal elections, P W Botha hurriedly convened a special session of parliament to rush through a crackdown on squatters and Group Areas Act offenders. At the time this move was widely viewed as a bone-throwing exercise for the benefit of right-wing constituencies. While this was an electorally successful strategy in the short term, it confirmed that any resolute attempts at meaningful political reform would drive the government's constituency into the waiting arms of the far right. Indeed, in the May 1987 general elections the privileged electorate had returned to office a right-wing Nationalist government and an ultra-right official opposition, thus endorsing either apartheid or ultra apartheid, not democratic change.

The 1983 constitutional referendum was an even clearer test of the privileged electorate's sentiment towards apartheid. In that referendum, the white electorate confronted a constitution that expressly excluded Africans, expressly subjected Coloured and Indian communities to a *baasskap* parliamentary regime of formal representation but actual powerlessness, and gave the State President in Council unprecedented personal powers amounting essentially to a state of martial law.

The 1983 Constitution would be incomprehensible without the key concepts of apartheid – how else would one make sense of the three racially separate chambers? It made apartheid a crucial ingredient of constitutional clearsightedness. Yet in a referendum this constitution was decisively approved by white voters, including a substantial number of English speakers, the business community led by Anglo American Chairperson Gavin Relly, and some leading publications such as the *Sunday Times* and the *Financial Mail*. They took this position even though they knew that the majority of the country's people opposed it. Once again, they thought they knew better.

In the build-up to this 1983 vote, the Minister of Community Development, Pen Kotze, made it clear that the Group Areas Act would not only remain but would be "relentlessly" strengthened by legislation that he promised to pass in the next session of parliament. Moreover, these assurances were not his own initiative, but were given in response to grassroots activism by the National Party's constituents in Jeppe and Langlaagte, displeased by the presence of Indians in Mayfair. Such moves continued a long tradition of white grassroots pressure for the intensification of apartheid, going back at least as far as the fifties, when the Swellendam Nationalists called on H F Verwoerd to curtail the Coloured franchise in the Western Cape.

Even the modest 1983 "power-sharing" arrangements, which actually entrenched apartheid in a baroque fashion, seemed too reformist for significant sections of the privileged electorate. A wave of anti-reformist dissidence, led by Dr Andries Treurnicht, split the National Party and led to the birth of the right-wing Conservative Party.

In 1981, in the midst of its attempts to cut into the support base of the liberal opposition by employing reformist rhetoric, the National Party government was forced into a rapid course correction to reassure its primary constituencies of its unwavering commitment to white supremacy. Agriculture Minister Pietie du Plessis shamelessly reassured voters in Greytown, Natal, that the government was spending twelve times more on educating each white child than each black one. Meanwhile Defence Minister Magnus Malan offered the reassurance that the South African Defence Force was sparing no effort to avoid racial mixing in its ranks.

Likewise the Minister of Police announced a white populist ruling that black police officers were forbidden to arrest whites except in cases of serious crime. And Minister Gerrit Viljoen broadcast in the Nationalist press that only the children of black diplomats were allowed at white state schools; and that, moreover, even that limited practice would be frozen at current levels (a total of ten black foreign children in the entire country).

These manoeuvrings were in part the result of the April 1981 election in which voters returned a National Party caucus that was several degrees to the right of its already repressive predecessor. A politically shrewd P W Botha willingly put his "reformist" agenda on ice in order to reassure his pro-apartheid constituents. He had learnt the lesson of the October 1979 by-election results, when his "reformist" agenda had triggered a substantial voter stayaway, resulting in significant ultra right-wing gains.

Foreign Minister Pik Botha confessed in 1977 that "there is no state, no government in the world which is our friend. They are all our enemies." And yet Mr Botha's National Party electoral bandwagon proceeded smoothly onwards, as though the whole world was just a small dog barking at the wagon wheels.

Die Burger's influential columnist, "Dawie," commented in 1972 that the white electorate would not tolerate "decisive non-White power in the white democratic structure." Four years later, in resisting calls for reform, Prime Minister B J Vorster said defiantly that *"you cannot ask me to accept policies which have been rejected by the electorate"*[13] (emphasis added).

At an earlier phase of his career, during his outward-looking policy designed, for propaganda purposes, to secure the collaboration of African states and the world, Vorster found that intensified repression inside the country was necessary to placate his white constituency; the latter interpreted the mildest flirtation with black African states as a dangerous form of liberalism. He had to show that his foreign dalliances with blacks were not signs of weakening on the precepts of white supremacy at home. This led one newspaper to conclude in 1973 that "white public opinion, expressed not only through the HNP but within the National Party and, to a certain extent, the United Party, will carry much of the blame for not making it politically easier for Mr Vorster to be bolder."[14]

While the Nationalists themselves suffered the vagaries of a right-wing backlash and splintering of their party, these pressures were even more acute for the liberal constituencies that were marginally to the left of the Nationalists. When the Natal congress of the Progressive Federal Party (the Democratic Party's forerunner) voted in 1978 for a mildly reformist agenda of equal franchise rights for all within a plainly undemocratic "federal" system, right-wing opponents of the party found a rich harvest of votes in conjuring up pictures of nonracial democracy (which was, sadly, not what the PFP advocated) and then terrifying voters about what such a society would look like.

The small constituency of mild liberal reformers in the old South African parliament had only anaemic electoral support. From 1962 to 1974 they had literally a single representative. Within the white electorate, the liberals were not the tip of an anti-apartheid iceberg, but rather the whole of their own ice cube. (White adherents of the resistance movement scorned apartheid's racially exclusive elections and so were no part of apartheid's all-white electoral politics.)

Individuals like P W Botha, who vigorously captained apartheid, might, facing a different electorate, have remained marginal figures railing against the tide of history, as Botha has only lately become in his Cape retreat, a place appropriately called Wilderness. But because of the pervasive white-supremacist logic of old South African institutions at every level of society, wild white tribalism found an enthusiastic mass base.

Contrary to what is often suggested, this white-supremacist world view was not confined to Afrikaners or to Afrikaner nationalists. It was part of the very structure of white electoral politics. Former Prime Minister J C Smuts said in September 1948, shortly after his defeat at the hands of Afrikaner Nationalism and at a time when resistance to apartheid might have seemed quite an urgent necessity: "We have always stood and we stand for social and residential separation in this country, and for the avoidance of all racial mixture . . . There is a great deal about apartheid which is common to all [white] parties in this country."[15]

As apartheid's legislative juggernaut gathered momentum in the 1950s, the United Party opposition in parliament did not break with the logic of white supremacy. In June 1957, at the height of the most nakedly white supremacist period of apartheid, Sir de Villiers Graaff, leader of the opposition United Party, commented: "When we get into power again there will also be discrimination." United Party frontbencher Douglas Mitchell, from Natal where the white electorate was overwhelmingly English, commented that "the United Party would never allow effective political control of the country to pass into the hands of the non-Europeans." Free State United Party leader, Senator Swart, added that "under our policy the white man will remain master."[16] With parliamentary enemies like these, the apartheid government needed no friends.

It is possible, as was the case in Nazi Germany, for individuals to oppose a vicious government for a variety of reasons, while yet sharing in its contempt for those who are its principal victims. Thus some prominent opponents of the Nazis and liberal objectors to certain of Hitler's policies held views that were saturated with the prevailing anti-semitism of German culture. German anti-Nazi sentiment often revolved around aspects of Nazism other than its anti-semitism (e.g. its ham-fistedness or its militarism).

Even the great historian Friedrich Meinecke, a political liberal and democrat, was anti-semitic. Karl Barth, a bitter opponent of Nazism for theological reasons, nevertheless in a 1933 sermon described Jews as "an obstinate and evil people." The brother of Claus von Stauffenberg, the man who in July 1944 placed the bomb that was intended to kill Hitler, testified as follows: "In the sphere of internal politics we had welcomed the basic tenets of National Socialism for the most part" and objected merely that its "implementation was carried too far."[17]

In South Africa, the progressive wing of white parliamentary politics for most of the duration of apartheid never advanced beyond Cecil Rhodes's old idea of "Equal rights for all civilised men," a qualified franchise based on property or education requirements. This was actually the agenda of the opposition Progressive Party as late as 1978.

Such postures bring to mind the notorious 1809 Emancipation Edict of Baden which granted Jewish people "equality" subject to the condition that "this legal equality can become fully operative only when you [the Jews] in general exert yourselves to match it in your political and moral formation." In the interim, Jewish people were subject to a host of restrictions that excluded them from full citizenship and that remained in force for the entire period between the edict and the holocaust.

3. The Professions and Business

Outside the parliamentary sphere, professional institutions and business groupings cast aside their expected independence in order to serve the apartheid state. Hitler had emphasised, in *Mein Kampf,* the need to "adopt all available means for winning the support of long-established institutions" in order to enlist "those old sources of power" for the movement.[18]

In South Africa, this was the logic of the secretive Afrikaner Broederbond grouping which had actively sought since the 1920s to develop tentacles at every level of public, private, cultural and economic life in South Africa. In 1925 it had 160 members; by the late 1980s, its membership roll had risen to an estimated 20,000. H F Verwoerd, a Nazi supporter during the war, moved swiftly after becoming Prime Minister to integrate the Broederbond firmly into apartheid governance, actually granting it "co-responsibility with the party to prepare the electorate" for Nationalist policies.[19]

Even without direct and conspiratorial arrangements (of which there are in fact ample examples), apartheid's strategies to enlist powerful South African professional and business institutions had impressive impact. In the medical profession, a striking example of this was the finding of the Medical and Dental Association (MASA) in 1980, that the inquest into the death in detention of Steve Biko did not merit reopening. At the inquest, a district surgeon had explicitly conceded that the interests of his patient had been subordinated to the alleged interests of state security. Yet this explicit confession was deemed insufficient to trigger a public investigation by the Association until years later, after sustained calls for review by a few brave individuals.

In 1985, apartheid's police brutality was challenged by a young doctor, Wendy Orr, who was employed by the district surgeon's office in Port Elizabeth. Courageously, she went to the courts to try to stop detainees being tortured and assaulted, and succeeded in obtaining an interdict; but the very same day that the interdict was published she was banned from seeing people in prisons and was re-assigned to work in homes for the aged and for children. This led to her eventual resignation from the Department of National Health. The healthcare bureaucracy, ostensibly independent and needs-driven, was drafted into an ugly and partisan set of functions in defence of apartheid. Moreover it was systematically blind to the medical needs of the majority. It for instance researched infant mortality rates among whites but not Africans.

The legal profession did not lag far behind. The Transvaal Law Society initiated a move to strike Nelson Mandela off the roll after he was convicted of organising the 1952 Defiance Campaign. The Supreme Court refused the application on this occasion but, as outlined in pages 87–88 of this book, the courts themselves were soon drafted into the service of apartheid.

For present purposes the single example of *R v. Pitje* may suffice to illustrate the pro-apartheid enthusiasm of the courts. In that case the country's highest court upheld a contempt citation against Barney Pitje, a young law clerk and colleague of Nelson Mandela and Oliver Tambo. Mr Pitje had questioned, as had Tambo himself, a magistrate's voluntary initiative establishing separate "European" and "non-European" tables for counsel of these respective racial classifications.

The magistrate's voluntarism went unambiguously beyond the strict requirements of the Reservation of Separate Amenities Act. Yet the country's highest court held that the magistrate's voluntary initiative was a legitimate exercise of judicial policy and had, in principle, been sanctioned by legislation governing other spheres of life. Apartheid had cheerleaders on the bench, despite the frequent assertions of its enthusiasts that South African common law was an unshakable bastion of liberty.

Outside the professions, the scarcity of skilled labour presented real dilemmas for apartheid policymakers and tempted them to agree to the use of black labour. But the deep-rooted prevailing social norms were consistent obstacles to an efficiently (and equitably) integrated labour market.

The business community, whether of local or foreign origin, was likewise reluctant to rock the profitable boat of apartheid. Indeed, many of them banded together in the 1960s to support the South Africa Foundation, which they used to promote the allegedly bright side of apartheid to foreign politicians and industrialists. The Foundation's membership roll included such business luminaries as Harry Oppenheimer of Anglo American, Anton Rupert of Rembrandt, and Charles Engelhard.

The Foundation was a consistent opponent of anti-apartheid sanctions and also had other unmistakably political views, despite its protestation to the contrary. In 1975, for instance, it insisted that "the pace of advance in abolishing discrimination cannot be speeded beyond what the politicians can get their followers to accept."[20] The Foundation, which remains an active group in today's South Africa, matched the electorate's complicity with its own.

As the Defence budget grew rapidly in the 1970s and 1980s apartheid's repressive war machine became good business. By the end of the 1970s, the state-owned arms manufacturer, Armscor, was the country's third biggest industrial group. Moreover, although nominally state-owned, it actually subcontracted 60 per cent of its production to the private sector. At the end of the 1970s, some 5,600 private business operations were linked to the Defence establishment, including subsidiaries of virtually all South Africa's major private sector conglomerates. Military contracts accounted for much of the production in the seemingly non-military areas of textiles, mechanical engineering, electronics, and construction. It is insufficiently noted that the apartheid economy, especially in the seventies and eighties, was in significant part a war economy.

In 1981, the liberal Barlow Rand conglomerate consented to P W Botha's request that they second a key executive, Johan Maree, to run Armscor. This fulfilled Botha's often-stated desire to "unite business leaders behind the South African Defence Force." As executive vice-chairman of Armscor, Maree sat on the influential government Defence Planning Committee and, according to the *Financial Mail*, one of his achievements was to galvanise "heavy private sector involvement, both at board and production levels, in armaments production."[21]

The concept of the corporate war criminal remains underexplored in South African debates about the past. In the Tokyo trials of Japanese war criminals, companies as well as individuals were prosecuted. Among the former was the Kajimi Gumi company, which had paid the Japanese Imperial Army for the use of war prisoners and kidnapped Chinese civilians. Nine hundred and eighty-six Chinese slaves were brought in this way to a copper mine in Hanaoka, owned by the Dowa Mining Company. They wore only rags, even in snowy winters, and were fed rotten apple skins. Only 568 survived the war.[22] Their plight was echoed in the fates of the South African prison labourers rented out to apartheid farmers.

In South Africa, an accurate account of the number of deaths through apartheid's private and public industrial labour regimes and its prison labour arrangements is unavailable even today. Yet in the late middle 1980s, Anglo American directors privately discussed the fear that their company would be "remembered as the I G Farben of Apartheid," a reference to the company that, through slave labour, became the industrial backbone of the Third Reich.[23]

This is not to suggest that the South African mining and industrial corporations under apartheid used prison labour. But they exploited the cruel migrant labour system and made unabashed use of apartheid labour, and actively peddled its availability as an advantage to international investors.

Today it is gradually becoming possible to count the costs. In July 1994, a commission of enquiry into health and safety standards in South African mines heard that in the past 94 years more than 69,000 workers died on apartheid mines; over one million were injured.[24] For purposes of comparison, throughout the entire apartheid period, 68 political prisoners died in police detention. The mines killed one thousandfold more people than the police torturers did.

Yet in a paid advertisement in the *Sunday Times* of 14 May 1967, L B Gerber, the Director of the South Africa Foundation, the international mouthpiece of apartheid business, urged that privileged South Africans should stop apologising for apartheid and instead "substitute a tone of confident self-assertion" which publicised "the *opportunities*" that apartheid offered to international investors (emphasis original). This was the South Africa Foundation placing its best foot forward, with a deliberate eye on attracting elements within the international investment community.

By 1971, the Foundation could claim that through its propaganda efforts it had helped to "stem the tide of ignorance, criticism and misrepresentation against the Republic."[25] The Foundation propagated the view that economic growth would cause apartheid to wither away of its own accord, a view which was highly influential abroad – yet it was demonstrably a hoax. Black wages did not rise to reflect the booming apartheid economy of the 1960s, a period during which South Africa's rate of GDP growth was second only to Japan's.

In fact between 1957 and 1967, the percentage increase in average wages for Africans was less than that for whites, indicating that the apartheid wealth gap was actually widening. In one investigation, Dr Francis Wilson, the well-known authority on poverty from the University of Cape Town, found that African real wages in the gold mines were no higher in 1966 than they had been in 1911. He found that the white-to-black wage ratio, which was roughly 12:1 in 1911, had widened to roughly 18:1 in 1966.[26]

It was only when the disruptive tide of resistance to apartheid rose and threatened profits that the stance of apartheid business began to change. According to his approved biographer, Anthony Hocking, Anglo American conglomerate magnate Harry Oppenheimer, a perceived opponent of certain aspects of apartheid, "never subscribed to the view that apartheid was morally wrong. In his view it was at root an honest attempt to cope with overwhelming racial problems."[27]

Oppenheimer's objections to apartheid were practical ones, that it was not really possible to separate blacks and whites, and that the repression necessary in order to enforce separation was stirring up rebellion and endangering profits. "Nationalist policies have made it impossible to make proper use of black labour," he said in October 1978.[28]

Oppenheimer advocated a restricted franchise based not on colour but on education and property ownership; these ideas were also for decades the heart of the agenda of the liberal Progressive Party, which he personally financed and which initially could not have survived without him. By 1980 he had given up on that party ever winning the allegiance of the white electorate and had decided to focus on what he called "the reasonable people in the National Party" and their ideas of power-sharing; he acknowledged that this shift in his views would "shut out one man one vote in a unitary state."[29]

Upon Oppenheimer's retirement in 1982, his successor Gavin Relly announced himself to be, like Oppenheimer, "not in favour of one-man, one-vote in South Africa" because that "would simply be a formula for unadulterated chaos at this point in time in our history."[30] Anton Rupert, the leading Afrikaner businessman, agreed: "After many African countries became free they got dictatorships like [Idi] Amin's. We have to find a solution that won't end up giving us one man one vote."[31] This fear of black dictatorship was expressed, ironically, in the early 1980s, as the P W Botha dictatorship – intensifying the decades-long white electoral dictatorship over blacks – gathered momentum.

The entire ethos of the old closed apartheid system was one of autarchy, claustrophobia and corruption – a state of affairs captured by the familiar phrase "laager mentality." Within the circled wagons of apartheid rule, norms of good governance and ethics were not so much cast aside as simply forgotten. The economic survival of the country, it was felt, required that maximum levels of international trade be maintained in the face of international sanctions, even if this necessitated bribery and corruption. The 1980 National Keypoints Act effectively coopted companies into the militarisation of society by compelling them to take whatever security precautions the government deemed necessary; no information about the measures taken could be published. A government that actively encouraged and facilitated unlawful commerce, sanctions-busting, and illicit arms trade, and that financed hit squad activity through commercial front companies, was hardly in a position to insist on scrupulous business conduct more generally. Government and business slid down the twin paths of violence and corruption.

4. Sports, Culture and Recreation.

In the areas of sport, culture and recreation, most facilities were at one time or another strictly segregated, often at the request of their privileged patrons. Beaches, national parks, cinemas, theatres, zoos, restaurants, libraries, hotels and other amenities, were compelled, by local authorities or by their clienteles, to comply with a variety of apartheid laws, though these were often not laws specifically directed against the activities in question. For instance, no law spelt out the prohibition of mixed sport; instead, the authorities relied on expansive application of the logic of the Group Areas Act, the Separate Amenities Act and related legislation to prevent mixed teams playing together on the sportsfield.

Those rare local authorities that tried to alleviate the effects of apartheid edicts risked the intervention of Cabinet, spurred by considerations of national politics. In 1971, for example, the Pietermaritzburg Philharmonic Society was given local government permission for thirty Africans to attend their concerts – but the central Government was so shocked by this that after one concert the permission was withdrawn. The interaction between local and central governments, pandering in different ways to racist electorates, set up a lose–lose dynamic for black victims of apartheid.

Some local authorities spent long hours debating whether particular restrictions should be removed or lifted on certain special occasions. Durban, which gave its librarian discretion to admit blacks, nonetheless was much exercised as to whether the existing "Europeans only" sign should be removed or not. Other local authorities bowed to white civic pressure and voted to keep restrictions. Swimming pools were a particularly sensitive issue. Durban was less liberal on that subject than on libraries; it was prepared to de-segregate black pools, but not white ones.

In rare instances where nonracial access to amenities was implemented, local zeal insisted on the provision of separate toilets and entrances for whites so that they could avoid any chance of whatever pollution they feared. In the process, they sometimes ruined the very facility they sought to preserve. Today, the famous Cango Caves face serious decay because local apartheid enthusiasts insisted on hacking out a whole new entrance rather than letting blacks enter by the same entrance as whites.

The apartheid sporting community itself was for decades a model voluntary practitioner of apartheid. By the time the National Party won the 1948 election, sporting organisations already had racist rules governing membership. By the time the 1965 Group Areas Act excluded black spectators from designated whites-only matches, most municipal sporting facilities had beaten them to the punch, having already imposed the colour bar during the fifties. Thus apartheid policymakers were correctly comfortable relying upon (im)moral suasion rather than legislation in outlawing nonracial sports.

When the Minister of the Interior, Dr Dönges, said in 1956 that the government expected "whites and non-whites" to organise separate sports, his gentle nudging was avidly heeded. When Prime Minister B J Vorster, hoping to retrieve South Africa's international sporting relations, asked his Transvaal Party Congress for a mandate to relax apartheid in international sporting events, disgruntled ultra right-wingers left to form their own party. In 1971, the Students Representative Council of Stellenbosch University formally opposed the idea of a nonracial rugby match against the University of Cape Town. These policies bred absurdities. For instance, champion golfer Papwa Sewgolum received his trophy in pouring rain outside the clubhouse, because he was permitted only to play, not to fraternise afterwards, with his fellow-sportspersons.

Even after mounting international pressure induced some sporting organisations to relax white supremacist regulations in an effort to stave off the momentum of the boycott campaign, the changes were grudgingly implemented; old attitudes and practices remained. In Port Elizabeth in 1980, black cricketers from the Rainbow Cricket Club complained that while they were now allowed to play matches against white clubs, they were confined to separate entertainments afterwards. Moreover, in order to secure a wider circle of sporting engagements with white teams, the Rainbow Cricket Club team found that it had to purchase a portable toilet – so that it could reassure white hosts that they did not need to share their facilities.

Only after the 1994 election did all the formal barriers come down; even now, there are real and substantive barriers to black advancement in sports, such as the skewed availability of facilities and imbalances in available resources.

Predictably, apartheid's enthusiasts invoked these skewed resource allocations and patterns of exclusion in a circular fashion, to justify the further exclusion of blacks:

"There's no racial discrimination in South African sport; it's all lies; it's just that there are no blacks fit to take part in the Olympics. If there were they would be selected like everybody else. But they are running around wild," said Reg Honey, the South African member of the International Olympic Committee, addressing an IOC meeting in 1960.[32] This recalls – indeed it exceeds in its outrageous idiom – the view of Ritter von Halt, Nazi sports leader, commenting on the composition of the German Olympic team in 1936: "The reason that no Jew was selected to participate in the Games was always because of the fact that no Jew was able to qualify by his ability."[33] This was a relatively sober comment, compared to Honey's bitter virulence.

Despite espousing such political and racist views and practices, many white sports organisations objected that anti-apartheid campaigners who urged international boycotts were dragging politics into sport; they still thought there could be normal sport in an abnormal country.

5. Apartheid's (Un)Civil Society.

All of these instincts and micro-practices of apartheid were self-perpetuating in their effects, creating an extra-parliamentary momentum in favour of apartheid and forestalling democracy. As the *Cape Times* commented in June 1977, "The mere mention of one-man one-vote produces an instant laager among whites, which might give temporary satisfaction to the government, but will not further the country's long-term chances of peace."

The racially exclusive electorate and institutions of all kinds, as well as the media institutions that shaped their world views, were trapped in a vicious circle. They mistakenly identified their immediate self-interest with the survival of white supremacy; they did this at the expense of justice, international norms and, indeed, their own long-term self-interest. When one's head is stuck in the sand it is difficult to see trouble coming.

In the days and months before the 1976 Soweto uprising, for instance, the apartheid parliament, ignoring the burning issues of black urban poverty and political oppression, was instead occupied with the secondary and ideological matter of finalising the sham independence of a bantustan. Reality was someone else's business.

In 1969, newspapers reported that "local demand for moon news has been phenomenal," and families voraciously tuned in to radio broadcasts of words from the men on the moon, while crowds jostled for "lunar souvenirs." Alongside this, the problems of black fellow-citizens were wilfully ignored as though they were the remote concern of another planet. Today's equivalent of yesterday's moon news is the current desire of privileged South Africans to forget – or erase – the harsh facts about their past.

In the intellectual climate that gripped privileged South Africa under apartheid, and still grips many of its beneficiaries today, the lunatic fringe was at the centre of white culture and politics. Afrikaans writer W A de Klerk complained in 1967 that "the main consideration is – at least as far as Afrikaans authors are concerned – what the inner circles would say if writers were to tell the truth; just what is, without praising. Ultimately there is a general capitulation to the Idea. Approaches become timid, clever, and in the end evasive."[34] Insane ideas were taken as gospel and truth came to resemble insanity.

Thus Verwoerd's failed assassin of 1960, David Pratt, who spoke in open court the impassioned truth about the evils of Verwoerd and of apartheid, found himself certified mentally unsound. Verwoerd's successful assassin six years later, Dmitrio Tsafendas, would be similarly categorised. Meanwhile the architects of the Voortrekker Monument could build a straight-faced shrine to a mad idea – that they brought the guiding light of civilisation to a benighted land. Such was the complete inversion of madness and civilisation under apartheid.

Insulated from serious and sustained intellectual challenge, white supremacy and the correctness of apartheid became part of the basic fabric of common sense among beneficiaries of the system. In the 1970s 60 per cent of Afrikaners, according to one study, said that they would support the apartheid government even if they did not understand what it was doing.[35] But the grip of white supremacy was not limited to Afrikanerdom.

In 1982, commenting on the *Rikhoto* case which mildly lessened the effects of the pass laws restrictions, the *Natal Mercury* could not muster more than a cautious welcome, warning that "it would be foolish not to temper one's gratification over the human benefits with some sober reflection on the practical consequences."[36] Amidst widespread white fears of a massive black influx into "white" urban areas, it was left to Black Sash campaigner Sheena Duncan to emphasise the irrationality of those concerns since those affected by the judgment were not a new influx, but rather "have all been in town working legally and productively for a minimum of ten years." Even a small dent in the unnecessary bureaucratic obstacles that stood in the way of productive – indeed essential – black labour led to white fears of a *swart gevaar*.

The entire exercise of legislated white supremacy gained a momentum of its own. Among its beneficiaries, human nature being what it is, apartheid bred demands for more apartheid, not less. People's existential appetites were whetted and their inadequacies salved by the creation of a lowly caste of black serfs. Apartheid's beneficiaries developed a psychological dependence on the false and easy fragile self-esteem that goes with racial overlordship; it was a tempting addiction.

The well-known story of Sandra Laing illustrates the complexities – and power – of white supremacy within conformist civil society under apartheid. Laing was born into a white Eastern Transvaal family in 1955 and re-classified Coloured in 1966 after parents, students and staff at her school objected to her presence, and the headmaster expelled her (complete with a police escort) from the classroom.

In 1991 Laing recalled that, accompanying her father in the town of Ermelo in the 1960s, she was chased out of a café because the shopkeeper objected that she was Coloured. Laing had to wait outside while her father finished his meal. When Laing became involved with Petrus, a black labourer, her parents themselves threatened to shoot him if the relationship continued. So she and Petrus eloped.

When Laing's mother, who had not corresponded with her for decades, finally wrote to her in the early 1990s, it was to urge Laing to stop talking to the press because "everything that happened in the past is over and you have to look forward to the future."[37] Yet surely these truths, about the informal social conventions and the ostracism that gave apartheid its resilience, form an important chapter in any full picture of the past. We cannot just dismiss such truths by saying that the past "is over." The past will never be over unless we move deliberately and systematically to end it. In 1991, "black" Laing still lived in a derelict township house near Springs; her "white" family lived in comfort elsewhere. Nothing better captures both the caprice and the iron-clad consequences of apartheid.

Apartheid's crimes, and the international isolation that they bred, were not forced upon an unwilling privileged population. Rather, apartheid had a fan club. H F Verwoerd was greeted like a hero at D F Malan airport in 1961 when he returned home after leading South Africa's withdrawal from the Commonwealth as a response to anti-apartheid pressures within that body.

Apartheid survived because of a complex interplay among individual merchants of racism and their willing clientele. Dreams of perpetual domination and privilege, as well as genuine revulsion from those of a different skin colour, may have motivated the leaders such as Malan, Verwoerd, Vorster, and P W Botha. But they could not have imposed their will without the support of their loyal Cabinet and parliamentary phalanx; complicit institutions of the state and of civil society such as the security establishment and many professional organisations and sport and cultural organisations, as well as some churches, and the press; and, most important of all, the civic-minded champions of apartheid who went forth from their beds every day determined to score victories for white civilisation which was threatened, as they saw it, by the barbaric forces of racial equality.

Not all blame for apartheid can be shifted onto an evil government. The government was expressive of the core values of the privileged electorate. German philosopher Karl Jaspers has written that people must be held collectively responsible for the way that they allow themselves to be governed. Nowhere is that more so than among an electorate that had the option of throwing the racists out of office and yet failed to do so in forty-six years. The 1994 general election, the first in which blacks were allowed to vote, was also the first that the apartheid government lost.

The after-knockings of apartheid's wrong-headed canons of civic virtue are still with us in pockets today, for instance among those privileged in the Western Cape who voted solidly for the National Party in 1996 and among those white parents of Potgietersrus who resisted the admission of black children to the primary school. This was civic mobilisation of exactly the wrong kind, yet it had apparently deep roots.

Less strident, but just as wrong, were the objections of the white English-speaking residents of Rondebosch who in June 1990 opposed black students moving into quarters in the area that were previously occupied by white students. They claimed that their objections were not racist, but based on their fears of noise and disruption that the change could bring. An educational trust had planned to run a residential college in Rondebosch to teach science and maths to historically disadvantaged students. But the Cape Town City Council, caving in to the Rondebosch activists, refused permission to change the flats into classrooms. In reaching this decision the Council disregarded its own professional staff which found that the proposal would not have altered the land-use character of the area. As this example illustrates, the Potgietersrus phenomenon is not confined to rural Afrikanerdom.

Conformist civil society under apartheid is saturated with responsibility for what was done.

6. The Churches

When the National Council of Church leaders met in Rustenburg in 1990, Dr Willie Jonker, a leading theologian of the Dutch Reformed Church (NGK), confessed that this influential body had in the past "judged apartheid too superficially and uncritically, not taking into full account the pain, humiliation, suffering and injustices which the system of apartheid had caused the black community."

White adherents of the Christian churches have to face up to the problem of "why a group of people from an entirely orthodox religious background and with entirely orthodox religious convictions could have devised, implemented and justified to their own satisfaction an apparently glaring deviation from orthodoxy."38 Why, asked Father Trevor Huddleston in 1956, "does the European population of the Union, the English-speaking section especially, accept and live by the concept of apartheid if it is contrary to the teaching of the Church or denomination to which it belongs?"39

In all the churches, it is possible to single out white religious leaders and church members who stood up bravely to oppose apartheid in word and deed. Some of these individuals have already been named in this book. Many churches condemned apartheid, and church bodies played an outstanding role in the struggle to defeat apartheid. Nevertheless, although it was only the Dutch Reformed churches which formally established segregated churches, the general ethos of the Christian churches in South Africa did not discourage racism.

The Anglican Church in South Africa in 1954, while it opposed racial segregation, held that "both linguistic and geographic reasons make it natural that normally Africans and Europeans should worship in different places."40 Certainly, "in the vast majority of Anglican parishes in European areas, the presence in church of any number of Africans at any service would be greatly resented and cause trouble."41 Similarly when one of the first South African black Roman Catholic bishops was appointed in Natal in 1954, a circular was drawn up by the Catholic Church committee of Margate which called on the white Catholics of Margate to "unite in Protest" in order to "keep your Church white."42

While the English-speaking congregations had to fit racist practices to their nonracial church doctrines, the Dutch Reformed churches laid a doctrinal basis for socio-economic separation of the races. As late as 1987 the NGK – which in 1980 had 3.5 million members – remained strictly committed as a matter of formal policy and not just practice to exclusively white membership. More than that, the church became at times an active participant in, even an instrument of, apartheid. In 1962, for example, 70 black families were evicted form the western Cape Dutch Reformed Church mission farm, Elandskloof; they received no compensation, and the land was sold to white farmers.

In a formal statement in March 1988, the Dutch Reformed Church berated eminent cleric Desmond Tutu as a man on an "evil" path, because of his vocal support for sanctions against apartheid. And its decision in 1987 to open itself to all races triggered a breakaway church, the Afrikaanse Protestante Church, that remained committed to white exclusivity. Nevertheless, the eventual declaration of the NGK that racial discrimination could not be justified helped greatly to open a breach in the closed Afrikaner universe of which apartheid was an integral part.

Dr Jonker pointed out in 1990 that "rational reconciliation" required "the NGK to clear the ground by confessing its guilt for the support of apartheid." But Dr Jonker also made the further observation that, despite his own previous personal criticism of certain aspects of apartheid, "*I could not claim that I have had no part in the collective guilt that rests upon all of us in this regard.*" Jonker not only offered a personal confession but also confessed, vicariously, the guilt of the church as a whole. He thus took forward the 1982 Belhar Confession adopted by the synod of the Dutch Reformed Mission Church (the segregated Coloured "daughter church" of the Dutch Reformed Church), which denied that there could be any moral or theological grounds on which to defend apartheid.

Jonker's atonement exemplifies the form of acknowledgment required from the individual and institutional beneficiaries of apartheid, if reconciliation is to make real progress. Unsurprisingly, these confessions drew stern rebukes from the unreformed, while P W Botha questioned what right the church hierarchy had to confess on behalf of its members. Botha's rebuke recalled the Hervormde Kerk's earlier decision to place leading Afrikaner theologian Professor A S Geyser on trial for heresy after he joined Beyers Naudé in founding the anti-apartheid Christian Institute.

The major role of the dominant churches in legitimising the South African past is perhaps one of the most significant differences between Nazidom and apartheid. Hitler was hostile to all existing churches, which he subsumed under a "National Reich Church" founded by himself. Its thirty-point programme stipulated, among other things, that there were to be no crucifixes, Bibles or pictures of saints. It expressly provided that "on the altars there must be nothing but *Mein Kampf* (to the German nation and therefore to God the most sacred book)."

Rather than unseating God, Verwoerd's National Party for decades successfully co-opted Him – at least in the eyes of those millions of the South African privileged who, under the urgings of their church elders, saw in apartheid an earthly form of Calvinist destiny. Girded by this biblical certainty, Verwoerd could assure his political flock that "I do not have the nagging doubt of ever wondering whether, perhaps, I am wrong."[43] This expressed the hubris of an entire privileged population.

7. Moving Towards Acknowledgment and Catharsis.

It is not sufficient to dismiss criticism of white mass complicity in the hideous South African past as "reverse racism." It is not enough to blame evil individuals like Hitler or Verwoerd for terrible historical events. Totalitarian leaders are not omnipotent; they too face problems of governance. Despots like Hitler face institutional obstacles if not electoral ones; their armies, for instance, are always influential and need to be well fed. Under apartheid, those inside the burnished circle of electoral privilege predictably developed a fondness for the pleasures of racial caste. And so there are today attempts to preserve these benefits in updated and defensible rubrics.

Thus even now much of the debate over "standards" and "merit", over squatters and law and order, effectively places blacks on probation, in the style of the anti-Jewish Emancipation Edict of Baden (referred to above), a process in which the privileged remain complicit. The only way to escape this double-edged imprisonment of the privileged (locked in complicity) and the majority (put on probation) is for the privileged to recognise and grapple with the real burdens of their complicity in the past. It is easy to join, rhetorically, in the hosannas to a free democracy; it is more complex and it takes self-probing to figure out the levels of material, personal and political identity that remain freighted with the detritus of the past.

The sudden elusiveness of supporters of the prior regime and the fact that, today, most white South Africans put an anti-apartheid gloss on their personal histories, is not unique to South Africa.

In a fascinating study of the Argentine experience in facing a similarly terrible past, Guillermo O'Donnell noted, in returning to interview people to whom he had spoken years before under military rule, that all his respondents "remembered" their previous conversations with his team "in a way that sharply contrasted with what they had actually told us. They were wrong, but evidently sincere, as they had been sincere before, in telling us, in the reinterviews, that they had always strongly opposed the regime and had never accepted its injunctions."

However, on the previous visit, they had dismissed talk of abductions, murder and torture as only "rumours" or "exaggerations"; they had said that, anyway, "there must be some reason" why some persons were so victimised. In his revisit, O'Donnell found that they had rewritten their memories to fit what they now felt they should have believed during those years.[44]

Because of such wonderful – and perhaps sometimes involuntary – mind games, the beckoning task of facing up to complicity in apartheid is difficult, but not impossible. The range and culpability of that complicity is varied: from the eager shock-troops of apartheid who zealously wreaked havoc, ran the torture chambers and exulted in ideas of white destiny, to the journalist who did as instructed and killed a story of an activist assassinated, to the more diffuse mass complicity of the enthusiastically passive, those individuals and communities who eagerly swallowed half-baked propaganda and gratefully averted their eyes from the violent and depraved underside of their prosperous racial caste system.

But whatever the depth and scope of complicity, it was possible to overcome it. Bram Fischer was born into one of Afrikanerdom's leading families, but turned in adulthood fully against the old South African system and, as a brilliant lawyer, represented Nelson Mandela and the other Rivonia show trialists, among others set upon by the apartheid system. He suffered cultural excommunication, was disbarred from the legal profession and was imprisoned until within weeks of his death. By any measure, he was a towering figure in the anti-apartheid movement.

Yet, speaking from the dock in his own trial in the late sixties, he made it unflinchingly clear, in a speech of extraordinary honesty, what a distance he had travelled given the cultural indoctrination of his beginnings. As a young apostle of segregation, he had once met a group of Africans in order to convert them to ideas of separate development. To his horror, he was expected to shake hands with them. This, he said, "required an enormous effort of will on my part. Could

I really, as a white adult, touch the hand of a black man in friendship?"[45]

Thus was the distance that Bram Fischer fully travelled: from an outright adherent of Betsie Verwoerd's science of racial disgust to an icon of the anti-apartheid movement. Yet, facing criminal charges for no more than his human-ist beliefs, he chose to use his platform in the dock to reflect on his own prior complicity, rather than suppress it. His life was a lesson to history; it preserved the ideal of nonracialism from the chauvinist view that all South African whites are irredeemably racist. But here is the paradox: Bram did this by fully acknowl-edging, explicating, and then deliberately renouncing, apartheid's zoo of white-ness.

Bram placed himself vigorously on the correct side of history at a time when that was a dangerous thing to do and when it could mean nothing other than extreme personal sacrifice. In no sense can his example be equated with the individual and collective responsibility that is borne by South Africa's passive beneficiaries and practitioners of apartheid. For them, coming to terms, after the fact, with their gainful complicity in the past will necessarily be a different process. But it remains an imperative.

Perceptive guidance is furnished by *Account Rendered: A Dossier of My Former Self,* the confessional memoirs of Melita Maschmann, an intelligent and educated devotee of Hitler Youth, published in 1964 and addressed to her lost Jewish friend. Writing of her response to the November 1938 *Kristallnacht,* a nationwide orgy of anti-semitic violence during which 100 Jews were killed and thirty thousand more sent to concentration camps while hundreds of syna-gogues were razed or demolished, and the glass store-fronts of 7,500 Jewish busi-nesses shattered (hence the name "Crystal Night"), Ms Maschmann reflected:

> For the space of a second I was clearly aware that something terrible had happened there. Something frighteningly brutal. But almost at once I switched over to accepting what had happened as over and done with and avoiding critical reflection. I said to myself: The Jews are the enemies of the new Germany. Last night they had a taste of what this means. Let us hope that World Jewry, which has resolved to hinder Germany's "new steps towards greatness," will take the events of last night as a warning. If the Jews sow hatred against us all over the world, they must learn that we have hostages for them in our hands.

One reads this with a jarring recognition of the success with which the apartheid regime demonised the resistance; one recalls the eagerness with which the mass of South Africa's privileged joined in the invented ideology of a communist onslaught and thus justified to themselves the extermination of alleged "terrorists" and "communists," including children. Maschmann's reflec-tions eloquently recall the hysteria of the South African *Swart Gevaar,* the black threat, equivalent to the Jewish Problem that was constantly on German anti-semitic lips.

In 1996, there are still landladies in Johannesburg's opulent northern suburbs who refer to criminal car hijackings as sabotage, unconsciously echoing the apartheid regime's ludicrously vague Sabotage Act, which authorised ruthless detention and torture of persons associated with that amorphous embodiment of all evil: the anti-apartheid movement. So even today, that barbarous idiom springs from the tongue when the well-meaning privileged yearn for security. Meanwhile for others, insecurity and hideous violence characterised the whole body of sabotage and other laws.

Here lies the gulf that must be crossed. Crossing it will form a large part of the catharsis that must come about among South Africa's privileged. Mrs Nakaya Yasuko, a Japanese war widow, won a court case in 1988 preventing the inclusion of her husband's name in a shrine honouring the conduct of Japanese soldiers in World War II. She explained that she did not want to see future generations deceived into supporting participation by their loved ones in aggressive wars and war crimes; as such, she did not want to be part of commemorating such conduct of the past.[46]

How many of South Africa's privileged have as yet sloughed off the analogous propaganda that their conscripted children died in a worthy fight against an evil foe? The exercise of facing the past must reconcile the old complicit to such new truths about the apartheid past.

15

Apartheid and Its Neighbours

"This way of killing people indiscriminately should be put to an end. What I would like is to go to school and have clean exercise books, a pen, a pencil and a good eraser. Only that."

   – Anna Paula, 12-year-old Mozambican child, mid-1980s.

Throughout the 1970s, apartheid was not the only repressive racial system in Africa. Under John Vorster, it was the premier partner within the so-called "unholy alliance," including the Portuguese dictator Salazar, and the rebel British colony of Rhodesia under Ian Smith. The former British territories of Botswana, Lesotho and Swaziland were too small and poor to pose any serious threat. Apartheid was thus safely (in its view) insulated from the rest of Africa by the Portuguese colonies of Angola and Mozambique, by its own occupation of Namibia, and by Rhodesia. During this period, South Africa extended genuine good neighbourliness towards regimes with which it shared a kinship of repression.

This period of vicious tranquillity began to crumble in 1974, when the Portuguese dictatorship fell and the liberation movements of MPLA in Angola and Frelimo in Mozambique soon afterwards took power. With these changes of governments, apartheid's white supremacist co-religionists were replaced by determined opponents of racial hierarchy.

The apartheid regime thenceforth relied more and more on brute force to insulate itself from what it saw as hostile elements on its borders; elements that, actually, were friends of the majority of South Africans. It attacked its neighbours with impunity. As Julius Nyerere wrote in 1986:

> When is war not a war? Apparently when it is waged by the stronger against the weaker as a "pre-emptive strike." When is terrorism not terrorism? Apparently when it is committed by a more powerful government against those at home and abroad who are weaker than itself and whom it regards as a potential threat or even as insufficiently supportive of its own objectives.[1]

A full reckoning of the South African past must include an account of its regional massacres which accelerated after its secret invasion of Angola in 1975. In the first five years of the 1980s, South Africa:

   • invaded three capitals (Lesotho, Botswana, Mozambique) and four other countries (Angola, Swaziland, Zimbabwe and Zambia);

- tried to assassinate two prime ministers (Lesotho and Zimbabwe);
- backed dissident groups that brought chaos to two countries (Angola and Mozambique) and lesser disorder in two others (Lesotho and Zimbabwe);
- disrupted the oil supplies of six countries (Angola, Botswana, Lesotho, Malawi, Mozambique and Zimbabwe); and
- attacked the railways providing the normal import and export routes of seven countries (Angola, Botswana, Malawi, Mozambique, Swaziland, Zambia, Zimbabwe).[2]

Millions of people were displaced, killed and injured. The cost of South African destabilisation and aggression in the region amounted to US$ 50 billion, far outweighing the foreign aid that these countries received. Even a country such as Malawi, which was not in the front line of opposition to apartheid, suffered financially because of the huge numbers of Mozambicans (estimated to be almost 700,000, equal to almost 10% of Malawi's population) who fled their own country to take refuge there.

The new South Africa owes an enormous debt to the Front Line States of southern Africa, which in the face of intolerable economic and military pressure yet clung stubbornly to their support for a nonracial South Africa. That debt can never be repaid – or even reliably quantified – in monetary terms, but an acknowledgment of it is an important task of the country as it faces its past.

1. Namibia.

The people of Namibia, who had already endured a savage process of colonisation by Germany, were reduced again to *de facto* colonial status after the anti-Nazi war, this time under the rule of South Africa.

South Africa originally received a mandate over South West Africa from the League of Nations. Such mandates were like a form of curatorship – a "sacred trust of civilisation" as it was termed in the paternalistic idiom of the day – under which the mandated state had special responsibilities to ensure the wellbeing of the supervised territory. Such obligations were never observed, and instead Namibia was plundered of its wealth for the gain of South Africa and its privileged citizens.

South Africa repeatedly refused to relinquish the mandate when told to do so by United Nations resolutions and even when the International Court of Justice revoked the mandate in 1966. In 1969 the Security Council authoritatively decided that the "continued occupation of the Territory of Namibia by the South African authorities constitutes . . . a violation of the territorial integrity and a denial of the political sovereignty of the people of Namibia." The apartheid regime had effectively hijacked a whole country. International law was brazenly flouted in the process, the wealth of the land was looted, and the people themselves were repressed in the familiar apartheid fashion.

Defiantly, South Africa treated Namibia and black Namibians as it did its own people. Apartheid laws were introduced and with them apartheid's violence, abuse and waste. Over R4 billion (reckoned in 1988 money) was wasted on creating eleven parallel and wholly unnecessary racial and tribal authorities in order to ensure that Namibian governance complied with apartheid ideology.

The Namibian liberation movement, SWAPO (the South West Africa Peoples' Organisation), founded in 1960, was treated with the same contempt and repression as was the resistance in South Africa, although it was never actually banned.

In the early 1970s, the Security Council declared that "South Africa's continued illegal presence in Namibia constitutes an internationally wrongful act and a breach of international obligations and that South Africa remains accountable to the international community for any violation of its international obligations or the rights of the people of the territory of Namibia."

South Africa intensified its bloody repression of the Namibian people throughout the 1970s and '80s, imperfectly concealing these actions from South Africa's privileged electorate by heavy-handed military censorship. In one attack in 1978, South African planes bombed the SWAPO refugee camp at Kassinga in southern Angola for twelve hours. Some 600 people were killed and a thousand wounded, including many children. Two hundred prisoners were taken, of whom 137 were detained and held incommunicado without charge or trial; two years later over one hundred of them were still being held.

In 1984, relatives brought an action in Windhoek Supreme Court for the release of 37 named detainees, but the South African State President banned the court action under apartheid laws that gave him this extraordinary personal discretion. Only after an international campaign was launched were the detainees finally released later that year.

The Kassinga massacre – a raid on a refugee camp – may have been the single worst example of carnage inflicted on Namibians by South Africa. It graphically illustrates the way in which South Africa contravened humane standards of behaviour while also flouting its international obligations. In addition, the apartheid bureaucracy constantly used Namibia as, in the words of a UN Security Council resolution against the practice, a "springboard for armed invasions and destabilisation" of Angola, for which it was condemned by the Security Council and the international community.

2. Angola

Angola bore the brunt of South Africa's illegal military attacks on foreign countries, of which Kassinga was only one example. Its large reserves of oil were a tempting target, and South Africa embarked on a series of invasions designed to defeat the Angolan liberation movement, the MPLA, and to support the other Angolan movements, the FNLA and UNITA, which were better disposed towards apartheid.

Unlike other Front Line States, Angola was not economically dependent on South Africa and could not be controlled by trade and financial manipulation. South Africa therefore relied to a greater extent on more direct military measures to eliminate the MPLA, which was relentlessly opposed to apartheid, in the hope of installing one or both of the other two movements in power.

Major South African military involvement in Angola began in 1975, when the three movements were battling for control of the country. South Africa in that year began supplying and training UNITA troops, and South African forces, with covert US backing, were sent in to attack and capture Angolan towns. However, this period did not last long. The American Congress discovered the secret CIA military involvement and banned the use of US military funds in Angola for any purpose except the gathering of intelligence. Without American encouragement, the South African forces withdrew, bitterly complaining about the fecklessness of their erstwhile US ally.

The Angolan economy's tentative steps towards recovery were rudely interrupted by the parallel rise of P W Botha as South African Prime Minister and Ronald Reagan as President of the United States. South African aggression resumed in earnest, under the pretext of attacking Namibian rebels allegedly camped out in Angola. But such an excuse, even had it been factually accurate rather than disingenuous, would have had no validity under international law (see below pages 192–3). Moreover, its factual inaccuracy was made clear by the apartheid bureaucracy's attacks on economic targets such as the important Kassinga iron mine.

South Africa saw the MPLA government in Angola as a threat to its domination of the area, and therefore backed UNITA which was not so hostile to apartheid. Indeed UNITA's founder, Jonas Savimbi, attended the inauguration of P W Botha as State President. The South African government's backing intensified after the 1975 withdrawal of Portuguese imperial power. From early 1981 there was a permanent war in southern Angola accompanied by clear evidence of South Africa's intention to prop up UNITA. In 1983, for instance, South Africa stepped in to reverse the outcome of a failed UNITA assault on the government-held position at Cangamba. The Botha regime parachuted tons of weapons and explosives into Angola for the use of UNITA. Defence Minister Magnus Malan openly declared that South Africa, exercising its alleged prerogative as a "regional power," would not allow UNITA to be defeated.

This policy served the "interests of the free world," said apartheid's most violent ever Defence Minister. He announced that Savimbi "stands for the same norms and values in which we believe."[3] Uncharacteristically, Malan was quite accurate on this point. UNITA policy, as the London *Guardian* put it in October 1984, was one of "sowing terror and destruction," truly a page torn from the apartheid game plan.

UNITA's effectiveness in these terrorist strategies depended in large part on South African support. The South African Defence Force aided and abetted terrorism and war crimes, and committed them itself, in Angola.

The cost to ordinary Angolan citizens was extraordinary. When in 1981 for example 10,000 SADF troops invaded Angola and succeeded in capturing most of the key towns in Cunene Province, they displaced 160,000 civilians. The towns were reduced to rubble, and most of the province was laid waste.

At the end of 1983 the tide began to turn. In that year the UN Security Council, through its Resolution 545, condemned the continuing occupation of Angolan territory as a "breach of international law" and, specifically, of the United Nations Charter, a document which is in effect the constitution of the United Nations.

These irresistible international pressures induced South Africa to sign the Lusaka Accord, promising to withdraw its troops from Angola. But the apartheid government predictably ignored the agreement and continued its murderous aggression for several years, until its defeat by black Cuban and Angolan forces in the famous 1988 battle of Cuito Cuanavale, which punctured the myth of an invulnerable apartheid war machine.

The colossal expense of these military operations, the wasted lives of young South African conscripts, the appalling destruction and havoc wreaked, did not ultimately save the apartheid regime. They merely wrecked the burgeoning economy of a new country, just emerging from colonial domination, and destroyed the lives of hundreds of thousands of its inhabitants.

According to a study carried out by the United Nations Economic Commission for Africa published in 1989,4 well over one third of Angola's people were displaced from their homes with the result, among other things, that peasant agriculture was badly affected, primary health care and education facilities were reduced, and up to 75 per cent of small town and rural water systems were destroyed or damaged and out of operation. The country's transport system was wrecked. Angola estimated the total damage at $6.7 billion. Between 1980 and 1988 more than 500,000 people were directly or indirectly killed as a result of war.

The same study documented that over 40,000 citizens were handicapped through loss of limbs, mostly due to landmine explosions. Many of the victims were children, who will carry invisible limbs, blown to bits by apartheid, for the rest of their lives. Landmines were a South African speciality, and the least we can do in facing this part of our past is to acknowledge the appalling injuries caused to so many by supporting moves towards a complete ban on the manufacture, ownership, storage and use of landmines.

3. Mozambique

It was not only in Angola that South Africa fostered and supplied surrogate forces to carry out its policies and destabilise governments that were opposed to apartheid. The worst example of these practices was Mozambique, where the rebel Renamo forces killed, brutalised and terrorised hundreds of thousands of civilians.

The Robert Gersony report commissioned by the Government of the United States and published in 1988 documents the mass murder, rape, and arson carried out by Renamo. The Report provoked the United States Deputy Assistant Secretary of State for Africa to describe the activities of the South Africa supported rebels as "the most brutal holocaust against ordinary human beings" since the Nazis.5 South Africa's ambassador to Washington, Dr Piet Koornhof, attempted at the time to delay publication of the Report; or to have it copublished in the joint names of the US and South Africa.[6] He was both times rebuffed, but his vigorous attempts to repress the truth about apartheid atrocities demonstrates the evasiveness of the perpetrators and the need for a meticulous reckoning of apartheid's cross-border past.

Renamo had originally been encouraged, supported and controlled by the illegal Rhodesian regime. After Rhodesia held democratic elections in 1980, and after it had made the transition from the short-lived Zimbabwe–Rhodesia to Zimbabwe, the new government ceased to support Renamo, and South Africa stepped in to fill the gap. The pattern of sabotage continued and was particularly directed at the country's transport network, because this, with its access to good ports, was a vital necessity for the land-bound countries of southern Africa. Without these ports these countries would have been strangled in the chokehold of reliance on apartheid South Africa's infrastructure.

Renamo's efforts, funded and supported by South Africa, were supplemented by direct South African military attacks. The first direct South African raid was in 1981, when an apartheid commando team crossed the border in trucks disguised as Mozambican army vehicles and attacked houses occupied by South African guerrillas in Matola, a suburb of Maputo. Thirteen ANC refugees were killed.

Such raids not only destabilised Mozambique but also enraged and embittered South African refugees who saw their companions obliterated by these illegal strikes. Yet despite the appalling damage caused by Renamo, and despite the raids, the Mozambican government was never in danger of collapsing. It was, however, anxious to end the instability. The apartheid regime exploited its vulnerability to coerce it into a diplomatic agreement, the Nkomati Accord, in 1984, which pledged good-neighbourliness between the two adversaries. As a result of this Accord, ANC members were forced to leave Mozambique.

This should have ended South African interference in Mozambican affairs. Instead, although the Mozambican Government kept its side of the bargain, South Africa hastily rushed a six-months' supply of arms to the Mozambican anti-government forces of Renamo just before the agreement was signed, enabling them to continue their gruesome operations. Moreover, South African training and financial support continued, as was confirmed by the "Vaz diaries" captured by the Mozambique government in September 1985, which revealed deliberate SADF violations of the Nkomati Accord.

The Renamo operations also prevented the Mozambique Government from bringing relief to drought-stricken areas, which consequently suffered from famine. In mid-1989, the US State Department confirmed that South African support for terrorism in Mozambique was continuing. By that stage, over 4.5 million people had been driven from their homes and another million had become refugees in nearby countries. Due to the conflict, nearly 1 million Mozambicans died between 1980–88. Close to 40 per cent of rural water supplies were destroyed or severely damaged, with consequent severe effects for health, especially as in addition around 5 million people lost their access to medical services.7

It will take decades for this now poverty-stricken country to restore its economy, rebuild the shattered lives of its people and undo the damage inflicted by the regional impact of the apartheid past.

4. The Other Front Line States

Apartheid's violent attentions were trained upon Botswana, Lesotho, Swaziland, Zimbabwe, Zambia and Tanzania, as well as Namibia, Angola and Mozambique.

From its illegal military bases in the Caprivi Strip in northern Namibia, apartheid South Africa launched repeated attacks on Zambia and Botswana. It brazenly sent agents into Zambia and Zimbabwe to sabotage economic targets and to murder or attempt to murder ANC leaders.

Tanzania made huge financial sacrifices to resist apartheid. It sent armed forces to assist the Mozambican Government, and it accommodated thousands of refugees from that country. It also gave land and facilities to the ANC to build the Solomon Mahlangu Freedom College and the Dakawa settlement within its borders.

Lesotho, Botswana and Swaziland were so economically dependent on South Africa that they were sometimes referred to as the "captive states". They were bound to South Africa by the customs union as well as by less formal mechanisms of economic dependence. This relationship was manipulated by South Africa to pressure them whenever the apartheid regime detected signs of sympathy or support for the South African resistance.

Despite such pressures, all three offered sanctuary to South African refugees. Swaziland, being entirely surrounded by South African territory, had little room to manoeuvre when the apartheid regime demanded that it take action against the ANC. Lesotho and Botswana were better placed to resist such demands, but suffered as a result, both through economic reprisals and from armed raids into their countries.

One of the most shocking of these raids was conducted by SADF commandos, supported by helicopters and armoured trucks, which invaded Lesotho in December 1982. They attacked a number of houses in Maseru which they claimed were occupied by South African refugees. Thirty South African refugees and twelve Lesotho nationals were killed. Many were gunned down in their beds. The dead included women and children.

A similar operation carried out on Gaberone in June 1985, left twelve people dead. SADF soldiers burst into houses which they apparently thought were occupied by South African refugees, and sprayed the occupants with automatic gunfire. The President of Botswana, Dr Ketumile Masire, issued a statement calling the attack a "blood-curdling act of murder" and recalling that "the stated objective of South African strategy is expressly to cower [neighbouring countries] into submission to its will as a regional power."

In 1989 UNICEF issued a report on the political, economic and social effects of this policy on the children of the region. Entitled *Children on the Frontline*, it found that 25 children were dying every hour from the effects of war in southern Africa. About half the people of Mozambique were at some time displaced from their homes, with women and children bearing the brunt of the pain.

In the nine countries of the then Southern African Development Co-ordination Conference, some 750,000 children were dying before the age of five, out of approximately three and a half million annual births. The UNICEF report estimated that one fifth of this number could be attributed to the effects of the conflict. The impact was particularly devastating in Angola and Mozambique, where infant and child mortality rates were estimated to be the highest in the world.

The front line states, which became the flashpoint of the civilised world's revulsion with apartheid, bore an involuntarily large share of the costs of the global resistance. It is something we must not forget in current debates over regional cooperation – and when faced with xenophobic calls for the expulsion or demonisation of "illegal aliens" from next door. The culpability of the old South Africa, its continuing responsibility for ongoing suffering on our cross-border doorstep, cannot be so easily evaded.

16

Apartheid and the International Community

"Historic change has come about not least because of the great efforts in which the United Nations engaged to ensure the suppression of the apartheid crime against humanity."
– President Nelson Mandela, address to the United Nations General Assembly, October 1994.

Since apartheid was at once part, cause, effect and example of the world's varied forms of moral and political wrongdoing; and since it systematised disparate evils to a degree that was unparalleled in post-war experience, apartheid South Africa was confronted with a coordinated response from the international community that was unique in its stamina and intensity.

There is a long legal and political history of persistent international support for the resistance to apartheid, predating even the December 1962 Joint Appeal by ANC President Albert Luthuli and the Reverend Dr Martin Luther King Jr for "an effective international quarantine of apartheid."[1]

In 1946, one year into its existence and two years before the formal electoral victory of apartheid, the United Nations General Assembly was already dealing, at the request of the Indian government, with complaints of legislated racial discrimination against people of Indian origin in South Africa. As apartheid's legislative horrors gathered momentum after 1948, the United Nations and the global movement against apartheid expanded and matured together.

In 1953 the United Nations Committee on the Racial Situation in South Africa condemned policies based on racial superiority as dangerous to international peace and security, and inconsistent with the Charter of the United Nations and the Universal Declaration of Human Rights. After 1960, mutually reinforcing international processes arose. Freedom begat more freedom, as the recently decolonised peoples, like the sixteen newly independent African states admitted to UN membership at the 15th session of the General Assembly, added momentum to calls for the end of surviving pockets of colonialism and racism, and as the Organisation of African Unity gave voice to the sentiments of a previously silenced continent.

The global anti-apartheid movement even changed the face of international law itself, giving impetus to a developing international norm of nondiscrimination; to the linkages between racial equality, decolonisation and self-determination; and to the clear-cut acceptance of the principle of self-determination as a rule of international law, among other innovations.

As the International Court of Justice noted in the 1970 *Barcelona Traction Case*, the old view that states owe duties only to other states and that these duties can arise only out of specific bilateral obligations is no longer valid. The international anti-apartheid resistance played a substantial part in bringing about this welcome state of affairs. They helped to put flesh and blood on to the resolutions and declarations of international bodies.

During the decades of the anti-apartheid struggle, international jurisprudence developed to the point that states have lost their monopoly over law creation where matters at the fundamental core of international legal principle are involved. The range of policies that were definitive of the apartheid state all fell within that settled core of international law, the *jus cogens*, which no state may renounce or ignore.[2] As the International Court of Justice confirmed in its 1970 Opinion on the South African occupation of, and extension of apartheid to, Namibia: "Racial discrimination as a matter of official government policy is a violation of a norm or rule or standard of the international community."[3]

Ultimately, the very basis of the apartheid government – systematic racial discrimination – was recognised as a breach of the *jus cogens*, so that all its acts (with the exception of basic administrative functions like the recording of births, deaths, and marriages) lacked legal validity. As unanimously resolved by the United Nations Security Council in 1984, the apartheid machine had no authority to represent the people of the country. Its status as a state was questionable because it constituted a pirate bureaucracy, a pariah entity, having an apparatus of force at its disposal and exercising *de facto* control of South Africa, but without legitimacy.

However, it is important to note that this lack of legitimacy did not free the apartheid bureaucracy of accountability to international law since, as the International Court of Justice has held, "Physical control of territory, and not sovereignty or legitimacy, is the basis of state liability."[4]

Ironically, the existence of apartheid helped generate fundamental rules of international law that have profound effects on the definition of what it means to qualify as a state, and on the freedom of states to wage war, pollute the environment, enter into treaties denying self-determination, and adopt policies of racial discrimination or other gross violations of human rights.

The anti-apartheid solidarity movement gained from the global mobilisation against apartheid. But also, less obviously, it contributed to the international community by supplying an abundance of theoretical and practical arguments against blind deference to domestic political tyranny.

These broad international developments inevitably had direct consequences for the old South Africa itself. The apartheid bureaucrats were not allowed to go unperturbed about their favoured business of domestic repression. Even the reluctant US policymakers of the Nixon administration conceded, in a secret 1969 memorandum, that "because other countries have made it so, our foreign policy must take into account the domestic policies of the white regimes" in southern Africa.5

In 1984, the United Nations Security Council spoke directly on the proposed elections for a tricameral parliament, which would classically have been considered among the internal affairs of a state. The Security Council declared the new constitution "null and void" and dismissed the racist elections as a scheme to "entrench white minority rule and apartheid." It found that "only the total eradication of apartheid in a united and unfragmented South Africa" could lead to a "just and lasting solution."

To no other of its member states did the United Nations insist so extensively on reform of internal laws, policies and practices. The whole political system of apartheid was declared a crime against humanity. The internal lawlessness of the apartheid state and its external pariah status were like an unconcealable and reversible (meaning two-sided) strait-jacket of shame. The condemnation it attracted was unprecedented and has not been equalled since. Even the ongoing war crimes trials in the former Yugoslavia are concerned with the isolation and punishment of individual wrongdoers, not with the state as such.

Equally, South Africa's internal release from apartheid has met an echo of international euphoria. "We enter into a covenant that we shall build a society in which all South Africans, both black and white, will be able to walk tall, without any fear in their hearts, assured of their inalienable right to human dignity – a rainbow nation at peace with itself and the world . . . Never, never, never again shall it be that this beautiful land will again experience the oppression of one by another, and suffer the indignity of being the skunk of the world," said President Nelson Mandela upon his inauguration as the first genuinely elected President of South Africa on 10 May 1994. The indivisibility of internal democracy and international acceptability could not have been clearer.

Yet there are some, those whose heyday was under apartheid, who would question what the President said. They suggest, also indivisibly, that apartheid was not really a crime against humanity and that what took place in April 1994, under the full glare of international scrutiny, "was not an election but a battle to control turf in which violence and intimidation were frequently employed."6

We should pause at this coincidence: that those who seek to rewrite the international consensus on apartheid are also ill at ease with the new democratic politics: "the excessive dominance of the ANC may well turn us into a variant of a one-party dominant regime," warns this critic, hands awringing already.

In its panicked Eurocentrism – in its Eurosis – this perspective brings to mind J M Coetzee's brilliant rewrite of Robinson Crusoe in his novel *Foe*, where the European narrator observes the alleged ex-cannibal Man Friday – now dancing civilised in wigs and robes – and wonders: "Is it not only a matter of time before the new Friday whom Cruso created is sloughed off and the old Friday of the cannibal forests returns? Have I misjudged Cruso all this time: was it to punish him for his sins that he cut out Friday's tongue? Better had he drawn his teeth instead!"

As the new South African democracy finds its own tongue, South Africa's old voices, whose tongues were left intact by the old regime for its own purposes, are understandably anxious. They see a lurking sharp-toothed beast beneath, it seems, a mere veneer of humanism. As one Eurotic commentator puts it, "One could have joined the ANC to assist the battle for black dignity ... but to have bet on democracy and human rights would have been a long shot."[7]

Something called "black dignity" (the robes and wigs of Idi Amin?) can evidently exist and can even be struggled for, in the absence of human rights and democracy; the latter benefits have apparently arrived only by accident in South Africa and subsist only tenuously on the tip of the dark continent.

Apartheid's role as a microcosm of global injustice inevitably occupied the centre of the stage in the past; and in dealing with that past we must likewise not lose sight of these global issues. Eurotic commentators appear to forget that there exist global problems of power and powerlessness, of wealth and dispossession, which found a parallel in the domestic South African politics of looting and oppression.

There are no inherently "civilised" countries; only civilised and uncivilised politics. And international law, which like all law comprises congealed politics, was and is a site of struggle between civilisation and its opposite. At a pivotal moment in the recent film "The American President", the lead character (the President) came under attack from political foes for his association with a political activist whose commitments included the anti-apartheid resistance. At a 1986 rally she was observed burning an American flag as part of an anti-apartheid protest. The fictional American President expressed amazement that he could come under attack for someone else's decade-old activism against a system that was so evil that "it doesn't even exist any more."

In the case of the anti-apartheid resistance, this global battle had a firm basis in international law and norms. As early as 1965, the United Nations General Assembly called on "all States to provide material and moral assistance to the national liberation movements in colonial territories."

The authoritative International Law Commission of the United Nations suggested, in a 1982 report, that there could be an obligation on all states to "contribute" to a situation in which the author of an international crime such as apartheid could be "compelled" to stop the breach. As a minimum, the Commission suggested that such a contribution would include refraining from support of conduct constituting an international crime.

The practical effect of this development was to condemn virtually all forms of assistance to the apartheid regime as aiding and abetting the crime of apartheid. The Nuremberg Principles, which were adopted by the UN General Assembly in 1949 and which are now part of customary international law, imposed a duty on corporations and individuals not to assist in criminal conduct forbidden by international law. Thus there was a duty on corporations and other entities and individuals not to provide succour to apartheid.

Yet, ignoring the implications of this duty in international law, the apartheid parliament (including its liberal "dissenters") opposed the international movement towards comprehensive economic sanctions. Nevertheless, these international campaigns gathered enormous momentum, and played a vital role in bringing apartheid to an end.

Now the new South Africa is developing new links with those countries and peoples who took on the solidarity role. This represents more than self-interest (although it is that too); it is part of the new South Africa's own intimate identity and its definition of its place in the world. The idea that the successful countries of the "South" or the "Third World" should adhere anxiously to a world order determined wholly by the "North" or the "First World" may be dressed up as sophisticated *realpolitik*, but in reality it is merely the international relations equivalent of bantustan politics: a self-seeking pursuit of massive personal gain, inevitably ending in the disappointment of mere crumbs from the masters' table.

Only because different values prevailed in international debates did global resistance to apartheid – and its status as an outlaw system – arise. The member states of the international community recognised, long before the final death of apartheid, that the regime was based on a racist concept that contradicted the very notion of human rights; that contact with it was subversive of the values enshrined in the world legal order; and that preservation of these values required, in the international community's own self-interest, that action be taken to defend the fundamental basis of the international legal order.

Thus international law and norms provide us with a vital moral compass to steer through the wreckage of South Africa's past. Unfortunately those who believe that there was an equal balance of abuses on both sides of the conflict are often either ignorant or dismissive of these international norms. It is part of their dismissiveness of whole nations of the world and of whole peoples. They view international relations through an apartheid lens that identifies an ill-defined category of "free market" or "western" countries and governments with civilisation.

Yet, despite such calculated dismissiveness, these international norms and rules are a vital resource of the search for the truth about the South African past. The praiseworthy effort to attain impartiality cannot be a parochial exercise, nor does impartiality mean that one must be neutral towards the two sides. Rather, impartiality requires a return to the civilised norms of the international community.

If the Truth and Reconciliation Commission succeeds in holding up a clear mirror to the past, it will no longer be possible for anyone to take the view proclaimed by John Vorster in the 1960s that the United Nations was full of "weak-livered souls" or "traitors and morally rotten creatures"; or to call the United Nations "a stage from which anti-apartheid groups and non-aligned states could display their bitterness and launch their attacks," as did an article in *Salut*, the official journal of the South African National Defence Force, which appeared as late as January 1996.

Such attempts to dismiss the international human rights consensus are not unfamiliar in times of transition; the tactic is familiar to those who feel themselves uncomfortably close to the prior regime. For the Argentine military and much conservative and anti-semitic opinion in that country, the very concept of crimes against humanity lacked credibility because the Nuremberg precedents were seen not as the triumph of international human rights, but merely as the revenge of the Jews.[8]

Similarly, in South Africa, some now seek to deny the fact that apartheid was a crime against humanity by claiming, backhandedly, that only the Nazi holocaust qualifies for that designation. As will be clear from the more specific discussion below, this view is simply incorrect as a matter of legal doctrine.

The concept of a crime against humanity is an international legal one with a living presence, featuring for instance in the ongoing war crimes trials in Yugoslavia, in the proposed tribunal for Rwanda, and, as a newly recognised crime, in the national laws of Canada, France, Australia and even Britain.

Remembrance of the Holocaust is generally accompanied by the admonition "Never Again." This is not merely a statement of the inevitable – not a mere tautology, or an absurd guarantee that crimes against humanity could never in fact be repeated or that they are limited to Nazi German atrocities. Crimes against humanity cannot be avoided by conceptual *fiat* or by a semantic insistence that there can only ever, for all posterity, have been one such crime. This would be an invitation to repetition rather than avoidance.

Rather, the injunction "Never Again" is an appeal to the world to avoid, to recognise and to act against any recurrence. It is an appeal that the world has taken up by evolving the legal doctrine of crimes against humanity in remembrance of the Holocaust dead. Apart from the international law doctrine, several countries, including Britain, have enacted domestic law statutes criminalising crimes against humanity and employing definitions that have a general application and are not limited to the specific Nazi crimes; this is a concrete expression of their remembrance.

The attempt to contain the scope of crimes against humanity, and to deny the concept a living and admonitory presence is a device to smooth historical forgetting. A formal acknowledgment of the wisdom of the international community on the matter of apartheid is an essential part of reconciliation. It is also part of our indebtedness to the world's people who stood for truth, against apartheid.

The enormity of apartheid's malfeasance was such that it is possible to say, in several precise legal senses, that the apartheid regime was an international outlaw. It had no right to assure its survival and thus could not justify any acts whatsoever on the basis of a legal claim to self-defence, or related concepts of "necessity." This lack of any right to assure the survival of apartheid renders null and void a whole range of mundane and abnormal acts done in maintenance of its system of white supremacy. Equally, it deprives the apartheid state of any claim that it stands on the same moral and international legal plane as the resistance to it. The status of the apartheid government and its practices under international law are examined in the necessary detail below.

From that discussion, it emerges that apartheid was a form of colonialism; it was a pariah state, illegitimate in international law; it denied the majority its right to self-determination and thereby triggered that majority's right, in international law, to revolt; it was a criminal system in itself; in addition, it committed specific crimes of aggression and against peace; it committed crimes against humanity as well as war crimes; and it committed genocide. Much of this accumulation of horrors sits on a special shelf of criminality, without an expiry date. There is no statute of limitations in international law for most crimes of this nature.

1. Apartheid As Colonialism

It ought to be obvious that the coloniser and those resisting colonisation can seldom be placed on an equivalent legal footing, least of all where the kind of colonialism in question is that particularly vicious variant: apartheid. No significant international legal principle, nor any resolution or decision of the UN Security Council, the General Assembly, or the International Court of Justice, equates the acts of a national liberation movement with those of a colonial state, or treats these acts as providing a justification for the use of force by the colonial state.

Meanwhile, apartheid's nature as a form of colonialism was firmly established under international law. As early as 1965, the United Nations General Assembly stated by resolution that the preservation of colonialism in all its manifestations, including racism and apartheid, was incompatible with the UN Charter and with the UN Declaration on Decolonisation.

The apartheid regime and its allies argued in the 1970s that the South African situation raised no issues of self-determination because the oppressive governing class were South Africans who were living permanently in that country, and self-determination was relevant only to such colonial territories as Namibia and Zimbabwe. This self-serving argument was flatly rejected by the international community and by international law. The fundamental principle of nondiscrimination was recognised as a common denominator of anti-colonialism and self-determination alike.

For instance, the Preamble of the 1965 International Convention on the Elimination of All Forms of Racial Discrimination specifically condemns "colonialism and all practices of segregation and discrimination associated therewith" and invokes the famous 1960 Declaration on the Granting of Independence to Colonial Countries and Peoples.9 A wretched thread of discrimination binds apartheid to colonialism.

Moreover, the specific features of the apartheid system also bind it to colonialism. Under the 1961 apartheid so-called constitution, full legislative sovereignty vested in Parliament, yet only whites were eligible to be appointed members of the Senate (section 34) and the House of Assembly (section 46). Only a "white person" could become the President or a Minister. By statute, only whites were enabled to vote.

But nothing reflected the colonised status of the black majority under apartheid better than the section of the 1961 constitution, that set out the constitutional status of blacks. It provided that "the control and administration of Bantu affairs ... shall rest in the State President" (section 8(4)). By their own theory and law, the rulers of South Africa treated the majority of the population as a separate, inferior, people, to be kept at arms' length and under the strict supervision – without representation – of the white authorities.

This position – that apartheid constituted a form of "internal colonialism" was long emphasised by the anti-apartheid resistance. In its 1969 *Strategy and Tactics* document, the African National Congress pointed out that the apartheid system had "most of the features of the classical colonial structures. Conquest and domination by an alien people, a system of discrimination and exploitation based on race, techniques of indirect rule; these and more are the traditional trappings of the classical colonial framework."

Current arguments by apartheid's apologists that drastic and abnormal measures were necessary in the past, given the seriousness of the prior conflict, must be seen in the light of apartheid's status as a form of colonialism. Such claims are utterly unfounded, since that which the apartheid state sought to protect was wholly without legitimacy.

Equally spurious is the related claim that, prior to 1990, the old regime faced a "total onslaught" which it had to, and was entitled to, rebuff by all means. A democratic government under attack from outside forces would indeed be entitled to defend itself. But the apartheid regime was not legitimate, nor did it face external assault. Apartheid's enemy was South Africa's disowned citizenry, either within the country or on its borders. In a more direct and violent sense than James Joyce ever intended in applying the phrase to Ireland, the apartheid regime was a sow that ate its own farrow.

2. The International Illegitimacy of Apartheid

The opposing moral universes of apartheid and the resistance to it, the very different positions of coloniser and colonised, cannot both have enjoyed international legitimacy at one and the same time. The international community, no less than South Africans themselves, had to choose between the fruit of two radically different apple trees.

And even though the wheels of international justice turn infinitely more slowly than the very slow wheels of domestic legal systems, the General Assembly first endorsed armed struggle against the "illegitimate racist minority regime" in 1968 (Resolution 2396). By 1973, a United Nations General Assembly resolution recognised the national liberation movements as the "authentic representatives" of the "overwhelming majority of the South African people."

The formal intellectual rejection of apartheid by the international community had in fact occurred more than a decade earlier when, at its sixteenth session, the General Assembly voted to censure the egregious Eric Louw, a former Nazi sympathiser and then apartheid's foreign minister.

This was a move unprecedented in the annals of the United Nations. In essence, as described by one writer, the General Assembly found that South Africa had, by its brazen advocacy of abhorrent racial doctrines, "voluntarily placed itself outside the community of nations envisaged in the [United Nations] Charter and therefore had no grounds to ask for the normal respect of divergent opinions that usually marked UN proceedings."[10] South Africa was officially a pariah nation; a global outcast.

The international community also organised itself to move from condemnation, criticism and intellectual renunciation to unprecedented collective action against apartheid. The apartheid bureaucracy's representatives were either expelled or suspended or withdrew from various international organisations. A Special Committee on the Policies of Apartheid established in 1962 was soon significantly renamed the Special Committee Against Apartheid.

Collective UN actions, and unilateral actions by its members, steadily gathered momentum. In 1984 for instance, the Special Committee Against Apartheid held a seminar on the legal status of apartheid, which denounced as racist the 1983 tricameral constitution and appealed to "all South Africans to resist, *by all means*, the imposition of the new constitution"[11] (emphasis added).

In 1974 the General Assembly refused to accept the credentials of the South African delegation. This was, in the words of the President of the Assembly, "tantamount to saying in explicit terms that the General Assembly refuses to allow the delegation of South Africa to participate in its work."

In a landmark resolution in 1975, the UN General Assembly, by an overwhelmingly majority, passed what would become its traditional annual resolution on The Situation In South Africa. This resolution stated that "the racist regime in South Africa is illegitimate and has no right to represent the people of South Africa." The General Assembly at the same time reaffirmed "the legitimacy of the struggle of the oppressed people of South Africa and their liberation movements, *by all possible means*, for the seizure of power by the people and the exercise of their inalienable right to self-determination" (emphasis added). In 1979 the United Nations General Assembly's Resolution 183L condemned "the illegitimate minority racist regime."

The international community thus refused to accept that the South African regime could speak on behalf of the South African population. The world emphasised that the very basis of the South African state denied the vast majority of the population a rightful place in the political, administrative and economic life of the community which that state purported to represent. Other governments may suppress and outlaw opponents; the apartheid bureaucracy denied 80 per cent of the population minimal rights of citizenship, strictly on the basis of colour. This denial of citizenship was criminal in itself.

From 1960 until the formal death of apartheid in April 1994, the United Nations General Assembly and its Security Council moved from general to specific resolutions urging action against apartheid. Through these proliferating and increasingly specific resolutions and other legal developments, the international community explicitly recognised that the apartheid system and the situation in South Africa were special cases of particular criminality, requiring exceptional responses both from the world body and from international law itself.

The idea that apartheid had an early idealistic phase is belied by the atrocious acts and venomous historical utterances of the architects of apartheid; and it was repudiated by the longstanding and unequivocal international consensus on the subject. Apartheid was possibly the only issue that, on a planet divided by tactical and ideological rivalries, united world opinion.

As we have seen, apartheid's breach of the principle of democratic self-determination and its state policy of systematic abuse of human rights meant that it could no longer be considered as the "internal affair" of South Africa. The crime of apartheid and the response of the resistance had effects which were international as well as national.

The reasons for this were spelled out with particular clarity in April 1964 by Dr Conor Cruise O'Brien, a former Irish diplomat, writer and critic. He said:

It is only part of the answer to say that South African oppression is on a far greater scale and more rigorously and systematically applied than anywhere else. Others may repress minorities, they repress an actual majority. Others may unjustly deprive individual citizens of their rights; they deprive whole categories of citizens, simply identifiable by their physical characteristics, of all political and civil rights ...

... The South African regime asserts in its practice, if not in its official declarations, that those peoples which make up the majority of the population of the globe are not fully human.

On this premise they have erected a whole elaborate legislation and practice: a code which bears with crushing weight on the majority of the people of South Africa and which is, at the same time, felt as an intolerable insult by the population of their continent and by most of humanity. Their regime, denying as it does our common nature as men, is not merely inhuman in the loose sense, it is actually anti-human in a precise sense.

Arising from the illegitimacy of apartheid, people were freed of the bonds and obligations that normally emerge from citizenship. Thus apartheid laws compelling armed service were invalid.

Eventually, in response to the apartheid bureaucracy's severe crackdown on legitimate mass resistance to the 1983 apartheid constitution and subsequent elections, the Security Council announced a virtual constitutional blueprint for a legitimate South Africa. In its Resolution 554 in 1984, the Security Council declared that "the so-called 'new constitution' is contrary to the principles of the Charter of the United Nations [and] that the results of the Referendum of 2 November 1983 are of no validity whatsoever." The Security Council strongly rejected and declared "null and void" the so-called "new constitution" and rejected all such "insidious manoeuvres" by the regime "further to entrench White minority rule and apartheid."

In its further Resolution 556, the Security Council reaffirmed the "legitimacy of the struggle of the oppressed people of South Africa for the full exercise of the rights of self-determination and the establishment of a nonracial democratic society in an unfragmented South Africa." It tackled other matters such as the unbanning of political organisations and the dismantling of the bantustans, and finally demanded *"the immediate eradication of apartheid and necessary steps towards the full exercise of the right to self-determination in an unfragmented South Africa"* (emphasis added).

These were the minimum requirements for a constitution that would comply with international law. This was the international community's authoritative verdict on the apartheid regime's increasingly baroque attempts to deny basic rights of self-determination to the millions of people held under its lash.[12]

3. Self-determination and the Right to Revolt

It is now accepted that people denied effective political participation and basic human rights have, under international law, the right to "alter, abolish, or overthrow any form of government that becomes destructive of the process of self-determination and the right to individual participation."[13]

Any doubt as to the existence of this principle is demolished by the consensus Declaration on Principles of International Law concerning Friendly Relations and Cooperation Among States, which was unanimously adopted by the United Nations General Assembly in 1970. This landmark Declaration, which is declaratory of customary international law, placed a duty on states to refrain from "any forcible action" which would deprive people of these rights. It recognised that peoples resisting such incursions on the right of self-determination "are entitled to seek and receive support in accordance with the purposes and principles of the Charter."

The use of force against the legitimate exercise of self-determination clearly violates international law; and those seeking to exercise self-determination are entitled to fight for it in accordance with decisions by international or regional organisations. The two sides are not equivalent. Moreover, the right of self-determination is not merely a right at the level of customary international law, but is rather part of the basic and inviolable core, the *jus cogens*, of the international legal system. The landmark Declaration on the Granting of Independence to Colonial Countries and Peoples, adopted by the General Assembly in 1960 (Resolution 1514(XV)), "regards the principle of self-determination as part of the obligations stemming from the Charter . . . [and] is in the form of an authoritative interpretation of the Charter."

This inviolable principle of self-determination represents an important move away from the old view, according to which rights under international law were accessible only to states and governments, not to groups and individuals. The old view was based on the idea, central to the 1933 Montevideo Convention on the Rights and Duties of States, that recognition required the exercise of some degree of continuous power of government over relevant territory or the major parts of it. This view was, however, hard to square with the recognition of governments-in-exile during the Second World War. Additionally, the undoubted illegitimacy of the apartheid regime and the sheer brutality of its governance meant that its continuing hold on power could not be treated as an immutable criterion of recognition.

The recognition of the legitimate representative function of the South African resistance was part of a broader awakening to the legitimate claims of anti-colonial resistance movements in Angola, Mozambique, and Guinea-Bissau, as well as the recognition of the legitimate liberation movement in Namibia, the South West African Peoples' Organisation (SWAPO), whose effective governance of that territory was precluded only by the undeniably illegal apartheid occupation.

Apartheid, racially discriminatory in its essence, subverted the majority's right of self-determination. The customary rule of "non-discrimination" in international law is closely associated with the right of self-determination. Both the International Convention on Economic, Social and Cultural Rights and the International Convention on Civil and Political Rights begin their catalogues of human rights by reference to the fact that "all peoples have the right to self-determination. By virtue of that right they freely determine their political status and freely pursue their economic, social, and cultural development." (Article 1.1 of each Convention). The Conventions impose the further and important obligation that states shall "promote the realisation of the right to self-determination, and shall respect that right, in conformity with the provisions of the Charter of the United Nations" (Article 1.3).

The Defiance Campaign announced by the Mass Democratic Movement in August 1989, with its echoes of the famous Defiance of Unjust Laws Campaign of 1952 and its closeness to the spirit of the MK Manifesto of 1961, was an assertion of the people's legitimate right, rooted in international law, to disobey laws that have no moral or legal validity. This right was also an important basis of the armed struggle.

The landmark All-In Africa Conference held in Pietermaritzburg in March 1961, organised in the aftermath of the Sharpeville massacre, brought together all Africans "irrespective of their political, religious or other affiliations" so as to "unite to speak and act with a single voice."

The Conference formally declared "that no Constitution or form of Government decided without the participation of the African people who form an absolute majority of the population can enjoy moral validity or merit support either within South Africa or beyond its borders." The Conference formally called on "democratic people the world over" to isolate and impose sanctions on the country.

It was a remarkably explicit and formal statement of the domestic and international illegitimacy of the apartheid regime.

The actions of the liberation movement were based on the exercise of the right to self-determination and rooted in international law; in addition, they found widespread acceptance in the international community. In 1979 the General Assembly of the United Nations, by its Resolution 183L, affirmed "the legitimacy of the struggle . . . *by all available and appropriate means,* including armed struggle, for the seizure of power by the people" (emphasis added).

The armed struggle was not only legitimate and legal in the eyes of international law but, further, gave rise to positive rights to mobilise and receive international support. The General Assembly's consensus Declaration on Principles of International Law Concerning Friendly Relations and Cooperation Among States lays down that "in their actions against, and in resistance to . . . forcible action in pursuit of the exercise of their right to self-determination, such peoples are entitled to seek and receive support in accordance with the purposes and principles of the Charter."

In the words of a member of the International Court of Justice, the highest court of law in the world, while deciding the Namibia case during apartheid's Vorster era, the liberation movement's right to revolt was similar to "the struggle of the French national movement at the time when France was under the domination of Nazi Germany."[14]

In its 1977 Resolution 417 the UN Security Council unanimously and specifically affirmed "the right to the exercise of self-determination by all the people of South Africa as a whole, irrespective of race, colour or creed." The Security Council, including the Western powers, thus confirmed the view that the struggle against apartheid was a wholly legitimate and lawful struggle for self-determination.

The UN General Assembly in 1973 "solemnly proclaimed" that combatants struggling against colonial and alien domination and racist regimes enjoy a protected status under international law. "Armed conflicts involving the struggle of peoples against racist regimes are to be regarded as international armed conflicts in the sense of the 1949 Geneva Conventions," it said.

The 1977 Protocol to the Geneva Conventions further formalised this view, providing that "armed conflicts in which peoples are fighting against colonial domination and alien occupation and against racist regimes in the exercise of their right of self-determination . . . shall be included in the definition of 'armed conflicts' to which the 1949 Conventions apply."

This recognition of rights under the Protocol codified an existing rule of international law which demanded that minimum humanitarian standards be applied to such conflicts. The failure of the apartheid regime to ratify the convention therefore did not affect the protected status of liberation combatants in South Africa.

In November 1987, the General Assembly reaffirmed its "full support to the people of South Africa in their struggle, under the leadership of their national liberation movements, to eradicate apartheid totally, so that they can exercise their right to self-determination in a free, democratic, unfragmented and nonracial South Africa." Again on 22 November 1989, a General Assembly resolution reaffirmed "full support to the national liberation movements, the African

National Congress and the Pan Africanist Congress of Azania, which pursue their noble objective to eliminate apartheid through political, armed and other forms of struggle and have reiterated their preference for reaching their legitimate objectives through peaceful means."

Yet in recent litigation seeking an interdict against grants of amnesty by the Truth and Reconciliation Commission, the Supreme Court of the Western Cape pronounced (in a finding that was unnecessary for its decision) that the fight in South Africa was one for internal liberation and not one for self-determination against colonial domination or against alien occupation.

These conclusions are in fact faulty. First, they omit an important part of the usual formulation of the right to self-determination: a right to resist "alien, colonial *or racist*" domination. It is hardly a coincidence that a traditional South African court should omit the latter phrase.

Moreover, the approach of the Supreme Court ignores a central fact about the right to self-determination: that it reflects a form of self-assertion against any form of domination, hence its content is as varied as the ways of domination are varied. It applies as much to orthodox forms of colonialism as to colonialism of the special kind that prevailed in South Africa. The contrary conclusions of the Supreme Court illustrate both the new relevance of international law in South African domestic law and the sad fact that the inherited judiciary may still be ill-equipped to handle these new demands.

American international lawyer J J Paust has described the suppression of the political authority of the people as a form of political slavery constituting "treason against humanity." Armed and other resistance to apartheid's denial of self-determination was not only morally necessary and legitimate; it was also completely in accord with international law. The regime's conduct, which stood in the way of this right to self-determination, was not.

4. General Criminality of Apartheid

According to well-established principles of international law, apartheid was intrinsically illegal. "From the start," wrote Albie Sachs, presently a Judge of the new South Africa's Constitutional Court, the old South Africa's constitution "went beyond merely sanctioning or condoning racism and it expressly stipulated that South Africa should be a racist state founded on principles of minority rule."[15] This was unique. Injustice occurs in many countries, but only in South Africa was such a major injustice enshrined in the constitution.

This fact was formally acknowledged by the international community when in 1973 the UN General Assembly specifically adopted the International Convention on the Suppression and Punishment of the Crime of Apartheid (the Convention), which entered into force on July 1976 and by September 1984 had been ratified by or acceded to by 79 states.

The Convention defined "the crime of apartheid" to include the upholding of racial supremacy by: the denial of the right to life and liberty of the person; the infliction of "serious bodily or mental harm" or the infringement of freedom or dignity, or using torture or cruel, inhuman or degrading treatment or punishment; or the arbitrary arrest or illegal imprisonment of a racial group.

Additionally, the crime of apartheid includes the deliberate imposition on a racial group of living conditions calculated to cause the group's physical destruction in whole or part. It also includes legislative and other measures excluding racial groups from participation in the political, social, economic and cultural life of the country and the deliberate creation of conditions preventing the full development of such groups, including the denial of a range of basic human rights, such as for example the rights of free movement and residence, free assembly and association, or the right to a nationality.

The crime of apartheid also includes legislative and other measures designed to divide the population along racial lines "by the creation of separate reserves or racial ghettos," the prohibition of mixed marriages, or the implementation of a policy of race-based expropriations of property. The crime also includes the exploitation of the labour of members of racial groups, in particular by submitting them to forced labour; it includes persecution of organisational or individual opponents of apartheid.

The foregoing categories of acts are crimes under international law. While states were required by international law to make such types of behaviour criminal offences, apartheid's rulers institutionalised them.

The Convention did not bind only those who ratified it. Its effect was to confirm the existence of standards in international law, forbidding any state to deny individual or collective human rights solely on the grounds of race. The Convention confirms, in the specific context of apartheid, the well-established general principle of individual responsibility for crimes against humanity.

Such was the international revulsion at apartheid that it received the specific attention of the prestigious International Law Commission in its Draft Articles on state responsibility, which distinguished between wrongful acts by states (resulting in civil liability) and international crimes. The latter included every "internationally wrongful act which results from the breach by a state of an international obligation so essential for the protection of fundamental interests of the international community that its breach is recognised as a crime by that community as a whole." Among the specific examples of international crimes given by the commission was: "a serious breach on a widespread scale of an international obligation of essential importance for safeguarding the human being, such as those prohibiting slavery, genocide, *apartheid*" (emphasis added).

Likewise apartheid offends the *jus cogens* which according to the International Court of Justice constitutes "peremptory norms" and obligations that "derive, for example, in contemporary international law, from the outlawing of acts of aggression, and of genocide, as also from the principles and rules concerning the basic rights of the human person, including the protection from slavery and racial discrimination."[16]

The authoritative American Law Institute in its *Restatement of Law: Foreign Relations of the USA* has accepted since 1985 that a systematic policy of racial discrimination is a violation not only of international law, but also of the *jus cogens*.

According to the 1973 Convention, liability for the international crime of apartheid extends to those who "commit, participate in, directly incite or conspire in the commission of" acts constitutive of apartheid as outlined above. Moreover, international criminal responsibility applies, "irrespective of the motive involved, to individuals, members of organisations, and institutions and representatives of the state," whether residing within the state or elsewhere. It extends to those who directly aided, abetted, encouraged or cooperated in the commission of the crime of apartheid. This includes trade and industrial and financial collaboration.

Those who administered the Group Areas legislation and the mass resettlement schemes, those who denied basic rights of association and freedom of expression, those who carried out torture or operated the bantustan policy, those who invested in apartheid and traded with it, are guilty of the crime of apartheid under international law.

In addition, the apartheid bureaucracy systematically engaged in torture, which in itself is a distinct crime recognised in international law, in for instance the UN Convention on Torture.

Apart from this diverse pattern of systematic and generalised criminality, the principles of international criminality – codified in the Nuremberg Principles as adopted by the UN General Assembly after the anti-Nazi war – reveal several distinct strands of criminality, each of which is discussed in turn below in relation to apartheid.

5. Apartheid As a Crime Against Peace

Unsurprisingly for a warlord state, the apartheid bureaucracy fell foul of international norms and laws designed to secure peaceful co-existence among nations.

In its own defence, the apartheid regime demanded that "the West" recognise the vital role that South Africa was allegedly playing in the regional battle against communism, and hence that the West should refrain from imposing sanctions and accept apartheid.

The international response was, in general, unobliging. In 1980 the Security Council, in its Resolutions 466 and 475, condemned the apartheid bureaucracy's "unprovoked" acts in violation of the sovereignty, airspace and territorial integrity of Zambia and Angola. In 1984, the Security Council's Resolution 546 referred to the "unprovoked bombing and persistent acts of aggression . . . committed by the racist regime of South Africa." By 1986, it was said with every justification that

Southern Africa has become a battleground. To maintain itself in power the apartheid regime has engaged in a massive process of militarisation. This has equipped it to continue its illegal occupation of Namibia, to extend its hold over the region by attacking other states, and to deploy military and police forces in order to suppress resistance in South Africa itself.[17]

According to the Nuremberg Principles, "planning, preparation, initiation or waging of a war of aggression or a war in violation of international agreements or assurances" constitutes a crime against peace. The Principles specifically provide that the mere fact of acting or claiming to act as a government official on behalf of the state will not exculpate the criminal.

"Aggression" is a crucial element in the international crime of a threat to peace. The United Nations Charter gives the UN Security Council a key role in resolving the existence of this element of criminality. A Security Council finding of a "threat to peace" operates, as a trigger under Article 39 of the UN Charter, to bring into play a whole range of binding Security Council actions against the aggressor. The internal politics of the Security Council, which were not always representative of the views of the majority of UN Member States, and which could result in the use of veto powers by some members of the Council, enlarged the obstacles in the way of this specific finding. Yet the Security Council repeatedly made it clear that the apartheid regime was, in substance, a threat to peace.

The Security Council for instance described the South African situation as "one that has led to international friction and if continued might endanger international peace and security" (1960 Resolution 134). It pronounced itself "convinced that the situation in South Africa is seriously disturbing international peace and security" (1963 Resolution 181). It said that "the situation resulting from the continued application of the policies of apartheid . . . constitutes a potential threat to international peace and security" (1970 Resolution 282).

Ultimately, the Security Council straightforwardly determined in 1977 (by its Resolution 418) that the continued supply of arms to the apartheid regime constituted a "threat to peace" and it imposed an international arms embargo. This was an unprecedented action under Chapter VII of the Charter against a UN member state.

A related area of apartheid's disregard for international law was in the regime's cynical resort to an alleged right of "hot pursuit" as it crossed borders with impunity in order to attack or detain civilians, refugees and liberation soldiers alike. In fact, the doctrine of "hot pursuit" is a concept of maritime law, inapplicable to incursions over land borders. It only protects the right of a state to pursue offenders beyond its own territorial waters and into the open sea, that is, into a place where no state is sovereign. The right does not extend to incursions over a land border into the territory of other states.

Additionally, the right of hot pursuit cannot be seen as an aspect of self-defence because according to Article 51 of the United Nations that concept is confined to repelling "armed attack." A claim of self-defence cannot be used to justify a pre-emptive attack, but only to justify rebuffing an actual one. Valid acts of self-defence must be confined to measures reasonably necessary for repelling the alleged danger.

The South African version of hot pursuit was to eliminate or kidnap opponents of the regime and to attack camps run by the liberation movements (whether camps for training soldiers or camps for refugees) in foreign countries. The regime also attempted to damage the morale of the allies of the liberation movement and reduce their capacity to assist, even though this assistance never involved armed support of any kind. The apartheid regime's claims that its hot pursuit operations were covered by a broader right to self-defence have generally been met with disapproval.

In any event, the validity of such claims is nullified by the recognised illegitimacy of the regime, which deprived it of any right to self-defence. The soldiers of the resistance had every right in international law to take their armed activities across the borders of friendly states and into South Africa.

Finally, the apartheid bureaucracy's attacks on its neighbours cannot be justified on the grounds that those neighbours were giving aid and comfort to the anti-apartheid resistance, because such assistance was not merely permissible under international law; it was actually required.

Following the apartheid regime's 1982 attack on Lesotho, the UN Security Council unanimously reaffirmed (Resolution 527) "the right of Lesotho to receive and give sanctuary to the victims of apartheid in accordance with its international obligations." On 21 June 1985, following the apartheid bureaucracy's attack on a number of houses in the capital of Botswana, the Security Council passed a similar Resolution (568) affirming the right of Botswana to "give sanctuary to the victims of apartheid, in accordance with its traditional practice, humanitarian principles and international obligations."

The further unanimity of the Security Council on a number of similar occasions is significant. The Council's 1977 Resolution 411 unanimously condemned a number of allegedly "hot pursuit" raids by the illegal regime into the then Rhodesia and urged "all states to intensify assistance to the people of Zimbabwe and their national liberation movement in their struggle to achieve self-determination and independence."

Additionally, responding to an apartheid attack on, and occupation of, parts of Angola, the Security Council, in its Resolution 454 in the early eighties, expressed concern at the "premeditated, persistent and sustained armed invasions committed by South Africa on Angola." This was a flat rejection of the idea that the invasions were immediate responses in the nature of "hot pursuit," required by the exigencies of the situation. In its 1985 Resolution 568, the Security Council left nothing to conjecture. It explicitly "denounced and rejected" the apartheid bureaucracy's "practice of hot pursuit."

Resolution 454 also stated, unambiguously, "that these acts of aggression by South Africa form a consistent and sustained pattern of violations aimed at weakening the unrelenting support given by the front-line states to the movements for freedom and liberation of the peoples of Namibia and Zimbabwe." The United Nations Security Council thus explicitly attributed the fault for that conflict to the apartheid regime.

6. Apartheid's Crimes Against Humanity.

The concept of a crime against humanity is not merely a factual description of the Holocaust, confined forever to that atrocity alone. Rather it is a legal concept, containing conceptual and factual elements. Under international law, crimes against humanity include: "Murder, extermination, enslavement, deportation and other inhuman acts done against any civilian population; or persecutions on racial or religious grounds, when such acts are done or such persecutions are carried out in execution of or in connection with any crime against peace or any war crime."

Such acts remain crimes against humanity whether or not they violated the applicable domestic law.

Apartheid's functionaries, without lawful excuse, deprived many thousands of South Africans, Namibians and others of their liberty and property and even their lives. They robbed people of their dignity by perpetuating, without lawful excuse, a system of gross racial discrimination and inequality. They killed entirely outside of the law (and outside even of the mock "legality" offered by their own unlawful courts). They tortured and maimed and embarked on a programme of genocide and violent forced resettlements which could in no event be legal.

They are thus guilty of many crimes under several legal systems, but the scale and gravity of the atrocities require recognition of the fact that these disparate offences add up to a systematic whole that is more than the sum of its parts: a systematic crime against humanity.

Some have suggested that the alleged reluctance of certain Western states to acknowledge that apartheid was a crime against humanity throws the legal soundness of the claim into question. This actually misstates the overall voting record of the West on this question. But more importantly, it misunderstands the nature and sources of international law.

International law is built on a combination of the longstanding practice of states, international organs and multinational bodies. According to the founding statute of the International Court of Justice, international law is to be found in international conventions, customs, general principles of law, as well as in the teachings of learned authors. International law is a cumulative and gradual process in which binding customary rules arise through consensus over time, in the absence of persistent dissent.

Since apartheid offended the *jus cogens*, the inviolable core of international law which no state is competent to disregard, the persistent dissent of the apartheid regime itself is wholly beside the point. More important is the practice of the organs and member states of the United Nations as a whole. In this regard the position could not be clearer. United Nations member states, organs and multilateral forums and institutions at all levels were unambiguous and consistent in their characterisations of apartheid as a crime against humanity, as the following examples, which could be multiplied, illustrate:

In December 1966, for the first time, the United Nations General Assembly condemned "the policies of apartheid practised by the Government of South Africa as a crime against humanity." The General Assembly "reiterated" this position in December 1968; and in December 1970 it declared that apartheid policies "are a negation of the Charter of the United Nations and constitute a crime against humanity."

In November 1973, a General Assembly Resolution observed that the United Nations, in its Convention abolishing the statute of limitations in relation to war crimes and crimes against humanity, qualified "inhuman acts arising from the policy of apartheid" as crimes against humanity. The same resolution promulgated the International Convention on the Suppression and Punishment of the Crime of Apartheid. That Convention itself declared that "apartheid is a crime against humanity."

In November 1983, the General Assembly reaffirmed that "apartheid is a crime against humanity," a conclusion that was noted in – and that provided a basis for – the General Assembly's Programme of Action Against Apartheid, adopted by the General Assembly the following month. Similarly, the General Assembly's 1985 International Convention Against Apartheid in Sports noted that "sports exchanges with teams selected on the basis of apartheid directly abet and encourage the commission of the crime of apartheid" as defined in the 1973 Convention.

In November 1989, the General Assembly, in a formal resolution calling for comprehensive mandatory sanctions against the South African regime, reaffirmed that "apartheid is a crime against humanity." In December 1990, ten months after the release of Nelson Mandela, the General Assembly noted that in spite of the beginnings of political transition, "the system of apartheid and most of its main pillars, namely, the Land Acts, the Group Areas Act, the Population Registration Act, the Bantu Education Act and the acts establishing the tricameral Parliament and the bantustan system remain intact." The General Assembly expressly reaffirmed that "apartheid is a crime against the conscience and dignity of mankind."

In December 1989, the General Assembly adopted its comprehensive "Declaration on Apartheid and Its Destructive Consequences in Southern Africa," which affirmed that apartheid, "a crime against the conscience and dignity of mankind, is responsible for the death of countless numbers of people in South Africa, has sought to dehumanise entire peoples and has imposed a brutal war on the region of southern Africa, which has resulted in untold loss of life, destruction of property and massive displacement of innocent men, women and children and which is a scourge and affront to humanity that must be fought and eradicated in its entirety."

The UN Security Council also joined in such assessments of apartheid. On 19 June, 1976, following the Soweto uprising, it reaffirmed "that the policy of apartheid is a crime against the conscience and dignity of mankind." In October 1977 the Security Council strongly condemned "the South African racist regime for its resort to massive violence and repression against the Black people, who constitute the great majority of the country, as well as all other opponents of apartheid." In June 1980, the Security Council reaffirmed that "apartheid is a crime against the conscience and dignity of mankind" and condemned "the repression and killing of schoolchildren." And in article 1 of Security Council Resolution 556, passed on 13 December 1984, the Security Council declared that apartheid is a crime against humanity.

United Nations conferences and other international fora and organs of all kinds adopted consistent views and recommended action premised on explicit acceptance of the authoritative and prevailing assessment of apartheid as a crime against humanity. Thus the programme of action adopted by the UN's April 1973 Oslo Conference of Experts for the Support of Victims of Colonialism and Apartheid in Southern Africa was based on the express view that there was a need to respond to apartheid, "which is a crime against humanity, a flagrant violation of the principles of the United Nations and a massive and ruthless denial of human rights."

The Lagos Declaration for Action Against Apartheid, adopted in August 1977 by the UN World Conference for Action Against Apartheid, premised its action on the view that apartheid "is a crime against the conscience and dignity of mankind." The 1981 Declaration of the UN International Conference on Sanctions Against South Africa strongly condemned "the minority racist regime of South Africa for its criminal policies and actions" and declared that an international "consensus has emerged on the fact that apartheid is a crime against the conscience and dignity of mankind." The 1982 Brussels Declaration of the UN International Conference on Women and Apartheid declared "that apartheid, especially as it affects women and children, is an international crime and an intolerable affront to the conscience of mankind." It continued:

> The Pretoria regime has subjected the women of South Africa to oppression and humiliation, including forced deportations and separations of families. It has killed, imprisoned, restricted and tortured numerous women and children for opposing apartheid. It has committed repeated acts of aggression in southern Africa and even bombed refugee camps in neighbouring independent African states, killing women and children.

The 1983 Geneva Declaration of the UN International Conference of Trade Unions likewise recalled that "apartheid has been declared a crime against humanity" and condemned "employers and investors in South Africa who directly or indirectly help to maintain the apartheid system and are collaborating with the apartheid regime in the military and nuclear fields and with its security forces." Likewise the June 1986 Paris Declaration of the World Conference on Sanctions Against Racist South Africa declared that "apartheid is not only a crime against the people of South Africa and Namibia, but one of universal concern. The General Assembly has condemned the policy of apartheid as a crime against humanity."

The cumulative effect of this impressively consistent web of international practice is to place beyond the shadow of a doubt the conclusion that apartheid constituted a crime against humanity and against the conscience and dignity of mankind. Claims to the contrary are unscholarly and constitute, at best, a form of defensive political rhetoric designed to sugar-coat the unpalatable. The characterisation of apartheid as a crime against humanity was not an exotic idea propagated by a small group of Third World and communist states. Rather, over a long period, the conclusion reflected the deliberative processes and juridical conscience of humanity. It was the world's verdict on apartheid.

Moreover, the simple human truth, which should not be abandoned in an overly scholastic exchange, is that apartheid denied the equal worth of humans and treated vast categories of South Africans as sub-human; this implies that billions of people of similar colour all over the world are also sub-human. "That is why," Nelson Mandela said in addressing the UN Special Committee Against Apartheid in June 1990, it is "correct to characterise apartheid as a crime against humanity," a crime which he described at that time as a continuing one.

The Special Committee's Report in November 1992 concurred, pointing out that while many apartheid laws had at that stage recently been dismantled, "the legacy of apartheid continues to pose a threat to the process of democratisation."

A full factual picture of apartheid's crimes against humanity involves consideration not only of the direct physical acts of individuals, but also of legislative, judicial and administrative acts covering the period subject to investigation by the Truth and Reconciliation Commission. It involves, for instance, examination of the South African variant of the Nazi "desk murderers," the middle and low level officials who produced infamy out of a series of banal daily routines.

7. Apartheid's War Crimes

According to the Nuremberg principles, war crimes are defined as:

Violations of the laws or customs of war which include, but are not limited to, the murder, ill-treatment or deportation to slave labour, or for any other purpose, of the civilian population of or in occupied territory, murder or ill-treatment of prisoners of war or persons on the seas, killing of hostages, plunder of public or private property, wanton destruction of cities, towns or villages or devastation not justified by military necessity.

The applicability of the humanitarian rules of war to conflicts between an incumbent state and a national liberation movement fighting for self-determination is clearly accepted. The Protocols to the 1977 Geneva Conventions are intended to apply to such a conflict and were subscribed to by the ANC in 1980. Although the apartheid state did not ratify the relevant Protocol, that Protocol merely codified pre-existing contemporary law on the subject. Thus both belligerents in South Africa were under an obligation to treat the conflict as one governed by the laws of war. Under Article 85 paragraph 5 of the Geneva Protocol, "grave breaches" of the Convention and Protocol constitute war crimes.

Clearly, captured members of the ANC should have been treated as prisoners of war. This is confirmed by a number of resolutions of the United Nations

General Assembly, such as Resolution 2506(A) passed in 1969, which stated that anti-apartheid fighters who fell prisoner to the apartheid regime were entitled to humane treatment in line with the principles stated in the Geneva Convention relating to the treatment of prisoners of war. Later, on 12 October 1974, the General Assembly adopted a declaration on South Africa (Resolution 34/93) which, among other things, specifically demanded that the apartheid regime treat captured members of the anti-apartheid resistance as prisoners of war under the 1949 Geneva Conventions and Additional Protocol I thereto.

Yet the apartheid regime consistently refused to accept these obligations. It subjected ANC cadres to ill-treatment, interrogation, torture, criminal trial, punishment and even death, all of which were illegal under the Protocol, and most of which were repugnant to any true civilised standard. In addition, such conduct fell foul of the United Nations Convention against Torture and Other Cruel, Inhuman or Degrading Treatment or Punishment. Those who committed the crime of torture cannot claim in mitigation that they were acting on superior orders. Truth commissions in other countries have refused amnesty to those who committed this crime.

It was not only armed MK combatants who suffered illegal treatment. Apartheid's abuses of the civilian population were also war crimes. Responsibility here attaches not only to the security forces but also to the leadership of the executive, judicial and administrative branches of the outlaw state. Apartheid functionaries locked up young children in morgues in order to terrify them; brutalised and raped women detainees; indulged in crude physical violence, or learnt sophisticated methods of torture which left no physical mark. Others gave instruction in methods of torture, bought the electrical instruments and other implements, went out on random township sweeps to catch the detainees.

Prison doctors heard the accounts of torture, examined the victims, and sometimes treated them so that the torture could continue. Judges criminally legitimised entire structures of violence. They held "trials within trials" to establish whether confessions that had been extorted through detention could nevertheless be admitted as evidence; often, they were. A specialised corps of judges heard many of these so-called security and detention cases and presided over political trials.

Parliament facilitated all this through its legislation allowing first 60 days, then 90 days, then an unlimited period during which detainees could be held without access to their families, to a lawyer, to their own doctor. No reason for the detention had to be given, and in later years the practice was extended to cover not only those who were suspected of having participated in the resistance to apartheid, but also to any potential witness. All this was criminal under international law.

8. Apartheid's Genocide

Apartheid's systematic policies of forced removal and resettlement created dumping grounds for human beings, almost uniformly leaving them at a far remove from the normal incidents and necessities of social and economic life. These locations foreseeably bred disease and death. And even physical survival had its deadening side, since there was little possibility of well-functioning social institutions. There could be no community life in these places; there were no town squares. Those who survived the genocide faced the walking death, the empty life, of what one international lawyer has called "sociocide."

This sociocidal process was present also in the townships, where little effort was made to create cohesive communities; and where housing, schooling and recreation were segregated along tribal lines, in a manner designed to advance the divide-and-rule strategies of apartheid. But the dumping grounds took sociocide to particular extremes. The bureaucrats who decided where to site these camps seemed motivated by a desire to use the sheer uninhabitable qualities of the chosen terrain and the calculated lack of essential facilities as a distinct strategy for the subjugation of people placed in these camps.

At a more prosaic level, there was often simply no water. The nature and extent of disease were themselves the best indications of the shortage of water, or clean water, in these dumping grounds. A doctor's report on the Limehill resettlement camp, published in 1969, explicitly noted that "from the disease we saw it as self-evident that the water and waste-disposal facilities are inadequate."[18] It is common medical wisdom that the very proliferation of diseases such as typhoid reflects extreme dereliction of standards of hygiene; the disease speaks for itself. Likewise, nutritional diseases such as kwashiorkor reflect social conditions.

Since, according to the logic of apartheid, the camps themselves were facilities for the disposal of superfluous human beings, the need to provide this surplusage with means to dispose of its own waste must have seemed nonsensical – like supplying a rubbish dump with pretty dustbins.

The lack of water and sanitation led specifically to unnatural levels of disease and death. There was a high incidence of typhoid, bronchial pneumonia, the nutritional problems of riboflavine deficiency, pellagra, scurvy, as well as rickets, rabies, worm infestation, gastro-enteritis and tuberculosis. There was an absence of systematic immunisation against diseases such as diphtheria, whooping cough, tetanus and smallpox.

Diarrhoea, the cause of 50.9 per cent of total South African mortality from infectious disease during the apartheid years, was predominantly caused by a lack of satisfactory sanitation and clean water. One study found that there was a 47 to 48-fold greater risk of dying from diarrhoeal disease among blacks and Coloureds than there was among whites, reflecting the racially skewed provision of water and sanitation facilities.[19]

In such circumstances, even pregnancy could seem an ailment, raising the prospect of maternal death in childbirth – and, of course, unnatural levels of infant mortality. Maternity facilities – properly equipped places to go in order to deliver newborn human beings – were simply absent.

Ultimately, the resettlement camps not only proved to be death-inducing but also, deliberately, invisible. In 1968, the regime removed kwashiorkor from the list of notifiable diseases, thus removing the obligation of the medical profession to inform the authorities of all such cases. Government collected infant mortality data on white, Coloured and Asian babies; information on deaths of African infants was ignored, the job falling by default to the nongovernmental sector.

Similarly, the regime's invention of "national states" in depressed rural areas such as Transkei, Ciskei, Venda and Bophuthatswana, enabled it to remove embarrassing levels of the incidence of disease from the health statistics of its conveniently redefined "South Africa."

One analyst calculated in 1989 that if "currently available interventions for infectious disease had been equitably applied throughout South Africa, over 80% of deaths to date due to diarrhoeal disease, measles and poliomyelitis could have been prevented."[20]

A deadly wall of deliberate official blindness allowed responsible officials to boast, for instance, that not one African in South Africa was starving. Meanwhile, in reality, starvation was widespread. In 1976, for instance, 65 per cent of children under 5 years of age in the Eastern Cape township of Mdantsane were malnourished.[21] Camp dwellers urged visitors to photograph them – they offered themselves almost as pieces of evidence, yearning for a recognition of the true nature of the system in the face of official denials: "Take all of us, we are all starving. How could we be anything but starving in these conditions." One observer tells of meeting a 35-year-old woman who weighed 50 lb and who had been on the verge of killing and eating her sixteen-month-old baby when she was admitted to hospital.[22]

In 1979 infant mortality among whites was 16.6 per 1,000 live births.[23] For blacks in rural areas the comparable figure was at least 220 per 1,000, reaching many more in some areas.[24] According to a Grahamstown municipal report in 1977, African infant mortality rates in that urban area were 378 per 1,000 live births; the comparable figure for whites was 27 deaths per 1,000 live births.[24] In 1989, nearly one in five youngsters died before reaching the age of 5, with nine African children, two Asian and five Coloured children dying for every white child.[25]

While the appropriate standard for judging apartheid is to compare white luxury to the black deprivation and death on which it was directly parasitic, many apologists for apartheid preferred irrelevant comparisons of black living conditions in South Africa with those elsewhere in Africa. Yet even by this self-serving standard, the infant mortality figures tell a powerful story.

In countries where per capita income and national wealth were well below that present in apartheid South Africa, black babies were actually more likely to survive than in wealthier South Africa. According to a UNICEF Report in 1989, *Children on the Front Line*, infant death rates within the narrowly drawn boundaries of the apartheid Republic of South Africa (excluding the so-called homelands, where rural poverty and dumping grounds are concentrated) ranged from 94 to 124 per 100 live births. This was substantially worse than the national average in Botswana (72), Zimbabwe and Kenya (76), the Congo (77), Tunisia (78), Algeria (81) and Zambia (84). It is impossible to set the parameters more favourably to apartheid; and still it comes out wanting.

Rates of black death in the dumping grounds, the resettlement camps, were substantially higher than in traditional rural areas or urban areas. According to UNICEF, infants and children were subject to a threefold higher risk of dying in these camps than in traditional or urban areas. So the resettlement strategies – and the camps it bred – were an efficient killing machinery.

While whites were encouraged to breed more white babies, and white immigration from elsewhere was frantically encouraged, black women were offered contraceptive injections and even sometimes sterilised without their knowledge or consent, in a procedure reminiscent of Nazi eugenics.

It is not hyperbole, if anything it verges on understatement, to note that systems of apartheid are forms of genocide. And this is indeed the unambiguous verdict of international law. Eminent international lawyer and Professor at Princeton University in the United States, Richard Falk, noted after a 1987 Harare Conference on Children, Repression and the Law in Apartheid South Africa, that "the South African government has declared war on the black children of the country. This deliberate targeting of the young has *no precedent* in the sordid history of repressive politics"[26] (emphasis added).

The Convention on the Suppression and Punishment of the Crime of Apartheid of 1973 expressly notes, in its preamble, that several of the defining elements of apartheid conform also to the defining elements of the separate crime of genocide, as defined in the Convention for the Prevention and Punishment of the Crime of Genocide.

Genocide refers primarily to the planned, systematic extermination, on racial, ethnic or national grounds, of entire human groups such as Gypsies, Jews or Slavs. However, it extends to all kinds of measures that fall short of direct killing but that are calculated to destroy national culture, political rights, and national will in the context of a struggle for national liberation and self-determination. While the point has been heatedly debated, the sound view is that there need only be foresight that deaths will be a logical result of the genocidal act; there need not necessarily be a specific intention to cause deaths.

Article 11 of the Convention defines genocide to include: (a) killing members of the group; (b) causing serious bodily or mental harm to the group; (c) deliberately inflicting on the group conditions of life calculated to bring about its physical destruction in whole or in part; (d) imposing measures intended to prevent births in the group; (e) forcibly transferring children of the group to another group.

Liability extends to conspiracy, attempts and direct and public incitement to commit genocide as well as "complicity in genocide." The role of family planning authorities under apartheid would make an interesting study under this heading, especially in the light of the persistent and explicit concern of policy-makers, throughout the apartheid era, to contain what were seen as excessive fertility rates among blacks as compared to whites. The ordinary concerns of population control necessarily take on a sinister aspect where a government is, as the apartheid government was, specifically concerned to redress a perceived racial imbalance, adverse to white supremacy, in growth rates.

The violation of the right to life on an extensive scale by the apartheid bureau-cracy, the violations of the physical and mental integrity of black people, espe-cially through mass deportations and mass removals of citizenship, and the adoption of administrative and economic policies that resulted in the large-scale and early deaths of children, were integral parts of the policy of apartheid. The legal infrastructure of apartheid was such that it inevitably inflicted mental and bodily harm (including death) on targeted racial and ethnic groups.

A 1985 Report of an *Ad Hoc* Working Group of Experts appointed by the United Nations Commission on Human Rights reported on what it considered a previously "hidden aspect of apartheid" and concluded that apartheid was "not simply a crime against humanity but a series of acts of genocide" and was "insidiously assuming a number of the forms of genocide."

Both the Anti-Apartheid and Genocide Conventions impute criminal respon-sibility "irrespective of the motive involved, to individuals, members of organi-sations and institutions and representatives of the state, whether residing in the territory of the state in which the acts are perpetrated or in some other state." The genocidal effects of apartheid, and the culpability in international law of those who inflicted the acts and policies of apartheid, are beyond doubt.

9. Summing Up

The doctrines and principles of international law that are the basis for the above indictment of apartheid are no empty claims to be brushed aside now that the anti-apartheid struggle is largely behind us. As American jurist Robert Cover has astutely observed, law is always written in the currency of blood, and this is especially so in the case of South Africa. Members of South Africa's mass democratic movement, the grassroots anti-apartheid resistance of the 1980s, lit-erally paid for freedom in suffering and death. The Front Line States too sacri-ficed the blood of their people in order to see a new southern African, regional and international legal order brought into being.

Farther away, the anti-apartheid solidarity movement united masses of people in large protests in capital cities and small towns across the globe. Despite apartheid's best efforts to sow racial hatred and division, its actual effect was ironically to galvanise one of the century's most moving global and collective campaigns for a better world. The footprints of those times are left now in the legal principles that the international anti-apartheid resistance movement gen-erated and refined in coming to grips with the enormous evil that it confronted.

Not all lawyers accept the relevance of international law, or accept the bind-ing force of the utterances of the various international organs. However, it has long been recognised that international law is a decentralised system which must harmonise, as well as influence, the undoubted sovereignty of individual member states subject to it. There are also potential questions about what it means for a state to be "subject to" a system of laws where that system lacks compulsory jurisdiction over those it would govern and thus depends to an extent on voluntary compliance, or at least voluntary acknowledgment of its binding force. One feature of this relative voluntarism of international law is that the system lacks automatically applicable enforcement procedures.

Such observations raise complex jurisprudential questions that go to the heart of the concept of law. Even in domestic legal systems, enforcement of many laws (e.g. against bigamy, jaywalking, prostitution, tax evasion) is a selective process. So it is enough to say here that international anti-apartheid law and norms, especially in the area of the fundamentally core principles, the *jus cogens*, of which apartheid fell foul, had a normative (i.e. standard-setting) bindingness that was independent of the international community's actual resources of enforcement, or its fluctuating inclination to enforce them.

In fact of course the international community did mount a highly effective enforcement effort against apartheid in the form of the various boycotts and sanctions initiatives, including a UN Security Council-mandated arms embargo in 1977. The important point, however, is that the bindingness of international law and norms in relation to apartheid remained independent of, and did not fluctuate in tandem with, the efficacy of enforcement of those laws and norms.

Their validity was always a separate matter from their efficacy. Even in rare periods when, for whatever reasons of *realpolitik* or simple distraction, global anti-apartheid enforcement measures flagged, the laws and norms still spoke clearly. And they must speak clearly now, in the domestic law and politics of the new South Africa, where the resources of enforcement and of political will at the disposal of the former anti-apartheid resistance are unprecedented.

As to the relative weight of international institutions in international law, it is somewhat predictable that those international organs that wield the most authority (such as the UN Security Council) tend to be those that dispropor-tionately represent the powerful nations. There is for instance a well-established practice, in international neo-conservative circles, of belittling the determina-tions of the United Nations General Assembly. This was a practice at which suc-cessive apartheid governments themselves excelled; and which their apologists today still have not abandoned.

The apartheid regime attempted to deny the international authority of the United Nations. However, this attempt was rebuffed in a variety of ways. For instance, the International Court of Justice held in a 1950 Advisory Opinion that "the General Assembly of the United Nations is legally qualified to exercise the supervisory functions previously exercised by the League of Nations with regard to the administration of [Namibia] and that [South Africa] is under an obligation to submit to supervision and control of the General Assembly and to render reports to it."

The first attempt to end South Africa's mandate over Namibia failed when the International Court of Justice rejected the case brought by Ethiopia and Liberia, on the ground that these countries lacked the requisite legal standing. The 1966 Resolution 2145 (XXI) of the General Assembly of the United Nations, calling for the termination of South Africa's mandate, failed to have an effect.

However, in 1969 the Security Council decided that the "continuing occupation of the Territory of Namibia by the South African authorities constitutes an aggressive encroachment on the authority of the United Nations." Finally in 1970 the Security Council straightforwardly declared continued South African presence in Namibia illegal. No western power exercised its veto. Apartheid was virtually at war with the world.

The ICJ said that the Security Council's determination of the illegality of South Africa's occupation of Namibia "cannot remain without consequence" and that Member States had an obligation "to bring that situation to an end." Resolution 276 in 1970 imposed on Member States "an obligation to abstain from entering into economic and other forms of relationship or dealing with South Africa" that might entrench its authority over Namibia.

Security Council Resolution 301 in 1971 in turn "adopted" the ICJ's Advisory Opinion and, among other things, declared that franchises, rights, titles or contracts relating to Namibia and granted by South Africa after the General Assembly Resolution of 27 October 1966 would not be protected or espoused by Member States against claims of a future Namibian government. International developments in response to apartheid's expansionism thus touched on basic issues of property rights.

These developments also laid the groundwork for international legal endorsement of the comprehensive sanctions and coordinated boycotts that were aimed not only at South Africa's illegal cross-border adventures but also at apartheid itself.

So, as the United Nations effectively asserted normative jurisdiction over the conduct of the apartheid regime, a double battle was under way: it was as much a struggle for the heart and soul of the United Nations as it was a movement against the apartheid regime itself. With an important 1971 judgment of the International Court of Justice, the dust settled and it became clear that the anti-apartheid resistance had won significant gains. The ICJ's Advisory Opinion upheld the competence of the United Nations to terminate the South African mandate over Namibia because of South Africa's "deliberate and persistent violation of obligations" under that mandate.

Furthermore, in a finding that remains of extreme general importance for the institutional status and bindingness of the UN General Assembly's positions, the ICJ declared that it would not be correct to assume that "because the General Assembly is in principle vested with recommendatory powers it is debarred from adopting, in specific cases within the framework of its competence, resolutions which *make determinations or have operative design*" (emphasis added). In short, the ICJ declared that the General Assembly had real teeth; there were things that it could actually do. Apartheid's own international conduct gave impetus to the very institutional and legal developments that would be part of its eventual undoing. In December 1983, for instance, the General Assembly adopted an exhaustive "Programme of Action Against Apartheid," detailing and urging action by governments, specialised agencies and other intergovernmental organisations, by trade unions, churches, anti-apartheid and solidarity movements, other nongovernmental organisations, individuals, the Secretary General of the United Nations, the Special Committee Against Apartheid and the UN Centre Against Apartheid. The common theme of this detailed action plan was the complete isolation of apartheid in all business, cultural, sporting and other spheres.

Such was the atrocity of apartheid that opposition to it soared above smaller internecine bickerings; international institutions at all levels in the United Nations and elsewhere condemned it and acted in unprecedented ways against it. This cruelly fortunate circumstance should not, however, cloud the broader institutional issues.

A democratic South Africa owes a duty to enhance the stature and authority of international organs. The new international law, as one judge in the *Namibia Opinion* of the International Court of Justice described it, is "a law discernible from the progress of humanity, not an obsolete law, a vestige of the inequalities between man, the domination and colonisations which were rife in international relationships up to the beginning of this century but are now disappearing."

If South Africans, of all peoples, ignore or belittle the new law and institutions of the international community as we examine our past, then surely no one on earth need afterwards pay them the slightest heed. It would amount to the careless demolition of the very stepping stones that we used in order to get to where we are.

Our new constitution, expressly incorporating a basic floor of international laws and norms in its interpretation clause, doubly bolsters both our own constitutional security and also the authority of international law.

Similarly, the Truth and Reconciliation Commission, by looking to the wisdom of international precepts as a guide to its conclusions, will bolster its own domestic authority along with the authority of those global precepts that were a feature of the country's deliverance from what went before.

To preserve and keep faith with these fragile international footprints of idealism, the Truth and Reconciliation Commission needs to make a formal finding in each of the international categories of criminality into which apartheid fell. It should issue considered determinations in its final report that apartheid South Africa committed specific war crimes, such as the brutal post-surrender murder in the Western Cape of MK combatant Ashley Kriel, who was shot in the head, point-blank, while kneeling immobilised in his own home where he had been apprehended; or the point-blank slaughter, also in the Western Cape, of the resistance soldiers known as the Guguletu Seven; the crimes multiply.

The Truth and Reconciliation Commission should validate and acknowledge the right of resisters such as these to have risen up in exercising their right to self-determination. The parents of the Guguletu Seven, confronted in the mid-eighties by the apartheid government's accusations that their children were "terrorists" lying in wait to ambush the security forces, staunchly denied these allegations, insisting that their sons would not ever have committed crimes. Today those parents can, if they so wish, be openly proud of their sons, and in that way some of their pain may be alleviated. South African society must acknowledge, as the world has already, that their slaughtered children were simply not criminals.

The United Nations Commission on Human Rights adopted a formal resolution in March 1967 deploring the actions of the apartheid government as "contrary to international law and international morality." Behind that general and deceptively restrained statement hides the whole morass of international outlawry that has been catalogued in this chapter.

It is important that the Truth and Reconciliation Commission should issue findings that the old apartheid country committed crimes against humanity as well as acts of aggression against the front line states. It must reaffirm the nature of apartheid as a form of genocide and a crime against peace. It must validate the international community's verdict that apartheid itself, in its every embodiment, constituted a crime against humanity and lacked all legitimacy in the family of nations. Because, alas, it did.

Finding One South Africa

"There the victims parade with no mask to hide the brutish reality – the beg-gars, the prostitutes, the street children, those who seek solace in substance abuse, those who have to steal to assuage hunger, those who have to lose their sanity because to be sane is to invite pain ... Among us prowl the products of our immoral and amoral past."
 – Deputy President Thabo Mbeki upon the adoption of the new and final South African constitution in the National Assembly, 8 May 1996.

The renowned historian, commentator and critic, C L R James, wrote in 1944 of an earlier time when he had lodged in the West Indies with a woman of high propriety but little education. Mrs Roach "spoke English with the French *patois* accent of the peasant people." One day her brother, Francis, "a drinking, shuf-fling, guitar-playing idler," brought disaster to the fastidious household when his habits as a brothel-keeper came to light and to the attention of the police.

Mr Roach was the City Cashier, so this meant a terrific scandal. The constab-ulary's attention, the possibility of formal social sanction, it all seemed a confir-mation of her longstanding and accumulated doubts about the worth of Francis. Returning to his lodgings, James encountered Mrs Roach, standing in the yard outside the house, in torrential and public conversation with Francis:

She had never spoken like that before. I never heard her speak that way again. But for a moment she had uninterrupted fluency, a wonderful rhythm, dramatic pauses etc. I, a very literary person in those days, listened amazed. What caused it? Intense emotion, it was bursting in her, and a subject she knew well, had long meditated upon. At various times she had said this and thought that about Francis; other people had discussed it with her. Then under a powerful stimulus, this last disgrace, she became for the moment a poet. She was on a very high level of emotion and to batter Francis into some sort of discipline she needed a very high level of expression. She found it. Perhaps for once in her life.

This is the creative value of catharsis. Apartheid was an elaborate historical blindfold as well as a gag; its privileged were wilfully blinded, its victims forcibly muted. This is a familiar fate of the materially dispossessed: the dispossessors try to beggar them culturally too, as Bantu Education tried openly to do.

But as Edward Said has said, it is very rare for resistance to be completely sup-pressed. In apartheid South Africa cultural resistance never died; there were never smiling natives of the sort apartheid hoped to breed, content with injustice. Instead what happened was a damming up and a periodic release, as in Soweto in 1976, not an evaporation. The Truth and Reconciliation Commission should be a final cathartic dam-burst, unleashing tides of reconstruction.

This is not an unusual paradox, this idea of a flood that builds. The story of constructive floods is as old as that of Noah and his ark, except that, in today's South Africa, people must not perish. Only the old ways must get washed aside. And there must be a reuniting of the South African family with its prodigal elements. "Our parents brought us up together, Francis, spent time and money on us. But from youth you went your gambling guitar-playing way . . . You have disgraced yourself and disgraced us enough,"[1] said Mrs Roach, urging Francis to mend his ways. We must welcome Francis back, after his remorse. And after so long as a squanderer, he must help us build a real family for the first time. The whole past was a wasteful stain on South Africa's collective family name.

The custodians of apartheid were always pathetic in the strict sense of that word, despite the brute force they mustered. They longed childishly for the absence of whole groups of people, whole parts of the family, despite their manifest dependence on those same people. Despite its guns and bombs and other paraphernalia of military security, apartheid became a terrified and self-maiming flight from reality; its proponents resembled infants hugging porcupine pillows during extended nightmares.

Apartheid's moral and political surrealism had deep and longstanding roots in South Africa. In the mid-nineteenth century, one commentator noted self-reassuringly that "the history of the Cape is already written in that of America and the gradual increase of the white race must eventually though slowly ensure the disappearance of the black."[2] There was a striking anomaly: a belief that advancing civilisation would mean the certain and wholesale death of blacks. Civilisation and genocide could somehow seem two sides of the same coin.

Moreover, this advancing civilisation remained civilised even as it admittedly resorted to barbarism. In a perverse variant of the idea that all's fair in love and war, it was acceptable to stoop to barbarism in order to combat people conveniently defined as barbarians. "In dealing with barbarians such as those they were at war with [the Ndebele], the farmers had no scruples about adopting barbarous modes of attack," wrote George McCall Theal, the grand architect of traditional white South African history, in his 1902 work, *Progress of South Africa in the Century*. Theal's prolific historiography, avowedly designed to reconcile Boer and Briton in one white South African nation through a shared history, provides the governing perspective even today in many South African schools. It reinforced (and still reinforces) the intellectual roots of white supremacy, which systematic apartheid intensified but certainly did not invent.

Nobody should enter upon an analysis of South Africa's impunity in armed assaults upon its southern African neighbours in the 1980s without having at hand Theal's view, expressed one hundred years earlier, in the 1880s, that "in the nature of things, a petty barbarous government could not be allowed to do what it pleased, even within the limits of its own territory, in opposition to the interests of a powerful civilised neighbour."3

This rationale served the Cape Government in destabilising the African societies east of the Kei in the 1870s; and it served equally well a century later to justify attacks on independent nation states on the front line of the battle against apartheid. In fact, as several commentators have noted, the South African military strategy of the 1980s, the intention to play the role of regional boss, reached levels of ambition and arrogance exceeding those of the arch-imperialist Cecil John Rhodes himself.

The idea that South African history would be an unruffled replay of genocidal histories elsewhere; the fact that privileged South Africans could dream, well into the 1970s and in the teeth of vast contrary evidence, of an all-white South Africa; the fact that the short-sighted repression of the early 1960s could be duplicated in the 1980s; the fact that many privileged South Africans could view themselves as part of "western democracy" while surrounded, in Africa, by millions of voteless Africans; that they could feel themselves part of the First World threatened by the Third World barbarians at the gate; all these and other facts give force to the observation that white nationalism in South Africa "exhibits a profound, even pathological, spatio-temporal dislocation. In plain language, this nationalism prevents those in its ideological grip from understanding where they are and when they are living."4

Much of the racist legislation in South Africa early this century was common to colonies everywhere. What is intriguing about apartheid is its function as an historical time capsule and, in addition, its role in intensifying, rather than undoing, the widespread imperialist racism of earlier this century. At worst, elsewhere, repression became more subtle. Overt racism and imperialism gave way to covert racism and neo-imperialism. But not so in South Africa. Why? The privileged caste's collective unawareness of time and place is a large part of the answer.

In the 1930s, on the eve of new waves of apartheid, the liberal historian C W de Kiewiet noted that the eighteenth-century frontier lifestyle, of interracial dependence alongside virulent white supremacy, had somehow been carried over into the twentieth century. He suggested that South Africa's Union Constitution of 1909 represented "the triumph of the frontier ... It was the conviction of the frontier that the foundations of society were race and the privileges of race." He commented that "the equality which had been denied the natives in the churches of the rural Republics was again denied them in the temples of labour."5 This was a reference to the openly discriminatory labour legislation being implemented in the decades before the 1948 election, which accelerated the formalisation of apartheid.

In a grotesque spiral of forgetting time and place, the settler population (including the English settlers of Natal and elsewhere) believed itself to be re-creating Europe in a faraway land; thus the liberating possibilities of frontier existence were tainted with a corrosive racism. Africans, not part of the human landscape of Europe, could not be accommodated in this new Europe in Africa. This flaw sustained itself in the key cultural and constitutional assumptions of early twentieth-century South Africa, as well as in its land ownership regulations, labour laws, and electoral politics.

Then came the intensification of apartheid after 1948, a desperate and anachronistic lunge to recreate the imagined racial purity of the early frontier period. It had become clear, even to the mainstream media establishment in the late seventies and early eighties, that apartheid worshipped many fictions, including a belief that people could be bureaucratised out of existence, that the men and women who kept South African industry humming along, its roads tarred, and its water flowing were not people, but, as Verwoerd phrased it, units of labour.[6]

Under apartheid, black people were things; not human individuals but a collective tool for various jobs. This attitude to black workers – that they constitute more a natural than a human resource – is still with us. As recently as 1996, the Atomic Energy Corporation (AEC) attracted major controversy when, as was alleged, it had deployed casual workers to excavate a radiation-contaminated area without alerting them to the dangers and also without supplying them with protective clothing of any sort. The workers were viewed as mere disposable raw material. The AEC contracted them by way of Brits Arbeidsmakelaars, a so-called "labour exchange," whose proprietor, Piet Cronje, summed up his involvement in this way:

> It was like any other recruiting job. A company comes to me requesting a fixed amount of workers. I then go into the local townships and get the said number of workers . . . It is none of my business what their names are or where they come from or where they worked before. I just recruit workers on demand. After that they are in the hands of the company who demanded them."[7]

In March 1996, it was still possible for people to speak, with revealing bad grammar, of an "amount" of workers, as if from some human slag heap.

Even today in South Africa, the dead hand of white nationalism, with its forgetting of both time and place, remains with us. Exactly where (and when) are those few people living who still carry the old South African flag to sporting events in the new South Africa? Where (and when) are those pilots of our national airline living, still oblivious that the old H F Verwoerd dam in the middle of the country, a landmark they are fond of pointing out to passengers, is now called the Garieb in honour of the area's inhabitants. Where (and when) are those people living who proclaim grandly their property rights over land and water taken from blacks at fire-sale prices after violent forced removals?

What time are some of us living in when the former Police Commissioner urges the Truth Commission to adhere to the principle of "equality before the law" by judging his actions (and those of his subordinates) according to the moral standards allegedly prevailing in 1979, rather than 1996? What country is this when a small band of racial nationalists still seeks a race-pure Volkstaat, despite the wretchedness of the white supremacist experiment at Orania and the obviously thriving nonracial democracy that exists in a country that they are almost part of? What country (and which era) did the Conservative Party believe itself to inhabit when in 1992, at the height of the negotiations, it suggested rebanning the liberation movement and returning President Mandela to jail?

In early 1996, as already recounted, three black children turned up at a previously white school in Potgietersrus to find barricades and barbed wire and a parent with a gun blocking their way. One of these white parents commented, "It will be an uphill battle but we must fight. God warns us in the Bible about mixing race. It is only the communist government who wants this. Under no circumstances will my children mix with blacks."[8]

This woman inhabits a fanatically religious world firmly based on white supremacy and threatened by an unrepresentative communist government. Which country is this, and when? Another Potgietersrus parent, Elaine Esterhuizen, said that no one had expected change to come so quickly. They expected that tomorrow would be a different country; suddenly, today is.

Many privileged South Africans have long lived in what Dutch–American novelist Hans Koning might have called "The Almost World," a place of oblivion which exists, if at all, only in neurotic acts of rejecting reality. Some still live there. The old South Africa was, to its ideological adherents, always almost a racially pure country; it was always on the brink of that breakthrough. This old Almost World is sustained, even now in the new South Africa, by aggressive acts of denial and forgetting; by erased facts and manicured history.

White supremacist serial killer Barend Strydom, who set out in Pretoria one day in the early 1990s to shoot blacks at random, was not a lunatic, frothing at the mouth. He was a more complex phenomenon. He spoke at his trial of his early education at a veld school, one of the notorious bastions of white supremacist indoctrination. He was a natural, if hyperbolic, product of the apartheid vision.

In the mid 1980s, when the apartheid bureaucrats made a pivotal decision to fight to the end rather than seek a negotiated solution, a seasoned observer noted that "the Botha government, blind to Afrikanerdom's own history, still fondly believes it can wipe the ANC off the face of the earth, destroying it militarily and as a political force. There were British imperial pooh-bahs who held similar views about Afrikaner nationalism earlier this century."[9] It is a vicious and blind-sighted historical ailment.

The cure is loud doses of truth. As the poet Adrienne Rich has remarked, "silence can be a plan rigorously executed . . . Do not confuse it with any kind of absence." The best service that we can perform for those citizens still sadly trapped in this Almost netherworld, is to coax them towards us through public acknowledgment of what they have rigorously overlooked.

This coaxing cannot be an act of vengeance, but must rather be one of sympathy; perhaps it cannot avoid, though, being patronising. But we must try to avoid this last vice too. If there are real gestures of reconciliation from those still in the old Almost World, then the process of finding a shared history might even be exhilarating, rather than unattractive and hierarchical. But, as is the case in all actual historical processes, much will depend on the concrete actions that individuals, and groups of people, decide upon. The South African privileged must choose to leave the Almost World.

A central requirement for rejoining the real world is the unconditional renunciation of the horrendous apartheid past. There can be no equivocation, no residual pleading that apartheid was a system of well-meaning atrocity. Apartheid brought together the worst things that people everywhere have done to other people. Apartheid manipulated, relied upon, and even invented racial and ethnic categories in order to keep millions of people in persistent poverty and semi-slavery. It used a mighty state apparatus to satisfy the elemental land-lust of late-twentieth-century, peculiarly suburban, conquistadors who moved into places like Triomf, and every little dorp in the Western Cape, and dominated the economies even of designated "black" areas.

In a country of enormous material and human resources, apartheid deliberately generated the world's highest levels of inequality. In a century when the world was shedding imperialism, apartheid intensified colonialism of a special kind. In an increasingly globalised and multicultural world, apartheid looked obsessively inward, trying to pull the shutters down against the universe. As the world moved towards multi-national institutions and cooperative models of coexistence, apartheid rode roughshod over its neighbours with tanks and guns.

And in the process apartheid created something: its privileged population is one of the wealthiest in the world. In the last decade of apartheid, defending its honeypot of privileges, the regime resembled a wounded bear, lashing out furiously at all who came near its claws regardless of who was responsible for its wounds, and only aggravating those wounds in the process. P W Botha openly embraced this animalistic imagery by defiantly assuring the international community that apartheid South Africa "would fight like a little tiger."[10]

But what may be understandable behaviour in an animal is neither rational nor acceptable in a state, especially one which claimed to be the upholder of "civilised values." As Dr B B Keet, an Afrikaner and one-time head of the Theological Seminary at Stellenbosch, wrote in 1956:

> ... true civilisation can never go hand in hand with or be served by a denial of human rights; on the contrary that is precisely what would cause barbarism to prevail and all true culture to die out. The test of our civilisation is our treatment of the underprivileged. Everything which bears the stamp of oppression (and oppression of the personality is the worst) debases the oppressor just as it degrades the oppressed.[11]

Civilised Afrikaner voices like this were ignored in forty years of white nationalist frenzy that harmed blacks and whites alike. Today the Van Eden family, former supporters of the right-wing AWB in the former white supremacist stronghold of Brits, have burned their khaki uniforms and joined the ANC. The family's oldest daughter, Elize Vorster, and her husband "were told that if we did not sell everything the blacks would take it all. We were told the AWB was going to fight a war and needed the money."[12] So they sold their possessions and gave the proceeds to Eugene TerreBlanche's AWB; now, virtually penniless, they live with Ms Vorster's parents. It was a small confidence trick amidst apartheid's death throes, echoing the larger historical hoax that gave birth to that system.

In all this, apartheid was emblematic of the wrongs that people can do to other people. Joseph Conrad's *Heart of Darkness* cuts close to the core:

> They were conquerors, and for that you want only brute force – nothing to boast of, when you have it, since your strength is just an accident arising from the weakness of others. They grabbed what they could get for the sake of what was to be got. It was robbery with violence, aggravated murder on a grand scale.

Since so many kinds of violence are wrapped up in apartheid, South Africans have a responsibility to themselves, but also to histories and peoples beyond South Africa. If South Africa speaks in a muddled way about its past, the intellectual barriers against whole categories of violence in faraway places will be weakened, both now and in times to come. And also, of course, in South Africa itself.

So the South African exercise of facing the past will be far more than a legalistic exercise or a bureaucratic fact-finding mission. It must ask how living, breathing, political institutions could have so distorted and abused their duties to secure humane values. It must lay bare the immoral anatomy of apartheid and never again allow truth to be hostage to the few. Responding to the anti-apartheid resistance tactics of the End Conscription Campaign, the then Minister of Defence Magnus Malan objected that "No citizen can decide of his or her free will which laws to respect."[13] It was the call of an evil system for the abdication of the moral sense of the individual.

This call was freely answered by many who now claim exculpation, pleading that they were merely the puppets of people like Malan. Some, though, did manage to avoid the fate of collective moral puppetry that the apartheid regime sought to impose on the population. Charles Bester, an 18-year-old committed Christian and resister against conscription, objected that "I cannot go into the townships on the back of a Casspir and say as a Christian I have got good news."[14] In an atrocious system like apartheid, truth and morality itself were under-debated concepts; we were supposed to believe that only the received wisdom of officialdom was necessary.

But in fact, inexorably, "there is a battle for truth. The political question is truth itself."[15] This awareness must never leave us in the new South Africa. Everyone, together, must undo the fables, the old Almost World, of the apartheid history syllabus; we must also reject the philistine idea of a new state-sanctioned or organisationally orthodox official history.

Unfortunately National Party leader F W de Klerk comes close to repeating the wrong historiography of his party's past when he suggests that "a starting point for the commission should be to ask the major role-players of the conflicts of the past . . . to put before the commission a perspective as to what happened, why did it happen, what motivated the policies which were followed and what were the policy frameworks that were applied during those years of conflict."

This is a flexible book-keeper's version of history. It would produce a suspect balance sheet of alleged facts and opinions, a product of free-form addition, subtraction or multiplication towards convenient conclusions, without deference to relevant realities. Its use of the creepingly amoral language of "policy frameworks" essentially suggests that the Truth and Reconciliation Commission's work should give special weight to the story of apartheid as told by the Great Men who ran the system, rather than to the perspectives of the victims and of those who resisted the system on the ground. This approach, sacrificing the vernacular memory and oral history of the oppressed in favour of the paper sophistry of the oppressors, would sacrifice truth itself.

The South African Truth Commission is only one of the structures through which we should hope to dismantle the old regime of truth in order to replace it with new and multiple narratives. We must remain aware of the dangers of replacing apartheid's false utopian historicism with our own new orthodoxies. As we construct new historical narratives, it will be in the currency of *heterotopias*, multiple idealisms, rather than the singlemindedness of utopia; it will be with an awareness of the pain that is inflicted when one ethical world conflicts with others nearby. This exercise should not be confused with the cheap pluralism of live-and-let-live; accountability and ethical choice are inevitable parts of this process. There can be no indifference towards apartheid, nor towards its legacy. Rather, we must be driven by what Edward Said has called an "unstoppable predilection for alternatives" to the old order.[16]

Our state-sponsored Commission has no monopoly on processes of historical rectification. It is not the sole forum for the voices of the South African people, nor will it provide the only resource for the subsequent interpretive efforts of an unbounded range of historians, intellectuals and schools of thought. This is not to say that it can avoid making judgments of its own. It must judge. But also it will be judged.

We have suggested that, for a number of reasons, it is important to face the South African past. Such an exercise will ensure that we speak clearly about apartheid to the watching world. Its decades of unambiguous resistance have given way to celebration, but also to confusion about where apartheid went and whether it has genuinely already disappeared. Facing the past will also ensure that we achieve justice for those who did not live to see the new country. It will lay bare, in unambiguous terms, the illegitimacy of apartheid and of its legacy. It will provide a basis for genuine reconciliation built on a realisation, among the privileged, that they must face new facts about an uncomfortable past. It will clarify the need for decriminalisation of those who, in resisting apartheid, fell victims to its brutal apparatus of criminal courts. It will lay bare the roots of violence in South Africa, by clarifying how the old government used the rhetoric of law and order in order, actually, to spread lawlessness and chaos. It will disabuse many privileged South Africans of their still-distorted views about the nature of the anti-apartheid resistance. It will demonstrate the resilient humane values of that movement and the unimpeachable morality of its armed struggle. It will help create a political culture in which genuine equality before the law can be established for the first time, and it will ensure that apartheid's lawless process of private and public looting gives way to durable and legitimate institutions of property.

Perhaps most importantly, facing the past will mean that the South African privileged face up to – and resolve – their complicity in that past. Additionally, we will develop a real sense of the damage that was done to southern Africa in the name of this country; and we will, as a country, finally become reconciled to international human rights norms and civilised standards, by using those standards as the guiding light in judging our own past.

Afterwards we will be blessed with a complex, perhaps contradictory, set of narratives about our past. And our task, necessarily a ceaseless one, will be to reconstitute our political reality into something that is coherent but self-questioning, ethically decisive but not self-righteous.

For there is no glamour in suffering. Victims of an atrocious system are not purified through their pain. Art Spiegelman's brilliant pictorial tale *Maus*, illustrating the inevitably self-seeking – even sometimes squalid – forms of behaviour that were forced upon concentration camp inmates by their dire circumstances under the Nazis, is a useful reminder for us in South Africa that dehumanising systems dehumanise people. While unfettered power corrupts, powerlessness corrupts too. It was powerlessness that bred apartheid's bantustan leaders, often corruptly complicit with apartheid. It was powerlessness that fuelled paranoia and led certain ANC cadres into acts of wrongdoing at the expense of those in their custody in detention camps. There is a place in all this for introspection among the formerly oppressed.

Nevertheless, if we are successful in building this new and ethically decisive political culture, we will have performed a public intellectual, moral and political task of the first order. We will have demonstrated, to the political and the academic worlds alike, that seemingly remote investigative, academic and historical inquiry can perform dramatic livewire functions in the political realities of countries and of the world. We will have shown that new truths can build new worlds.

While it is a truism that those who forget their past are doomed to repeat it, the reverse comfort does not necessarily hold. A society may remember its past and nevertheless repeat it; or even surpass it in cruelty. Hitler was a history buff. He built his career in part on the resentment bred of the sudden and unexpected military defeat of Germany in 1918. Afrikaner suffering at the hands of British imperialism early this century actually fuelled the racial oppression of apartheid, rather than serving as an admonition against it.

Since the devil can quote history to his or her own purposes, a simple factual record of the apartheid past, devoid of an ethical basis, would be of little value. What matters is not merely the fact that we remember history but the way in which we remember it. There can be no room for sentimentality or nostalgia in remembering apartheid. It even exploited the youthful idealism of its own soldiers. It manipulated them and made them die for a bad cause. At the heart of remembrance must be a collective renunciation of apartheid by both sides – those who fought to defend it as much as those who fought for its overthrow. The post-apartheid South African identity should not be homogenised, but broadly inclusive; yet it can have no legitimate place for apartheid or the various contending neo-apartheids.

So often it appears that history teaches only despair; cynicism can seem to sweep all before it, as it did in the old South African governance. But in a new environment, one that takes unflinchingly the full measure of the past, South Africa can become a safe place for idealism, the sort of place that Seamus Heaney had in mind when he wrote, in "The Cure at Troy", of those rare times and places "when hope and history rhyme."

Notes

CHAPTER 1 (PAGES 1–5)
1. Ruth First, quoted by Auriol Stevens, *Manchester Guardian*, 30 October, 1970.
2. Nelson Mandela, quoted by J Frederikse, *The Unbreakable Thread* (London: Zed Books, 1990), 266.
3. Eugene de Kock, quoted in *Sunday Independent*, 17 March, 1996.
4. See, *Business Day*, 19 March, 1996.
5. Betsie Verwoerd, quoted in *Cape Times*, 20 November, 1973.

CHAPTER 2 (PAGES 6–11)
1. *Business Day*, editorial, 5 March, 1996.

CHAPTER 3 (PAGES 12–27)
1. Benita Parry, "Reconciliation and Remembrance," *Die Suid Afrikaan*, February, 1996, 12.
2. Desmond Tutu, *The Rainbow People of God* (London: Bantam Books, 1995), 246-47.
3. Judge Richard Goldstone, *Business Day*, 7 March, 1996.
4. Tutu, *The Rainbow People of God*, 21.
5. Tutu, quoted by *Sunday Independent*, 18 February, 1996.
6. H Suzman quoted in *Rule of Fear* (London: Catholic Institute of International Relations, 1989), 29.
7. See, Mark J Osiel, *Ever Again: Legal Remembrance of Administrative Massacre*, 144 U. Penn. L. Rev. 463, 546-47 (1995).
8. See, e.g., Ziyad Motala, "The Promotion of National Unity and Reconciliation Act," XXVIII CILSA 1995 1, 2.
9. See, Osiel, *Ever Again,* 144 U. Penn L. Rev. 463, 604.

CHAPTER 4 (PAGES 28–40)
1. From "The Chameleon Dance", by Michael Chapman, in *The Paperbook of South African English Poetry*, (Johannesburg: Ad Donker, 1986), 51.
2. F W de Klerk, quoted in *Citizen*, 10 December, 1992.
3. Gert Engelbrecht, quoted by *Washington Post*, 29 May, 1996.
4. Prof J C van Rooy, quoted in Ivor Wilkins and Hans Strydom, *The Broederbond* (London: Paddington Press, 1979), 59.
5. F W de Klerk, quoted by Allister Sparks, *Tomorrow Is Another Country* (Johannesburg: Struik, 1994), 12-13, 128.
6. F W de Klerk, quoted by *Time*, 3 January, 1994.
7. F W de Klerk, quoted by *Cape Times*, 19 March, 1992.
8. Melanie Verwoerd, *Hansard*, 17 May, 1995, col. 1401-2.
9. B J Vorster, quoted by B Bunting, *The Rise of the South African Reich* (London: Penguin, 1969), 96.
10. Eric Louw, quoted by Michael Roberts and A E G Trollip, *The South African Opposition 1939-1945* (Cape Town: Longmans, 1947), 174.
11. Adolf Hitler, quoted in Alan Bullock, *Hitler: A Study in Tyranny* (London: Penguin, 1962), 39.

12. William L Shirer, *The Rise and Fall of the Third Reich* (London: Mandarin, 1991 ed), 254.
13. *Die O.B*, quoted by Michael Roberts and A E G Trollip, *The South African Opposition 1939-1945*, 154, 237.
14. Dr P Koornhof, quoted by *Cape Times*, 10 June, 1968.
15. Government Printer, Summary of the Report of the Commission for the Socio-Economic Development of the Bantu Areas within the Union of South Africa ("Tomlinson Report"), 102, 103, 106 (1955).
16. Tomlinson Report, 211.
17. G D Scholtz, quoted in J Mervis, "A Critique of Separate Development," in N Roodie (ed), *South African Dialogue* (Johannesburg: McGraw-Hill, 1972), 72.
18. H F Verwoerd, *Debates* 23 January 1962, quoted in Barbara Rogers, *South Africa: The Bantu Homelands* (London: International Defence and Aid Fund, 1972), 4.
19. See, D J Goldhagen, *Hitler's Willing Executioners: Ordinary Germans and the Holocaust* (New York: Alfred A Knopf, 1996), 420.
20. Shirer, *The Rise and Fall of the Third Reich*, 233.
21. National Party MP Jan Steyn, quoted by Jack Simons, *African Women: Their Legal Status in South Africa* (London: C Hurst, 1969), 282, House of Assembly Debates, 17 March, 1964.
22. Quoted in M Savage, *Pass Laws and the Disorganisation and Reorganisation of the African Population in South Africa*, Carnegie Conference Paper 281, p. 50 (Second Carnegie Inquiry into Poverty and Development in Southern Africa, Cape Town, 13–19 April, 1984).
23. D F Malan's reply, in February 1954, to a letter from Rev. John H Piersma of Grand Rapids, Michigan, quoted by Leo Kuper, *Passive Resistance* (New Haven: Yale University Press, 1957), 217.
24. See, Gerald Shaw, *Cape Times*, 3 June, 1992.
25. Milan Kundera, *The Book of Laughter and Forgetting* (London: Faber and Faber, 1992), 216.
26. See, Deborah E Lipstadt, *Denying the Holocaust: The Growing Assault on Truth and Memory* (New York: Free Press, 1993).

CHAPTER 5 (PAGES 41–45)
1. J Maree, quoted by *Weekend Argus*, 25 March, 1995.
2. Desmond Tutu, *The Rainbow People of God* (London: Bantam Books, 1995), 177.
3. Donald Abenheim, *Reforging the Iron Cross: The Search for Tradition in the West German Armed Forces* (Princeton: Princeton University Press, 1988), 839 (quoting a German military officer).
4. Mark J Osiel, *Ever Again: Legal Remembrance of Administrative Measures*, 144 U. Penn. L. Rev. 463, 695 (1995).
5. Cosmas Desmond, "Truth Body Must See that the End Justifies the Means," *Business Day*, 1 December, 1995.

CHAPTER 6 (PAGES 46–53)
1. D J Boorstin, *Cleopatra's Nose* (New York: Vintage, 1995), 41-2.
2. F W de Klerk, quoted by *Star*, 22 November, 1992.
3. Magnus Malan, quoted by *Saturday Star*, 2 March, 1996.
4. Mark J Osiel, *Ever Again: Legal Remembrance of Administrative Massacre*, 144 U. Penn L. Rev., 645 (1995).
5. South African Police, Further Proposals by the South African Police on the Truth and Reconciliation Commission, 14 September, 1994.
6. B Bunting, *The Rise of the South African Reich* (Penguin: London, 1969), 525.
7. A Sachs, "Reparations – Political and Psychological Considerations," 2 *Psychoanalytic Psychotherapy in South Africa 16*, 25 (Summer 1993).
8. Desmond Tutu, *The Rainbow People of God* (London: Bantan Books, 1995), 100.
9. Jan de Klerk, *Hansard*, 15 March, 1968.
10. John Vorster, quoted in *Rand Daily Mail*, 8 July, 1968.

11. F W de Klerk, quoted by *Cape Times*, 2 October, 1995.

12. S Brucan, "Keeping the Books Closed: Eastern Europe Fails to Purge Past Lies," *The World Paper*, April 1995, 3.

13. W Faulkner, *Absalom, Absalom!* (London: Chatto and Windus, 1937), 9.

14. W A de Klerk, *Contrast*, December 1967.

15. M Behr, *The Smell of Apples* (London: Abacus, 1995), 198.

16. Theuns Eloff, unpublished notes from the Dakar talks (on file with the authors).

17. William Wordsworth, "Essay, Supplementary to the Preface," *The Prelude* (text of 1805), ed E de Selincourt, (Oxford: Oxford University Press, 1964).

18. S Cavell, *The Claim of Reason: Wittgenstein, Skepticism, Morality and Tragedy* (Oxford: Oxford University Press, 1979).

CHAPTER 7 (PAGES 54–63)

1. Statement by Mr Diallo Telli (Guinea), Chair of the Special Committee on the Policies of Apartheid, at a plenary meeting of the General Assembly on a resolution concerning the trial of Mr Nelson Mandela and others, in *The United Nations and Apartheid 1948-1994*, 267.

2. See, e.g., Vienna Convention on the Law of Treaties, UN Doc A/Conf 39/27 (1969) art. 53.

3. "Statement by Mr Thabo Mbeki, son of Mr Govan Mbeki, the African leader on trial in Pretoria, before a delegation of the Special Committee on the Policies of Apartheid," London, 13 April, 1964, in *The United Nations and Apartheid 1948-1994*, 277.

4. A Odendaal, "The Weight of History: Dealing with the Past in South Africa," paper delivered to the Justice In Transition Conference On Truth and Reconciliation in South Africa, 29 July, 1994.

5. Father M Lapsley, quoted in *Hansard*, Wednesday 21 October 1992, col. 12784.

6. Reported in *Weekly Mail*, 16 July, 1993.

7. Quoted by Rob Nixon, *Homelands, Harlem and Hollywood* (New York: Routledge, 1994), 138.

8. Jacob Zuma, quoted in *Business Day*, 15 January, 1996.

9. Interview with *Cape Times*, in Tony Heard, *Cape of Storms* (Johannesburg: Ravan Press, 1991), 240.

10. Editorial, *Sechaba*, August, 1995.

11. Dr F van Zyl Slabbert, Dakar 1987 (unpublished notes on file with the authors).

12. H Suzman, *Hansard*, 24 April 1963, reprinted in *Helen Suzman's Solo Years*, ed Phyllis Lewsen, (Johannesburg: Jonathan Ball and Ad Donker, 1991).

13. Rev. B Naudé (unpublished notes on file with the authors).

14. Quoted by Richard Abel, *Politics By Other Means* (New York: Routledge, 1995), 98, 100.

15. Joel Joffe, *The Rivonia Story* (Cape Town: Mayibuye Books, 1995), 213.

16. Quoted by Jacques Pauw, *In the Heart of the Whore* (Johannesburg: Southern Book Publishers, 1991), 116.

17. Quoted by Ian Buruma, *The Wages of Guilt* (London: Vintage, 1995), 269-70.

CHAPTER 8 (PAGES 64–73)

1. Quoted by Kader Asmal, *Victims, Survivors and Citizens – Human Rights, Reparations and Reconciliation*, Inaugural Lecture, University of the Western Cape (1992), 25 May, 1992.

2. F W de Klerk, quoted in *Citizen*, 24 June, 1996.

3. Adriaan Vlok, quoted by Jacques Pauw, *In the Heart of the Whore* (Johannesburg: Southern Books, 1991), 114.

4. *Race Relations Survey 1989/90* (Johannesburg: South African Institute of Race Relations, 1990), 175.

5. Pik Botha, speech of 31 August, 1984 to a conference of editorial writers, quoted in J Hanlon, *Beggar Your Neighbours* (London: James Currey, 1986), 41.

6. Quoted by J Pearce, "School Uses Constitution in Race Row," *Mail & Guardian*, 9 February, 1996.

7. Hernus Kriel, quoted by *Cape Times*, 13 March, 1991.

8. Constand Viljoen, quoted by *Citizen*, 6 May, 1996.

9. Saleem Badat, Zenariah Barends, Harold Wolpe, "The Post-Secondary Education System: Beyond the Equality Versus Development Impasse and Towards Policy Formulation for Equality and Development," paper presented at the University of Cape Town's Colloquium on Equity Policies and Practices: Restructuring in the Tertiary Education Sector, 16-18 April, 1993.

10. C van Onselen, Tertiary Education in a Democratic South Africa (1991), unpublished mimeograph quoted by Badat, Barens and Wolpe, above.

11. Nelson Mandela, quoted by *Star*, 23 December, 1991.

12. Anonymous white farmer, *Wall Street Journal*, 30 March, 1988.

13. Pik Botha, quoted by Hazlitt, *Cape Times*, 16 July, 1977.

14. Pik Botha, quoted in *Cape Times*, 31 August, 1976.

CHAPTER 9 (PAGES 74-110)

1. Reported by *Sunday Independent*, 11 February, 1996.

2. Quoted by B Bunting, *The Rise of the South African Reich* (London: Penguin, 1969), 522, 529, 416.

3. Quoted by Alan Bullock, *Hitler: A Study in Tyranny* (London: Penguin, 1962), 161.

4. Nelson Mandela, quoted in *Guardian*, 7 September, 1991.

5. John Vorster, *Star Weekly*, 19 August, 1967, quoted by Bunting, *The Rise of the South African Reich*, 142.

6. Japie du P Basson, quoted by Bunting, *The Rise of the South African Reich*, 147.

7. Kelsey Stuart, *The Newspaperman's Guide to the Law* (Durban: Butterworth, 1986), 110, 121.

8. William L Shirer, *The Rise and Fall of the Third Reich*, (London: Mandarin, 1991 ed.), 233.

9. Jill Wentzel, *The Liberal Slideaway* (Johannesburg: South African Institute of Race Relations, 1995), 96.

10. General van den Bergh, quoted in *Die Transvaler*, 30 September, 1966.

11. Quoted by Daniel J Goldhagen, *Hitler's Willing Executioners*, (New York: Alfred A Knopf, 1996), 142.

12. *Die Burger*, February 1963, quoted in Bunting, *The Rise of the South African Reich*, 197.

13. Bullock, *Hitler: A Study in Tyranny*, 116, 130.

14. Message issued by defendants convicted in the Delmas Trial, quoted by R Abel, *Politics By Other Means* (New York: Routledge, 1995), 364.

15. Justice van der Walt, quoted by Abel, *Politics By Other Means*, 369.

16. Shirer, *The Rise and Fall of the Third Reich*, 274.

17. This ouster clause was eventually disregarded by the courts. See, *Momoniat & Naidoo* v. *Minister of Law and Order*, 1986 2 SA 264 (W).

18. In Bloem and Ar. v. *State President of the R.S.A. and Ors*, 1986 (4) S A 1064, quoted by N. Pillay, Political Role of the South African Judiciary (unpublished Harvard Law School JSD thesis on file with the authors), (1988), 105.

19. Shirer, *The Rise and Fall of the Third Reich*, 274.

20. Pik Botha, quoted in Abel, *Politics By Other Means*, 296.

21. Quoted by Rob Nixon, *Homelands, Harlem and Hollywood* (New York: Routledge, 1994), 49.

22. John Laurence, *The Seeds of Disaster* (London: Victor Gollancz, 1968), 181.

23. SABC, quoted in Laurence, *The Seeds of Disaster*, 195-6.

24. Pik Botha, quoted in Abel, *Politics By Other Means*, 296.

25. Pik Botha, quoted in *Mail & Guardian*, 3 May, 1996.

26. Edward Heath, quoted by S Kanfer, *The Last Empire: De Beers, Diamonds and the World* (New York: Farrar, Straus & Giroux, 1993), 355.

27. Steyn Report, 181, 71, 35, 36.

28. Steyn Report, 1187.

29. P W Botha, *Hansard*, House of Assembly Debates, Weekly Edition no. 1, col. 103.

30. Steyn Report, 838-39, 945.

31. F W de Klerk, quoted by *Mail & Guardian*, 3 May, 1996.

32. Mother of victim, quoted by *Citizen*, 3 May, 1996.

33. Steyn Report, 1038.

34. Defence Minister Magnus Malan, quoted in Nathan, *Marching to a Different Drum* (Belville: University of the Western Cape Centre for Southern African Studies, 1991), 317.

35. *Citizen,* quoted in Abel, *Politics By Other Means*, 105-6.

36. Department of Defence, White Paper on Defence (1977), 35.

37. Publications Appeal Board, Grassroots (200/83), quoted by K Stuart, *The Newspaperman's Guide to the Law* (Durban: Butterworth, 1986), 77.

38. Anti-apartheid church leader, quoted by International Commission of Jurists, *South Africa and The Rule of Law*, ed Geoffrey Bindman (1988).

39. SADF Special Forces Directive, quoted by Report of the Harms Commission of Inquiry into Police Hit Squads (1990), 35.

40. Harms Commission Report, 42, quoting witnesses Botha and Van Zyl, who were members of the Civil Cooperation Bureau's Region 6 – the division responsible for CCB activities within South African borders.

41. Human Rights Watch, *The Killings in South Africa* (New York: Human Rights Watch, 1991), 11.

42. Joe Mamasela, quoted by E Koch, *Mail & Guardian*, 23 February, 1996.

43. Gerald Shaw, "How the Emergency Can Cut Off the News," *Cape Times*, 16 June, 1986.

44. See, generally, D Davis and D Foster, *Detention and Torture in South Africa* (Cape Town: David Philip, 1987).

45. Haroon Aziz, quoted in *Citizen*, 10 May, 1996.

46. Reported in *Mail & Guardian*, 19 April, 1996.

47. Gerald Shaw, "Urgent Need To Rebuild Trust Between the Parties," *Cape Times*, 14 September, 1990.

48. Reported in *Sunday Independent*, 16 June, 1996.

49. Interim Report of the Commission of Inquiry Regarding the Prevention of Public Violence and Intimidation: on the Conduct of Members of 32 Battalion at Phola Park on 8 April, 1992, 4, 5.

50. Report of the Harms Commission of Inquiry into Police Hit Squads (1990), 37.

51. Supplementary indictment of KwaZulu Natal Attorney-General, quoted by *Sowetan*, 1 March, 1996.

52. Quoted and reported in *Mail & Guardian*, 8 March, 1996.

53. Brig. Mostert, quoted in Harms Commission Report (1990), 32.

54. Brig. Jan van der Hoven, quoted by Jacques Pauw, *In the Heart of the Whore* (Johannesburg: Southern Books, 1991), 13.

55. Secretary of the State Security Council, quoted by Dan O'Meara, *Forty Lost Years* (Randburg: Ravan Press, 1996), 345.

56. Kit Bawden, letter to *Cape Times*, 10 September, 1992.

57. Defence Minister Magnus Malan, quoted in *Argus*, 3 March, 1990.

58. A L Jordaan, *Hansard*, col. 1620, 26 February, 1990.

59. Supplementary Report of the Commission of Inquiry into Alleged Irregularities in the Former Department of Information (1979), para 12, V.11.386.

60. Gerald Shaw, *Cape Times*, 30 August, 1990.

61. Douw Willemse, quoted by *Business Day*, April 16 and 17, 1996.

62. *Mail & Guardian*, 5 July, 1996.

63. Justice Harms, Harms Commission Report, 6.

64. Justice Harms, quoted by *Mail & Guardian*, 23 February, 1996.

65. P W Botha, quoted by R Davies, "The Fight of the Little Tiger," *Sanctions Against Apartheid* (Cape Town: David Philip, 1989), 219.

66. NSMS document, quoted by Jacques Pauw, *In the Heart of The Whore*, 118.

67. Military intelligence report, quoted by *Mail & Guardian*, 8 March, 1996.

68. Adriaan Vlok, quoted by Human Rights Watch, *The Killings in South Africa*, 23.

Notes

69. Brig. Jacques Buchner, quoted by Abel, *Politics By Other Means*, 198.

70. South African Commission of Enquiry regarding the Prevention of Public Violence and Intimidation (Goldstone Commission), 32-33.

71. F W de Klerk, quoted by Greg Myre, "SA Government to Investigate Police Violence," Associated Press, 3 September, 1990.

72. Report to the Commission by the Committee Appointed to Inquire into Allegations Concerning Front Companies of the SADF and the Training by the SADF of Inkatha Supporters at the Caprivi in 1986 (the "Goldstone Caprivi Report"), 12.

73. SADF legal counsel, reported in Goldstone Caprivi Report (June 1993), 20.

74. President Nelson Mandela, quote reported in *Star*, 27 January, 1995.

75. *Washington Post*, quoted by Abel, *Politics By Other Means*, 447.

76. *Sunday Times*, 18 February, 1996.

CHAPTER 10 (PAGES 111-19)

1. See, J Frederikse, *The Unbreakable Thread* (London: Zed Books, 1990).

2. South African Police, Further Proposals by the South African Police on the Truth and Reconciliation Commission, 14 September, 1994.

3. South African Police, 14 September, 1994, 5.

4. South African Police, Memorandum by the South African Police on the Desirability and Implications of the Truth and Reconciliation Commission as Envisaged in the Promotion of National Unity and Reconciliation Bill, 1994, 2-3.

5. Reported by *Business Day*, 4 March, 1996.

6. Quoted by *Sunday Independent*, 5 May, 1996.

7. Pik Botha, cited by Rob Davies, *Hansard*, 17 May, 1995.

8. Pik Botha, quoted in *Hansard*, 9 May, 1994, cols 6099-6101.

9. State Security Council minutes, quoted in *Mail & Guardian*, 3 May, 1996.

10. John Vorster, quoted by B Bunting, *The Rise of the Third Reich* (London: Penguin, 1969), 227.

11. David Dalling MP, *Hansard*, 6 November, 1986, col. 7957.

CHAPTER 11 (PAGES 120-25)

1 *Mail & Guardian* 5 July, 1996.

2. Joe Slovo, "South Africa – No Middle Road," in Basil Davidson, Joe Slovo, Anthony R Wilkinson, *Southern Africa: The New Politics of Revolution* (London: Penguin, 1976), 205.

3. "Resolutions of the All-In African Conference held in Pietermaritzburg, South Africa, 25-26 March 1961," in *The United Nations and Apartheid 1948-1994*, 247.

4. "Manifesto of Umkhonto weSizwe," in *The United Nations and Apartheid 1948-1994*, 250.

5. Howard Barrell, *MK: The ANC's Armed Struggle* (London: Penguin, 1990), 4.

6. Joe Slovo, quoted in *Hansard*, 7 May, 1990, col. 8187.

7. Joe Slovo, "South Africa – No Middle Road", 115.

8. Victor Molefe, quoted in *Sunday Independent*, 31 December, 1995, 10.

9. Ken Owen, *Sunday Times*, 22 March, 1992.

CHAPTER 12 (PAGES 126-130)

1. Navi Pillay, Political Role of the South African Judiciary (unpublished Harvard Law School JSD thesis on file with the authors), 4.

2. Magistrate's reasoning, in T Karis and G Carter, *From Protest to Challenge: A Documentary History of African Politics in South Africa 1882-1964*, vol. 3 (Stanford: Hoover, 1977), 726 (cited by N Pillay, *supra*).

3. A white farmer, quoted by *Cape Times*, 17 November, 1989.

4. Reported in *Weekend Argus*, 30/31 March, 1996.

5. See, Richard Abel, *Politics By Other Means* (New York: Routledge, 1995), 24.

6. Conversation with the conscript, December, 1994.

7. Reported by *Associated Press*, 4 June, 1984.

8. A Sparks, *Tomorrow Is Another Country* (Johannesburg: Struik, 1994), 93.

CHAPTER 13 (PAGES 131-42)

1. Reported in *Business Day*, 16 May, 1996.

2. Daniel J Goldhagen, *Hitler's Willing Executioners* (New York: Alfred A Knopf, 1996), 136.

3. Dan O'Meara, *Forty Lost Years* (Randburg: Ravan Press, 1994), 69.

4. *Economist*, 20 May, 1995.

5. J Nattrass, "Approaches to the problem of unemployment in South Africa" (1984) 2 *Indicator South Africa*, 3.

6. B T Schoeman, *Hansard*, House of Assembly debates, 19 March, 1942.

7. Minister Coetzee, quoted in *Rand Daily Mail*, 8 October, 1968.

8. Professor Renfrew Christie, quoted by K Asmal, *Victims, Survivors, and Citizens – Human Rights, Reparations and Reconciliation*, Inaugural Lecture, University of the Western Cape (25 May, 1992), 14.

9. See, International Commission of Jurists, *South Africa and the Rule of Law* (ed G Bindman) (London: Pinter Publishers, 1988), 24.

10. Impala Platinum executive, quoted in *Sunday Times, Business Times*, 12 May, 1996.

11. See, *Star*, 22 February, 1996.

12. Justice van Reenen, quoted by *Sunday Times*, 12 July, 1992.

13. P Krost, "Children of Triomf Never Knew Their Tidy Suburb Was Built on Misery," *Sunday Independent*, 26 January, 1996.

14. Tony Leon, quoted in *Saturday Star*, 9 March, 1996.

CHAPTER 14 (PAGES 143-67)

1. Editorial, *Star*, 7 May, 1996.

2. John Yeld, *Weekend Argus*, 29 June, 1996 (quoting another journalist who allegedly detected cynicism; and quoting truth commissioner Mapule Ramashala).

3. Cosmas Desmond, *The Discarded People* (London: Penguin, 1971), 6-7 (quoting M C Botha, Minister of Bantu Affairs and Development, in 1968).

4. Constand Viljoen and Magnus Malan, quoted by J Pauw, *In the Heart of the Whore* (Johannesburg: Southern Books, 1991), 107, 120.

5. Rob Nixon, *Homelands, Harlem and Hollywood* (New York: Routledge, 1994), 119.

6. See, e.g., Caroline Hamilton (ed.), *The Mfecane Aftermath* (Johannesburg: University of the Witwatersrand Press, 1996).

7. See, e.g., Rob Nixon, *Homelands, Harlem and Hollywood*.

8. Western Cape voters, *Mail & Guardian*, 17 May, 1996.

9. Prime Minister J C Smuts, quoted by C Desmond, *The Discarded People*, 222.

10. Free Settlement Board Chairperson H Kruger, quoted by SA Institute of Race Relations, *Quarterly Countdown*, Third Quarter, 1989, 18.

11. A Hitler, *Mein Kampf*, quoted by Alan Bullock, *Hitler: A Study In Tyranny* (London: Penguin, 1962), 69.

12. F W de Klerk, quoted by *Cape Times*, 19 March, 1992.

13. John Vorster, quoted by *Cape Times*, 20 October, 1976.

14. "Midnight: Time For South Africans To Wake Up," *Cape Times*, 27 August, 1973.

15. J C Smuts, House of Assembly Debates, 21 September, 1948, col. 2905.

16. Quoted by B Bunting, *The Rise of the South African Reich* (London: Penguin, 1969), 151.

17. See, Goldhagen, *Hitler's Willing Executioners*, 83, 112, 113, 115.

18. Alan Bullock, *Hitler: A Study In Tyranny*, 46, 186.

19. See, Dan O'Meara, *Forty Lost Years: The Apartheid State and the Politics of the National Party: 1948-1994* (Randburg: Ravan Press, 1996), 46, 48.

20. *Cape Times*, 14 March, 1975.

21. The foregoing discussion of private-public arms links relies heavily on D O'Meara, *Forty*

Lost Years, 226-28.

22. Ian Buruma, *Wages of Guilt* (London: Vintage, 1995), 276-77.

23. Stefan Kanfer, *The Last Empire: De Beers, Diamonds and the World* (New York: Farrar, Straus & Giroux, 1993), quoting comments of Anglo American executive Gordon Waddell at an executive meeting.

24. A Odendaal, "The Weight of History: Dealing With the Past in South Africa," paper delivered at the Justice in Transition Conference on Truth and Reconciliation in South Africa, 29 July, 1994.

25. Quoted in Anthony Sampson, *Black and Gold* (London: Hodder & Stoughton, 1987), 90.

26. Quoted in A Hepple, *South Africa: Workers Under Apartheid* (London: International Defence and Aid Fund, 1969), 53.

27. A Hocking, *Oppenheimer and Son*, quoted by S Kanfer, *The Last Empire: De Beers, Diamonds and the World*, 324-25.

28. Harry Oppenheimer, interviewed by Brian Hackland, quoted in David Pallister, Sarah Stewart and Ian Lepper, *South Africa Inc.* (London: Simon and Schuster, 1987), 55-6.

29. Harry Oppenheimer, quoted by Dan O'Meara, *Forty Lost Years*, 187.

30. Gavin Relly, quoted by Stefan Kanfer, *The Last Empire: De Beers, Diamonds and the World*, 347.

31. Anton Rupert, quoted by Dan O'Meara, *Forty Lost Years*, 187.

32. Reg Honey, quoted by Joan Brickhill, *Race Against Race* (London: International Defence and Aid Fund, 1976), 44.

33. Ritter von Halt, quoted by Peter Hain, *Don't Play With Apartheid* (London: Billing, 1971), 45.

34. W A de Klerk, *Contrast*, 1967.

35. See, T Hanf *et al, South Africa: The Prospects for Peaceful Change* (London: Rex Collings, 1981), 400-402.

36. *Natal Mercury*, 2 June, 1983.

37. Letter from Jan Kruger to S Laing, quoted by *South*, 19 September, 1991.

38. Martin Prozesky in "Implications of Apartheid for Christianity in South Africa," *Christianity in Southern Africa*, ed Martin Prozesky (Johannesburg: Southern Book Publishers, 1990), 125.

39. Trevor Huddleston, *Naught for Your Comfort* (London: Fontana Books, 1957), 54.

40. Quoted by Huddleston in *Naught for Your Comfort*, 58.

41. Huddleston, 59.

42. Garth Abraham, *The Catholic Church and Apartheid* (Johannesburg: Ravan Press, 1989), 87.

43. H F Verwoerd, quoted by Bunting, *The Rise of the South African Reich*, 148.

44. Guillermo O'Donnell, "On the Fruitful Convergence of Hirschman's Exit, Voice and Loyalty and Shifting Involvements: Reflections of the Recent Argentine Experience," in Alejandro Foxley, *et al, Development, Democracy, and the Art of Trespassing: Essays in Honour of Albert O Hirschman* (Notre Dame: University of Notre Dame Press, 1986), 249, 264-65.

45. Bram Fischer, quoted by Julie Frederikse, *The Unbreakable Thread* (London: Zed Books, 1990), 21.

46. Quoted by Mark J Osiel, *Ever Again: Legal Remembrance of Administrative Measures*, 144 U. Penn. L. Rev. 463, 607 (1995).

CHAPTER 15 (PAGES 168-75)

1. J Nyerere, foreword to P Johnson and D Martin, *Destructive Engagement – Southern Africa at War* (Harare: Zimbabwe Publishing House, 1986), 1.

2. J Hanlon, *Beggar Your Neighbours: Apartheid Power in South Africa*, (London: James Currey, 1986), 1.

3. General Magnus Malan, quoted by London *Times*, 23 September, 1984.

4. *South African Destabilisation: The Economic Cost of Frontline Resistance to Apartheid* (New York: United Nations, 1989).

5. US Deputy Assistant Secretary of State for Africa, quoted in *Weekly Mail*, 5 May, 1988.

6. See, Dan O'Meara, *Forty Lost Years*, 378.

7. *South African Destabilisation*, 21.

CHAPTER 16 (PAGES 176–206)

1. Joint Appeal, in *The United Nations and Apartheid 1948-1994*.
2. The American Law Institute in its *1985 Restatement of Law: Foreign Relations of the USA*, completed at the height of the Reagan era, concluded that a systematic policy of racial discrimination breaches the *jus cogens*.
3. Legal Consequences for States of the Continued Presence of South Africa in Namibia (South West Africa) Notwithstanding Security Council Resolution 276 (*Namibia Opinion*) (1970), A.O. 1971, International Court of Justice, 16, 57 (Judge Padilla Nervo).
4. *Namibia Opinion*, [1971], 54.
5. "National Security Study Memorandum 39," in M A El-Khawas and B Cohen, eds, *The Kissinger Study of Southern Africa* (Conn: Lawrence Hill & Company, 1976), 89.
6. Hermann Giliomee, *Saturday Star*, 24 February, 1996.
7. Hermann Giliomee, *Cape Times*, 26 February, 1996.
8. M J Osiel, *Ever Again: Legal Remembrance of Administrative Massacre* 144 U. Penn. L. Rev. 463, 620 (1995).
9. General Assembly Resolution 1514 (XV).
10. David Kay, *The New Nations at the United Nations* (New York: Columbia University Press, 1970).
11. Special Committee Against Apartheid, *Report of the Seminar on the Legal Status of the Apartheid Regime in South Africa and Other Legal Aspects of the Struggle Against Apartheid*, 10 (1984).
12. See, further, on the international illegitimacy of apartheid, K Asmal, *The Illegitimacy of the South African Regime: International Law Perspectives*, 1990 International Review of Contemporary Law, 21.
13. J J Paust, *The Human Right to Participate in Armed Revolution and Related Forms of Social Violence: Testing the Limits of Permissibility*, 32 Emory L J (1983), 545.
14. Judge Ammoun, *Namibia Opinion*.
15. A Sachs, World Conference Against Apartheid, Lisbon 1977 (unpublished conference documentation on file with the authors).
16. *The Barcelona Traction Case* (Second Phase), ICJ Reports (1970), 3, 32.
17. Gavin Cawthra, *Brutal Force: The Apartheid War Machine* (London: International Defence and Aid Fund, 1986), 3.
18. Doctor's report on Limehill, reproduced in Desmond, *The Discarded People*, 240.
19. Hoosen M Coovadia, in *Children of the Front Line*, 1989 Update (UNICEF), 110.
20. Coovadia, in *Children of the Front Line*, 101-102.
21. *A Survey of Race Relations in South Africa 1976* (Johannesburg: South African Institute of Race Relations, 1977), 381.
22. Desmond, *The Discarded People*, 217.
23. *Survey of Race Relations in South Africa, 1979* (Johannesburg: South African Institute of Race Relations, 1980), 71.
24. *Survey of Race Relations in South Africa, 1979* (Johannesburg: South African Institute of Race Relations, 1980), 564–5.
25. Kader Asmal, quoted in *Star*, 17 June, 1996.
26. Richard Falk, *The Nation*, 7 November, 1987.

CHAPTER 17 (PAGES 207–16)

1. C L R James, Letter to Constance Webb, collected in A Grimshaw, (ed), *The C L R James Reader* (Oxford: Blackwell 1992), 136-37.
2. Quoted in J S Galbraith, *Reluctant Empire* (Berkeley: University of California Press, 1963), 257-58.
3. G M Theal, *History of the Boers in South Africa* (London: Sonnenschein, 2nd ed, 1888), 10, 299-300, 305.

4. A Holiday, "White Nationalism in South Africa as Movement and System," in *The National Question in South Africa*, (London and New Jersey: Zed Books, 1988), 78.

5. De Kiewiet, *History*, 150-51, 212, quoted by C Saunders, *The Making of the South African Past* (Cape Town: David Philip, 1988), 92.

6. House of Assembly Debates, 20 May, 1959.

7. Piet Cronje, quoted in *Sunday Independent*, 3 March, 1996.

8. Potgietersrus school parent, quoted by *Star*, 2 February, 1996.

9. Gerald Shaw, "Government on Course for a Fight to the Finish with the ANC," *Cape Times*, 28 October, 1988.

10. Prime Minister P W Botha, quoted by R Davies in Mark Orkin, ed, *Sanctions Against Apartheid* (Cape Town: David Philip, 1989), 220.

11. B B Keet, *Whither South Africa* (Stellenbosch: Stellenbosch University, 1956), 85.

12. Mrs Elize Vorster, quoted by *Sunday Times*, 3 March, 1996.

13. Defence Minister Magnus Malan, quoted by *Citizen*, 5 August, 1988.

14. Charles Bester, quoted by Richard Abel, *Politics By Other Means* (New York: Routledge, 1995), 106.

15. Michel Foucault, *The Foucault Reader* (New York: Pantheon Books, 1984), 74-75.

16. Edward Said, *The World, the Text and the Critic* (London: Vintage, 1991), 247.

Index

James, C L R, 207–8
Japan, 10, 21
Jaspers, Karl, 162
job reservation, 138–9
Joffe, Joel, 61
Jonker, Dr Willie, 162; apology for apartheid, 163, 164
Joubert, General, 98
journalism: and transition, 6
Joyce, James, 183
Kahn, Sam, 130
Kajimi Gumi company, 155
Keet, Dr B B, 212
Khotso House, 105
Khanya House, 105
King, Martin Luther, 32, 176
kitskonstabels, 109
Koevoet, 98
Kohl, Helmut, 15
Koning, Hans, 211
Koornhof, Piet, 33, 72, 172–3
Korea, 10
Kotze, Pen, 150
Kriel, Ashley, 205
Kriel, Hernus, 68
Kruger, Jimmy, 43
Kundera, Milan, 39
Land Acts, 7, 129, 131
labour, 128–9, 136–7, 139, 210, *passim*
Laing, Sandra, 161
Lapsley, Fr Michael, 57
Lancet, 100
League of Nations, 169
legal interpretation: generally, 14; international law, 202–3; and history, 20;
Lekganyane, Bishop, 108
Lesotho, 168, 174
Liberal Slideaway, 81
liberals: and violence, 120; and sanctions, 179
"Little House on the Prairie", 139
Louw, Eric, 32, 183
Lubowski, Anton, 106
Luthuli, Albert, 1–2, 3, 30
MacArthur, General, 21
Macmillan, Harold, 9
Malan, D F, 31, 38, 161; and apartheid electorate, 151, 161; and press, 92
Malan, Magnus, 23, 43, 47, 48, 102, 104, 105, 106, 107, 108, 117, 145, 151, 213; southern Africa, 171
Malawi, 168–9
Mamasela, Joe, 99
Mandela, Nelson, 1, 3, 6, 8, 39, 50, 54, 55, 58, 59, 64, 65, 66–7, 71, 89, 107, 114, 116, 117, 121, 122, 124, 126, 154, 165, 178, 211; on apartheid as crime against humanity, 176, 197
Mangope, Lucas, 137
Maree, Johan, 155
Marquez, Gabriel Garcia, 50

Marx, Karl, 1
Masaryk, Thomas, 52
Maschmann, Melita, 166
Maus, 215
Mayibuye Centre, 147
Mbeki, Govan, 62
Mbeki, Thabo, 55; on pre-colonial past, 147; on apartheid legacy, 207
McBride, Robert, 59–60
Medical and Dental Association, 154
Meinecke, Friedrich, 153
Mein Kampf, 153, 164; anti-semitism plus negrophobia, 32
memory: and history; nature of, 9–10
metonymy, 1, 4
Mhlawuli, Nombwyselo, 146–7
Mitchell, Douglas, 152–3
Mkhonto, Sindiswe, 147
Mlangeni, Bheki, 103
Mohapi, Nohle, 100
Molefe, Victor
morality: favouritism, 7, 44; of the resistance, 14; relativism, 7, 14–16; anachronism, 48, 207–16
Mostert, Brigadier Floris, 102, 103
Motsuenyane Commission, 115
Mozambique, 168, 172–4
MPLA, 170–1
Mxenge, Griffiths, 103
Nagasaki, 15
Natal Mercury, 160
Nato, 21
National Party, imposing suffering, 31; Nazi tendencies, 32; bills of rights, 114; Geneva Conventions, 116; 1983 Action Plan, 150; continuing racist support of, 147
National Security Management System, 108
Naudé, Beyers, 31, 144, 164
Namibia, 66, 98, 168–70, 177
Namibia Opinion, 205
Nazi Germany, 3, 7, 15, 20, 55, 89; anti–Nazi plotters, 14; collaborators, 21, 63, 153; compared to apartheid laws, 132–3; 37; desk murderers, 147; enthusiasts, 143–4, 148; facing its past, 143; Jewish unemployment,
Ndebele, Njabulo, 146
Newspaperman's Guide to the Law, 78
Netherlands 14, 40
Ngqulunga, Brian 99
Nixon, President, 177–8
Ntombela, David, 108
Nuremberg: laws, 37, 62; trials, 3, 18–20; principles, 179
O'Brien, Conor Cruise, 185
O'Donnell, Guillermo, 165
Okri, Ben, 4
Oslo, 39
One Hundred Years of Solitude, 50
Oppenheimer, Harry, 155, 156–7
Orania, 4

Orr, Wendy, 154
Ossewa Brandwag, 33
Oxford Paperback Dictionary, 33
Pan Africanist Congress, 8, 122
patriotism, 58, 94, and apartheid Special
  Forces, 104
pass laws, 31, 37–8, 80–1, 129
Pauw, Jacques, 11
Pekane, Peks, 140
petty apartheid, 145
Pietermaritzburg Philharmonic Society, 158
Pillay, Navi J, 126
Pitje, Barney, 154
Ponti, Tulio Halperin, 48
Population Registration, 8, 129; absurdity,
  28–9; contrasted with U.S. "one drop rule,"
  130
post-colonialism, 3–4, 8, 29, 180, 182–9, 213
Potgietersrus, 29, 67, 68, 162
Pratt, David, 160
Progress of South Africa in the Century, 208
Progressive Party, 76, 121, 152; equal rights
  for civilised men, 153; conglomerate fund-
  ing, 157
Project Echoes, 101
Promotion of National Unity and
  Reconciliation Act (1995), *see* Truth and
  Reconciliation Commission
property, 131–42
prosecution, 21
Rainbow Cricket Club, 159
Ramashala, Mapule, 145
Rand Daily Mail, 38
Rapport, 90
Reagan, Ronald, 15; and southern Africa, 171
reconciliation: and amnesty, 17–18; meaning
  of, 46–53
Rediscovery of the Ordinary, 146
Relly, Gavin, 150, 157
Renamo, 2, 98, 172–3
reparations, 17
*Restatement of Law: Foreign Relations of
  the United States*, 190
revenge: rejection of, 20–1, 23, 48–9
reverse discrimination, 65, 139
Rhodes, Cecil, 153, 209
Rhodesia, *see* Zimbabwe
Rich, Adrienne, 211
Rise of the South African Reich, 89
Rivonia Trial, 54–5, 61, 65, 165
Roberts, Ronald Suresh, 3–4
Rosmus, Anja, 62
rugby, 58
Romania, 51–2
Rupert, Anton, 155, 157
SABC, 58, 90, 91–2
SADF, 98, 101, 102, 103, 108; and Front Line
  States, 168–75
Said, Edward, 207, 214
Salazar, 168

SAP, 115, 117
Sachs, Albie, 49, 104, 189
Schoeman, B J, 134
Scholtz, G D, 35
Seed is Mine, 146
separate development, *see* apartheid
September, Dulcie, 103
Sewgolum, Papwa, 159
Sharpeville, 8, 31
Shepstone, Sir Theophilus, 36
Shirer, William, 143
Simonstown Deliberations, 117
Shole, Lulu, 138
Slabbert, Dr van Zyl, 60
Slovo, Joe, 12–13, 50, 62, 83, 121, 123
Smell of Apples, 44–5, 50
Smith, Ian, 168
Smuts, Jan, 7, 112; support of apartheid, 148,
  152
sociocide, 199
South Africa Foundation, 155–6
South African Law Commission, 67–8
Soweto, 13; uprising, 16, 160
Spiegelman, 215
Steyn Commission, 92–4, 95
Steyn, M S, 37
Steyn, Tienie J, 92
Strijdom, 4, 32
Strydom, Barend, 59, 211
Sunday Independent, 139
Sunday Times, 150, 156
Suzman, Helen, 18
subpoenas, 22
Suppression of Communism Act, *see* com-
  munism
SWAPO, 170, 187
Swaziland, 168
Sweden, 40
Tambo, Oliver, 59, 89, 123, 154
TerreBlanche, Eugene, 105, 213
terrorism, 97–110
Theal, George McCall, 208–9
32 Battalion, 101
Tokyo Trials, 19–20, 155
Tomlinson Report, 34–5, 36
torture, 99–101
Treason: Trial (1960), 8; trials (1988), 85
Treurnicht, Dr Andries, 151
Trinidad and Tobago, 3–4
Triomf (and Sophiatown), 139–40
truth: and justice, 10, 12–27; manipulation
  of, 4; uses of, 10–11
Truth and Reconciliation Commission:
  amnesty cut-off point, 9; functions, 2; history and, 19, 26, *passim*; vengeance and,
  2–3; terms of reference, 7; interpretation of
  act, 14–27; judicialisation of proceedings,
  18–25; structural human rights abuse, 25;
  legal challenges to, 22–3; legal representation before, 24; duration of work, 26.